THE DEFINITIVE CYBERSECURITY GUIDE
FOR DIRECTORS AND OFFICERS

NAVIGATING
THE DIGITAL AGE

SECOND EDITION

Navigating the Digital Age:
The Definitive Cybersecurity Guide for Directors and Officers
Second Edition

Publisher: Palo Alto Networks

Editors: Aleksandra Miljus, Mike Perkowski, and Al Perlman. **Copy Editor:** Rupal Shah

Design and Composition: Tim Heraldo and Jeffrey Rennacker

Produced With Grateful Thanks to: Kristen Batch, Deirdre Beard, Paul Calatayud, Christopher Coccagna, Elizabeth Cockett, John Davis, Greg Day, Sean Duca, Karine Gidali, Rick Howard, Danielle Kriz, Dana Loof, Rossana Monzon, Sean Morgan, Aryn Pedowitz, Michaline Todd, Alison Varela, and Sara Verri.

Navigating the Digital Age: The Definitive Cybersecurity Guide for Directors and Officers, Second Edition is published by: Palo Alto Networks, 3000 Tannery Way, Santa Clara, CA 95054, USA
Phone: +1 408-753-4000 | www.navigatingthedigitalage.com

First published: 2018

© September 2018

Disclaimer

Navigating the Digital Age: The Definitive Cybersecurity Guide for Directors and Officers, Second Edition contains summary information about legal and regulatory aspects of cybersecurity governance and is current as of the date of its initial publication May, 2018. Although the Guide may be revised and updated at some time in the future, the publishers and authors do not have a duty to update the information contained in the Guide, and will not be liable for any failure to update such information. The publishers and authors make no representation as to the completeness or accuracy of any information contained in the Guide.

This guide is written as a general guide only. It should not be relied upon as a substitute for specific professional advice. Professional advice should always be sought before taking any action based on the information provided. Every effort has been made to ensure that the information in this guide is correct at the time of publication. The views expressed in this guide are those of the authors. The publishers and authors do not accept responsibility for any errors or omissions contained herein. It is your responsibility to verify any information contained in the Guide before relying upon it.

GLOBAL CYBERSECURITY EDUCATION FUND

Navigating the Digital Age, Second Edition, is published by Palo Alto Networks. As a company, alleviating the problem of cybercrime is at the heart of everything we do.

Our goal is to offer cybersecurity education and training to students of all backgrounds around the globe through the Global Cybersecurity Education Fund.

Which is why every action we take, and your readership of this book, gets us one step closer to our mission—protecting our way of life in the Digital Age.

Preface

From the Editors

Welcome to the all-new second edition of *Navigating the Digital Age*. We emphasize "all new" because none of the content in this edition is repetitive of what was written in the first edition. How could it be? The first edition was published three years ago. Welcome to the Digital Age, where three years feels like a millennium.

This edition brings together more than 50 leaders and visionaries from business, science, technology, government, academia, cybersecurity, and law enforcement. Each has contributed an exclusive chapter designed to make us think in depth about the ramifications of this digital world we are creating.

An important focus of the book is centered on doing business in the Digital Age—particularly around the need to foster a mutual understanding between technical and non-technical executives when it comes to the existential issues surrounding cybersecurity.

This book has come together in three parts. In Part 1, we focus on the future of threat and risks. Part 2 emphasizes lessons from today's world, and Part 3 is designed to help you ensure you are covered today. Each part has its own flavor and personality, reflective of its goals and purpose. Part 1 is a bit more futuristic, Part 2 a bit more experiential, and Part 3 a bit more practical. We hope you find each to be thought-provoking and valuable.

One of the pleasant surprises we discovered in editing these chapters was how seamlessly and, at times, brilliantly our authors were able to connect the business and technology challenges of cybersecurity to the broader issues facing the world at large.

But, in retrospect, we probably shouldn't have been surprised. After all, what makes this book so necessary and, we hope, so compelling is the reality that digital technologies are completely embedded in every aspect of our lives. And, as you will discover in the pages ahead, we're still only at the beginning of our journey in navigating the Digital Age.

Unless otherwise stated, all $ amounts are in U.S. dollars.

Table of Contents

How Work Requirements and Ethical Responsibilities Come Together

Part 2 – Lessons From Today's World
Introductions

Cybersecurity Awareness, Understanding, and Leadership

The Convergence and Divergence of Compliance and Cybersecurity

Part 3 – Make Sure You're Covered Today

Introductions

Language

Strategy

People

Process

Technology

Conclusion

Contributor Profiles

PART 1
The Future of Threat and Risks

Part 1 — Introductions

1

Prologue

Tom Farley — Former President, New York Stock Exchange

"No issue today has created more concern within corporate C-suites and boardrooms than cybersecurity risk."

That was how I introduced the previous edition of *Navigating the Digital Age* and, if anything, the sentiment is perhaps even more profound and urgent today, three years later. In that time, we have seen just how fundamentally we rely on connected digital technologies, and how on-guard we must be to prevent cybersecurity attacks.

We have witnessed attacks on data privacy and infrastructure, interference with elections, the rise of ransomware, and the potentially crippling impact of cyberattacks on businesses all around the globe. We have learned through hard experience that the status quo in cybersecurity is not giving us the trust and confidence we would like to feel as we continue to ramp up the pace of innovation in the Digital Age.

There is much that *can* be done to address the challenges of cybersecurity, and much that *must* be done. That's where this book comes in. Starting with the opening chapter about the concept of a "cybersecurity moonshot" and extending to nearly 50 expert-written chapters, this edition strives to foster a much greater understanding of the challenges we face in navigating the Digital Age, and the steps we must take to protect and enable our digital way of life, for now and the future.

You will see several recurring themes that resonate like a beacon across these pages:

- Connected digital technologies are at the foundation of every aspect of our lives—our business infrastructures to be sure, but also our power grids, water supplies, air traffic systems, electoral systems, and national security apparatus, to name just a few.

- We are still at the early stages of our journey in the Digital Age. The expansion of the Internet of Things, artificial intelligence, and other "exponential" technologies will drive dramatic innovation over the next few years, while at the same time expand our attack surfaces and therefore our risk.

- Because we are on the leading edge of this rapid expansion of data and technology, we must move quickly and comprehensively to address the cybersecurity challenge before it becomes too unwieldly. A deep sense of urgency felt by many of our authors comes through time and again in the chapters ahead.

- Effective cybersecurity is a combination of people, processes, and technologies. Our business and technology leaders must be on the same page, speak the same language, and adhere to best practices in governance. We must use advanced, automated technologies to level the playing field with our adversaries, fighting machines with machines.

- We *can* do something about cybersecurity. It will take a coordinated, concentrated effort. It will take cooperation across private industry and government. It will take training, education, experimentation, innovation, invention. It will take a lot, but it is something that can be done.

As leaders in business, technology, cybersecurity, government, and academia, it is our job to ensure that what *can* be done actually *is* done—and more, when possible. Several authors point to cybersecurity as the most important issue of our times, and it is hard to argue with that assessment. If we fail on the cybersecurity front, we put all of our dreams and aspirations for the Digital Age at risk.

If there is a single takeaway we can glean from the collected wisdom shared in these pages, it is this: When it comes to cybersecurity, failure is not an option. We must succeed, and we must succeed collectively, because ultimately we are all connected one way or another in the Digital Age.

At the New York Stock Exchange, we are fully committed to the task at hand. We strongly encourage our listed client community to do everything in their power to address the cybersecurity challenges within their organizations and to participate in some of the broader initiatives discussed in this book. As we all become more interconnected, we become increasingly reliant on our external relationships, whether partner, vendor, regulatory, or anything else. Cybersecurity is our collective responsibility, not only to our employees and shareholders, but also to society at large. The more we can do to cooperate, the more effectively we can reduce risk for all of us. The world is not only watching, it is counting on us to do our best.

2

To Protect Our Way of Life in the Digital Age, We Must Reach for a Cybersecurity Moonshot

Mark McLaughlin — Vice Chairman, Palo Alto Networks

The Digital Age provides us all with the privilege of being at the forefront of the ongoing endeavor that has the potential to uplift and shape the lives of people around the globe for future generations. Whether we come from business and industry, academia, or government, we, as entrusted leaders, have a vested stake in protecting our way of life in a world that increasingly relies on connected digital technologies.

If we do our jobs well, we can help address some of the biggest issues of our time: climate change, hunger, poverty, population explosion, and disease. We can make the lives of individuals better in thousands of ways, big and small—improving their healthcare, how they communicate, how they learn, what type of work they do, where they live, how they consume entertainment, and how they make their hopes and dreams come true.

But with our privilege comes responsibility. In order to see our own hopes and dreams come true, in order to ensure that our work is truly uplifting and not a broken promise, we must overcome a signifi-

cant obstacle that threatens to slow or halt this progress. That obstacle, of course, is cybersecurity. The future depends on getting it right.

How will history judge us?

The Challenge of Our Time: A Cybersecurity Moonshot

I believe that, if we are to be judged favorably, we have to shoot for the moon. I use the term "shoot for the moon" purposefully because it is not just a metaphor for the task at hand but, in some ways, it is representative of both a model and a mission statement. In our lifetimes, and even before many of us were born, humankind has shot for the moon—and made it. And it changed the world.

On Sept. 12, 1962, U.S. President John F. Kennedy pledged in a speech at Rice University to put a man on the moon by the end of the decade. He did so, recognizing that it was an audacious goal that would be viewed skeptically, at home and abroad. But he also knew it was a worthwhile and necessary endeavor, and he believed it could be done. He also had the vision to know that coalescing around a single, clearly articulated objective would have tangible, measurable, and long-lasting benefits. As he stated in his iconic speech: "That goal will serve to organize and measure the best of our energies and skills."

We are now in a similar place. The unlimited promise of the Digital Age—and the existential threat that cybersecurity poses to that promise—demands that we advocate, evangelize, and undertake a comparable type of effort today: organizing and measuring the best of our energies and skills around the vision of solving the world's cybersecurity challenge.

Our goal must be ambitious, simple, and direct. Real moonshots have clear and unequivocal goals, such as President Kennedy's goal of putting a man on the moon and bringing him back safely. I believe our "cybersecurity moonshot" should have a similarly simple, yet powerful goal: Make the internet safe within 10 years.

It is audacious, I know. I also know there will be naysayers, skeptics, and nitpickers: "It's too ambitious." "What does 'safe' even mean?" "How will we ever forge cooperation across the global cybersecurity ecosystem?"

Asking these questions, in many ways, addresses the very purpose of stating the goal. These questions articulate for us some of the most perplexing obstacles we need to address and overcome. Answering these questions and overcoming these obstacles is, I believe, one of the biggest challenges of our lifetimes, particularly for those of us in a position to effect change.

Understanding the Urgency

Before offering specific ideas on how we can organize and coalesce our energies and skills to achieve the cybersecurity moonshot, we should all understand the unequivocal urgency of the task at hand. Cybersecurity is not just about our future; it is our present. The fundamental underpinnings of our security and economy now depend on digitally connected technologies: our electrical grids, financial markets, military systems, and our infrastructure for water, food, communications, and everything else we need to live our lives.

While digitally connected technologies have enabled us to break barriers and achieve what was initially thought to be impossible, today's reality is that they are also under attack—constant, sophisticated, unyielding, innovative, and, in some ways, merciless attack. Today, hackers, criminals, and nation-states can—and do—shutter hospitals, halt business operations, and create political instability on a global basis.

The commercial internet has been around for more than 20 years, and the truth is we have never taken the fundamental steps to ensure its foundational long-term safety and security. We haven't yet done this as a global community, as individual nations, as industries—including the cybersecurity industry—as scientists, educators, government officials, business leaders, or activists. You could say the system is broken, but it's hard to break something that never truly existed in the first place.

It's not for lack of effort or interest. We desperately want the internet to be safe and secure; but, fortunately and unfortunately, technology has been moving at lightning speed for a long, long time. It's hard to keep up. The immediate steps that government and private industry often take to harden our defenses against potentially crippling attacks are, by their nature, short-term, incremental, and insufficient. Even some of the security technologies that we now consider to be state-of-the-art may be obsolete within the next year.

We are, frankly, at the edge of a precipice. The potential for a catastrophic event or series of events is very real. Our current incremental, piecemeal approach to addressing cybersecurity threats after they happen is simply not sustainable. Left unaddressed, the growing and increasingly destructive nature of cyberattacks will undermine our digital way of life and threaten the societal and economic gains new technology has helped us realize. If we don't achieve our goals within 10 years, it will be too late. Only by thinking big can we achieve a significant and enduring result.

Understanding the Challenge

There are two elements to the proposed cybersecurity moonshot. The first is: Make the internet safe. At its core, we are talking about safety and trust: People must feel safe online without the fear—whether it's top-of-mind or in the backs of their minds—that they are engaging in an activity that holds any real personal danger to them.

We shouldn't, at the outset, get too deep into the weeds of defining the statement, "Make the internet safe." Rather, we should let the process define it, using the best of our energies and skills to determine which characteristics are required to make people feel safe when using the internet. I can pretty much guarantee this: We will know it when we have achieved it.

The second element of our mission is: within 10 years. Why put a time frame on our efforts? First is the urgency we discussed earlier: We can't afford to be complacent in any way about solving the cybersecurity challenges of the Digital Age. The potential to make the world better is too important, and the risks are too great. Each day that we don't have a safe internet, there is potential for an event that can cause damage. And every time there is such

an event, it can cause even more damage to our confidence, our psyches, and our will.

A second reason for the 10-year time frame comes from what we learned from the original moonshot. When President Kennedy said that the goal was to put a man on the moon, he stated very clearly and very specifically: "By the end of the decade." This is what made the moonshot mission so audacious and generated such skepticism: "Ten years? How is that even possible?"

But the time frame became a galvanizing force. It empowered the U.S. to marshal unprecedented resources, brainpower, passion, and commitment behind a single goal. To achieve the 10-year time frame, the country had to unite and inspire the best energies and skills across a broad coalition, including government, education, technology, science, and private industry.

And it worked. Not only did the country put a man on the moon and bring him home, but the energy and efforts behind the endeavor also created a wave of innovation that changed the world. Inventions that emerged as a result of the original moonshot include solar panels, heart monitors and pacemakers, fire-resistant materials, cordless instruments, and dozens of others. These innovations have improved all aspects of our daily lives, from healthcare and safety to alternative energies and entertainment.

Actions We Can Take Now

Just as we should not proscribe what we mean today by "make the internet safe," we should not proscribe the models by which we can achieve our cybersecurity moonshot. The original moonshot model proved it could be done with a single country providing leadership, vision, and resources. That may be a successful model for the cybersecurity moonshot, or perhaps we will discover other models.

However, while we don't want to pre-determine a specific model for the cybersecurity moonshot, we do know that it will take a concentrated, collaborative, and coordinated effort among many forces to make it happen, including many "rooftop shots" along the way. Government, private industry, and academia all have a part to play. As leaders in our fields, we can provide vision, passion, leadership, and commitment. We have the opportunity, as President Kennedy said, "to organize and measure the best of our energies and skills."

Each of us—whether in private industry, government, or academia—can take action right now. And we can be secure in the knowledge that every step we take will bring us incrementally closer to our ultimate objective. We must begin thinking of it as a shared journey, working in our own areas of expertise, exploring what we can do to help, now and in the future. What areas should we be looking at, and what kinds of goals can we set? Here are five thoughts about critical disciplines that will be foundational to the success of the cybersecurity moonshot:

1. **Technology:** Let's face it. Our current consumption model for cybersecurity is fundamentally broken. We must develop a new model for how we protect our digital assets and interactions. We must evolve from the conventional model, which increasingly uses people to fight machines. We must, instead, promote and promulgate a progressive alternative, built on a prevention-oriented approach that will allow us to maintain trust in the digital world. Key elements of this new model include:

- **Automation and orchestration:** We need software to fight software. Humans facing off against machines have little to no leverage.

- **Coordinated and cooperative intelligence:** Sharing information is critical to our shared future. We can achieve this through an automated global information-sharing ecosystem.

- **A flexible security model:** We need the ability to choose the best solutions and access them when we need them, leveraging cloud computing and other models that are simple to deploy and economical to use.

2. **Privacy:** Privacy and security are mutually reinforcing. When we talk about trust—about assuring users that the internet is safe—privacy must be top-of-mind. People will be reluctant to use technology if they believe their financial or health records are in jeopardy of being exposed or used in a way that would cause them harm. At the same time, there may be circumstances in which the greater good can be achieved through the strategic sharing of information, without exposing the private records of individuals. Could we stop a terrorist attack or prevent a major security breach that would affect the lives of millions? Striking the right balance between convenience, safety, and privacy concerns is an essential element of protecting our way of life in the Digital Age.

3. **Education:** Education is not just about building the next generation of cybersecurity experts, although that is,

indeed, an essential element. It is also about building a society that is much more aware of the challenges, opportunities, and risks endemic to the use of digital technologies in the 21st century. Our children are beginning to use technology at younger ages, and that provides an opportunity to teach them while they're young. We need to think disruptively about how we educate our children, integrating technology and cybersecurity at all levels. We also must do a better job of integrating STEM education—science, technology, engineering, and math—into our curricula. We must also ensure that our schools have access to modern technologies, including broadband. And we must realize that education is not just for the young. We must make sure our leaders in government and business are more cyber-aware, and we must build and train a more cyber-aware workforce.

4. **National security:** Cyber is a democratized threat wherein the targets are not always visible and not always identifiable. And they are not just aimed at government. Attacks against financial systems, healthcare, energy—you name it—can have a devastating impact on the security of any nation. Viewing national security strictly as the purview of government significantly expands the risk profile. Governments are not wholly responsible for or wholly capable of making the internet safe. In fact, you would be hard-pressed to argue that governments are at the leading edge of technology in any area. Therefore, cybersecurity requires a coordinated, cooperative, and joint effort between the private and public sectors to address the national security concerns of any and all nations.

5. **Diplomacy:** The fundamental reality of the Digital Age, the reason why it can be a tool to uplift and inspire, is that we can all be connected, wherever we are in the world, with whatever technology we are using. The inherent power of a connected world is staggering. But it is also imposing and scary. Not every nation has the same interests. How do we address these challenges? How do we ensure, for example, global standardization of communications protocols? How do we move toward some level of rules that guide how nation-states operate in this brave new world? As I said earlier, it won't be easy, but confronting the difficult challenges is why we must shoot for the moon.

Taking the Next Step

These are not just idle thoughts, fortunately. They are reflective of actions that are already being taken today by businesses, governments, institutions, agencies, and individuals to address the cybersecurity challenges of the Digital Age.

On a global level, participating in events such as the World Economic Forum is a vital and important step we can take to heed the call for strengthening cooperation in a fractured world. On the national level, individual governments are moving forward. In the U.S., I am privileged to co-chair a subcommittee within the President's National Security Telecommunications Advisory Committee, tasked with further defining the cybersecurity moonshot vision and recommending a strategic framework for how government, academia, and private industry can jointly operationalize it. The NSTAC work is a critical milestone; it's also a catalyst for a much broader national conversation and collaborative effort, built around a common organizing principle, which we know needs to happen.

On an industry level, organizations such as the Cyber Threat Alliance are bringing vendors together to improve the cybersecurity of our global digital ecosystem by enabling near real-time, high-quality sharing of cyber threat information. On individual and company levels, all of us can do our best each day to be more collaborative and innovative in ways that will establish the building blocks of a cybersecurity moonshot outcome. We can make sure we are informed, aware, and action-oriented. We can ask the cybersecurity experts on our teams what steps we can take to make our digital interactions safer. We can educate and encourage the people we work with to be aware of the opportunities and risks of living in these challenging times. We can be advocates for change and progress.

As I said at the start, it is a privilege for each of us to be in a position to contribute our leadership, vision, talents, and knowledge to help deliver on the promise of the Digital Age. We must use, as President Kennedy said so aptly, "the best of our energies and skills." But with that privilege comes a responsibility to solve the cybersecurity challenge. It won't take a miracle, but it will take leadership.

Seizing the Opportunities, Understanding the Challenges

3

Why Our Digital DNA Must Evolve— Quickly

Salim Ismail — Founder, ExO Foundation; Board Member, XPRIZE

Our world is about to go from less than a billion connected sensors to 20 billion to more than a trillion, all in a time frame that will, in retrospect, seem like the veritable blink of an eye. In many ways, we are moving faster than our ability to keep pace with the change. Thus, we are seeing a disconnect between what we *can* do and what we *want* to do.

Here are two small, but illustrative, examples: Nearly two-thirds of executives say boards of directors have a vital role to play in digital transformation, yet only 27% say their boards are advocates for current strategies.[1] At the same time, 70% of CEOs say the move to the cloud and digitization is outpacing their ability to understand and define the risks.[2]

The opportunity before us is too important for these types of gaps to continue. The entire human race is at the threshold of an era of exponential change, when technology will transform all aspects of humanity into a digital environment—right down to our very DNA and cerebral cortexes. Moreover, as data continues to grow exponentially, it will become interconnected in the cloud to form a cyber mesh of data.

Our Immune Systems Are Causing Disconnects

We are experiencing these disconnects because, fundamentally, our systems are not designed to absorb this amount of dramatic and rapid change. We all rely on protective measures to adapt to change and mitigate risk, whether we are talking about the biological systems in our bodies or the cultures and processes we have built into our organizations. I refer to these protective measures as immune systems, and they are built into our business and institutional practices just as surely as they are built into bodies.

In business, these immune systems comprise governance procedures we've put in place, restrictions on how we utilize personnel, processes or technologies, or rules that specify how new ideas are presented within the organization. Whatever they are, they serve the purpose of slowing down and regulating our corporate metabolism. And, in many ways, they work for us. Until they don't.

In today's environment, these immune systems are contrary to our need to move quickly and keep up with technology innovation, particularly as we embrace exponentially accelerating technologies, such as artificial intelligence and quantum computing. If we are to fulfill the promise of the Digital Age, we must overcome the limitations caused by our organizational immune systems.

To Fix Cybersecurity, We Must Remove Roadblocks to Innovation

We must also, finally and fundamentally, address the immense cybersecurity challenges of this new world order and ensure that our immune systems don't slow us down or stop us from making the necessary changes. We must remove roadblocks to cybersecurity innovation.

For example, many organizations still have a large number of point products in place that are not connected with one another and don't offer sufficient security against modern attack methods. The organization may think they are protected, when they actually have gaps. Relying on older technologies and not getting rid of solutions that don't work is an obstacle to innovation. The cyber mesh is growing exponentially; cybersecurity must keep pace.

Why? Here's the reality: As we expand our cyber mesh of data, as we transform to a world of more than a trillion sensors, we are exposing ourselves to a potential cyberattack surface the likes of which we have never seen. We are already struggling to deal with the world's existing attack surface. If we don't figure out the cybersecurity challenges of our expanding cyber mesh of data, we run the risk of being victims of our progress, rather than beneficiaries.

How do we move forward? How do we embrace progress? How do we create a new digital DNA that our immune systems won't reject? And, perhaps most importantly, how do we ensure that our digital interactions and activities are suitably safe in a world where our very bodies are exposed to the potential of a cyberattack?

Getting Ready for Exponential Disruption

Data has already become our most valuable currency and will remain the defining differentiator between organizations that thrive in the Digital Age and those that disappear. We've seen virtually every industry disrupted by connected digital technologies—transportation, media, advertising, healthcare, music, photography, communications, finance, entertainment, retail. The list goes on—and we're still at the beginning stage.

As we move from less than a billion sensors to 20 billion to a trillion and beyond, the potential for dynamic disruption expands exponentially, accelerated by the shift from the read phase of digitization to the write phase. In this next phase, we are talking about the capability of writing code to our bodies, brains, and genomes. From a biotech standpoint, we are probably within two years of more widespread deployment. From a neuroscience standpoint, we are perhaps five or six years away.

Real-World Examples, Real-World Risks

We are already seeing examples of how this next advance in the Digital Age will affect our lives, health, leisure, and work. Think about healthcare in an age when we can each have a tiny sensor injected into the fatty area between our thumb and forefinger, whereby clinicians can easily access identity data, medication information, and emergency information. Or when an alert automatically sends a message to our physician at the first sign of a clogged artery or a leukemia cell entering into our bloodstream.

Look at what has been accomplished by Neil Harbisson, who had a "cyborg antenna" implanted in his brain to help him deal with an extreme form of color blindness. The antenna allows him to feel and hear colors as audio vibrations inside his head.[3] Think about extending the capabilities of our human memories with petabytes of data stored somewhere deep within the cortexes of our brains.

We are also, unfortunately, seeing some of the risks of this new world. In 2017, the U.S. Food and Drug Administration recalled nearly half a million pacemakers because of security flaws that made them vulnerable to cyberattack.[4] Nations are already collecting the DNA of government leaders to prepare for the possibility of a targeted cyber-based bio attack.[5] And before we see self-driving cars on the road, we have to be comfortable that the level of vulnerability is acceptable. We can only imagine the potential chaos and harm a fleet of unmanned vehicles could create if they were controlled by adversarial forces.

It's Time to Think Big

Yet, forward we progress. We are creating exponentially more volume and variety of data, seemingly by the second. If we go about our business without making any changes, we are heading for disaster. In his chapter, Mark McLaughlin of Palo Alto Networks talks about the need for a "cybersecurity moonshot."

As Mark suggests, if you want to address big problems, you need to think big. Our organization has studied common traits among the world's fastest growing startup companies and has identified that each of these organizations is able to articulate a Massive Transformative Purpose. This is defined as the higher aspirational purpose of the organization.

If data is a resource like oil, then we need to start thinking about it that way. Do we have a Massive Transformative Purpose? Can we create one? What would it be? One thing is clear: When it comes to cybersecurity, our current frameworks, mindsets, and immune systems hamper us and need to be addressed.

Can We Break Down Our Immune Systems to Empower Innovation Securely?

Immune systems protect us against radical change. They are wired to give us time to adjust and figure out the right outcomes. Governance is designed to be compliant with process and regulation because we know it is necessary. But what works in one context doesn't work so well in another. Immune systems can sometimes be roadblocks to innovation.

To move forward with cybersecurity in the Digital Age, we need to break down our current immune systems so that we are encouraging, embracing, and empowering rapid change and innovation.

It is certainly possible to engineer our immune systems to respond quickly. When a doctor performs a kidney transplant, she administers an immunosuppressant drug so the new kidney has time to bed down. Can we create similar results in our organizations, whereby the normal attack on the status quo is suppressed and new ideas have time to find a foothold?

Can We Create a Process to Solve the Immune System Problem?

The simple answer is "yes." I know because our organization has created and implemented a successful model that works. The process works as follows:

- Bring together senior management from across the organization. Showcase new technologies, threats, and opportunities—very much shock and awe—to show that disruptive threats are on the horizon and something must be done. This creates a burning platform for change.

- Gather 25 young leaders/future lieutenants to do the real work over 10 weeks. Divide them into two streams:

  » One stream looks at disruptive new ideas in adjacent industries that could grow the business by 10x or more;

  » The second stream examines the existing organization and chooses mechanisms to improve the status quo.

At the end of the 10 weeks, they present their ideas. Senior management funds the ideas that they believe are worth it. We have seen conclusively that management, leadership, and culture can leapfrog three years ahead in that 10-week period.

In analyzing why it works, we found that the opening workshop acts like an immunosuppressant drug, similar to a doctor performing a kidney transplant. By having the future leaders create new ideas (with coaching support), they champion and own those ideas, increasing chances of adoption in the future. In the past, disruptive ideas got funded about 10–15% of the time; now, when you break down the immune systems, we find more than 90% of new ideas get fully funded.

Can We Apply the Process to Cybersecurity?

Absolutely. There are many different ways to approach and implement the process. Individual organizations could take one approach, regulatory bodies could take another, and organizations in different industries can implement the model based on their own challenges. Heavily regulated industries, such as financial services and healthcare, have different challenges than organizations in industries where regulation is less of a factor. While the same basic processes and principles apply, the specifics of each engagement can change, based on the organization and its goals.

An approach we took in the public sector provides an illustrative model that could be applied to cybersecurity. We set a deliberately aggressive objective: Drop the cost of an existing problem by 10 times. Perhaps this is not as audacious as making the internet safe in 10 years, but it is a worthy and difficult goal, nonetheless. We formed teams to take a problem space—such as transportation, healthcare, or affordable housing—through four phases:

1. **Technology layer:** The goal was to examine breakthroughs that will drive the future, looking at new technologies and working with maker spaces, biohacking labs, and fabrication laboratories. Areas explored included sensors, 3D printing, robotics, artificial intelligence, synthetic biology, and eco-friendly technologies, such as green building construction and low-carbon energy sources.

2. **Design layer:** The goal was to picture, imagine, design, and describe technology solutions. We worked with artists, science fiction writers, designers, and media experts to envision and paint a future with technologies in mind. Design experts then used human-centered design techniques to integrate that vision into possible products and services.

3. **Entrepreneurial layer:** The goal was to ensure economic sustainability. We

looked at developing funding mechanisms to help entrepreneurs raise money; created models to ensure the sustainability of potential solutions (via business or taxes); and designed business models to solve major problems through the combination of design and technology.

4. **Social layer:** The goal was to ensure that the solutions could be implemented into society. We worked with sociologists, anthropologists, regulatory experts, and legal thinkers. We explored public-private partnerships, conducted experiments and trials, and incorporated community leaders representing different social groups, classes, and interests.

In the City of Miami, we were able to create four components to address the specific problem of traffic congestion. Perhaps most important, funding has been made available for immediate development and employment.

Are We Ready to Transform Our Cybersecurity DNA?

We know the model works, and we know it can work in the cybersecurity space. First, we need the motivation to change, which should be well apparent to everyone reading this chapter and this book.

As Mark McLaughlin states in his chapter, cybersecurity represents an existential threat to navigating the Digital Age. If we don't fix it, and fix it now, we expose ourselves to exponential risks we must avoid at all costs. Mark proposes a cybersecurity moonshot as a Massive Transformative Purpose: Make the internet safe in 10 years. That is certainly a viable starting point.

One of the characteristics that makes this era's progress exponential is hyper-connectivity. Because we are all digitally connected, ideas and innovations can spread quickly. This can be used for the greater good and, as we have seen, can also serve malevolent purposes. As we deploy models to transform our immune systems, hyper-connectivity can be used as a point of leverage. For example, it gives us the opportunity to work at the edges, where immune systems are less likely to create insurmountable obstacles.

Another important point is that we don't have to solve the problem all at once, all of us at the same time, all in unison. Although there is a definite urgency to the cybersecurity challenge, we can adopt the principles we have developed in specific organizations and then share them across a broader spectrum. For example, what we learned from our engagement in Miami can be applied to other cities, thus accelerating change by providing ideas, inspiration, and proven implementation techniques.

Finally, we have to recognize that when it comes to cybersecurity, we all share a collective purpose, whether we define that as a Massive Transformative Purpose in capital letters, or whether we collectively and individually create a pathway, step-by-step, toward a more secure future—a future in which we can fully embrace the Digital Age without fear that a cyber mesh will entrap us, rather than empower us.

Conclusion

In some ways, the journey ahead of us is clear. We *will*, without doubt, move forward in our inexorable march toward exponential digitization: We *will* go from a billion to more than a trillion sensors; we *will* leverage artificial intelligence and other exponential technologies; we *will* digitize our brains and bodies; we *will* transform all aspects of humanity into a digital environment. As a species, we are programmed to proceed, always seeking to embrace innovation and progress.

At the same time, however, the volume, velocity, and pace of change in today's Digital Age is without historical precedent. We are moving at a speed that threatens to overwhelm us if we don't put the proper protections and safeguards in place. To fulfill the promise of the Digital Age, we must overcome the limitations of the immune systems we have built to protect us. In particular, we must transform our digital DNA so we can move forward creatively and innovatively to address the cybersecurity challenge before us. Now's the time.

---

1   "The Board of Directors You Need for a Digital Transformation," Harvard Business Review, July 13, 2017

2   "Cybersecurity and the cloud," Vanson Bourne 2018

3   "Neil Harbisson: the world's first cyborg artist," The Guardian, May 6, 2014

4   "Three reasons why pacemakers are vulnerable to hacking," The Conversation, Sept. 4, 2017

5   "Hacking the President's DNA," The Atlantic, November 2012

4

The Exhilarating, Exciting, and Sobering World of the Internet of Things: Imagine the Opportunities, and Realize the Risks

Jennifer Steffens — Chief Executive Officer, IOActive

Few technologies have the potential to impact the way we work, live, play, shop, and interact like the Internet of Things. Imagine the ability to use sensors, embedded chips, process inputs, and other ways to "smarten" everything, from our cars and our health to our physical communities.

At the same time, let's keep the excitement of connected things in perspective. Smart cities, intelligent dialysis machines, and self-replenishing retail shelves all are examples of using IoT to enhance our lives at work and at home. An IoT-enabled hairbrush is not.

Capturing, analyzing, and leveraging seemingly infinite volumes and varieties of data are exhilarating and can help fuel innovation for more life-enhancing IoT products. But it also can cause well-founded alarm for executives and consumers if care is not taken to account for bad actors and other threats to intelligent devices and processes.

Fortunately, best practices are emerging to address these IoT issues today, even as the technology is still in its infancy. The successful organizations will be the ones

that can stay ahead of the curve in spotting opportunities. They will need to open their minds to find innovative ways to stop threats and build a safe digital environment for consumers.

Can You Imagine It?
Imagine the Heady Stuff

There's no need to recite gaudy statistics—and there are oceans of them—about the explosive growth of IoT market expenditures, the number of connected devices, and the economic impact of an IoT-infused market ecosystem. Forget about clichés like "the tip of the iceberg." We're looking at the Marianas Trench—which is deeper than Mount Everest is high—of IoT market development. Many of us can't begin to imagine how big IoT is going to become because, like the Marianas Trench, we really don't see it. Stuff like computerized automotive emissions controls, cashless tolling systems, and retail loss prevention packaging are so much a part of our everyday lives that we don't even think of them as IoT applications.

For people like me, the heady stuff is trying to figure out where IoT will take us in the future, and what it will mean for society—for better or for worse.

Obviously, there are tons of business-to-business applications where IoT has only scratched the surface, such as inventory control in retailing and wholesale distribution, manufacturing floor workflows, RFID in third-party logistics, and smart power grids. And consumer applications are even more plentiful and fanciful because of the way they impact our lives, including sensor-controlled traffic management, intelligent medical devices, smart homes, and connected cars. These and similar applications are fast becoming commonplace, and our children will have trouble imagining a time when they didn't download music from the internet to their GoPro camera while gliding down the mountain on auto-leveling skis.

And then, there are the odd, eccentric, and downright weird (to some people whose imaginations don't always stretch that far), like "bovine management" (AKA, smart farming), internet-connected toys and, yes, even intelligent hairbrushes.

But, let your imagination run wild, and you'll begin to consider the vast array of possibilities to make things more efficient, affordable, and interesting for us. And for business executives and board members who care less about the technology behind those solutions and more about the financial opportunities it affords, these are exciting times.

Just imagine it:

- Machine-learning-enabled telemedicine (think of it as digital house calls on steroids), where doctors can receive real-time updates on a patient's heart condition before the patient even feels anything, and the doctor can fix the problem remotely using a smartphone.

- Store managers who uncover an organized retail-theft plot by matching an employee's digital ID with merchandise removed from a shelf, but not accounted for as a sale.

- Consumers who learn that their credit card numbers are being used 1,000 miles away—before their banks' fraud departments notify them and cancel their cards.

- City officials who spot a terrorist's attempt to poison municipal water sources from across the world using malware uploaded from a burner cell phone.

Undoubtedly, business executives and board members reading this chapter can envision countless other applications and use cases—if they can just let their imaginations run free.

Of course, there are significant implications for these and other soon-to-emerge IoT applications. Regulatory, legal, privacy, and cultural concerns weigh heavy on everyone's minds—and they should. Still, it's important for decision-makers to not let fear, uncertainty, and doubt cloud innovation and opportunity.

And that's why it's crucial that executives and boards keep in mind their leadership responsibilities: to question and to ensure their organizations stay ahead of rapidly emerging threats, at all stages of IoT product innovation and development.

IoT Threats and Risks: Look Before You Leap and Make a Connection

Here's a two-part premise for business executives, government leaders, and board members about IoT:

Part 1: Let's agree that just because something *can* be connected doesn't mean it *should* be connected.

Part 2: If something is connected because it has the potential to improve our work or personal lives—or generate revenue for our businesses—we need to understand that there are always risks involved.

In Part 1, my point is that we now have the ability to embed, attach, or integrate technology with everything from industrial equipment and our municipalities' most important services to household devices and our children's toys. Our electronics are smaller and more functional, our algorithms more intelligent and flexible, our packaging more inconspicuous and even attractive. But organizations and their leaders need to really think twice about whether intelligent food or robotic office plants—although technically feasible—are what we all need. We all know that consumers, in particular, love shiny new things. But the "if you build it, they will come" philosophy has never proven to be a sound and profitable business strategy.

But Part 2 is where we need to really put our energies, talents, and imaginations. Any time you connect something to another device, a computer network or the internet, you are opening up potential new avenues for intrusions and breaches. As business leaders, we naturally worry about the financial, operational, and legal impact of hacking IoT systems.

But what about other kinds of more personal risks? How about the risks to our children when their smart toys are hacked by bad actors to track their locations? *The New York Times,* in a lengthy article about smart toys for the recent holiday season, pointed out numerous instances of chip- and sensor-based toys that exuded vulnerabilities; some of them were even banned by various European government regulators.[1]

And then there are even potentially more widespread, insidious, and cata-strophic risks. What if hackers were to access a city's water purification system through Wi-Fi-based controllers? Or if someone's electronic pacemaker was corrupted through an RFID-enabled watch? Or foreign powers manipulated a country's national voting systems by downloading malware from a smartphone to an electronic voting booth? Or if computerized braking systems on our cars and trucks were disabled over the internet?

These are not hypothetical scenarios. Our company has long been involved in testing security vulnerabilities of IoT-based systems, and our experts have determined that all the scenarios—and more—are not only possible, but in many cases have actually happened.

Our researchers have repeatedly demonstrated that cars can be disabled while they are being driven, vulnerabilities of internet-connected toys can be exploited, and pacemakers can be maliciously hacked. And as for smart cities—well, let's just say our researchers have determined that those cities aren't always as smart—or as "digitally safe"—as they'd like to think.

Therefore, it's important to remember a few undeniable facts about IoT risks:

- The more "things" we connect to our network and the public internet, the more vulnerabilities are created. This is particularly true with what our technical colleagues call "unmanaged endpoints," which often lack the robust and automated security our traditional computer endpoints now include as second nature.

- The bad guys are working together, sharing information, tips, tricks, and shortcuts. They are even jointly funding efforts through their own flavor of crowdsourcing on the dark web.

- The good guys, by comparison, are usually going it alone. Companies and governments around the world rarely feel comfortable collaborating on security because it exposes their risks to others, presumably eroding what they see as competitive advantage.

- The potential for more and more risks is going to expand in direct proportion to the dramatic increase in connected devices, systems, and business processes.

In short, doing nothing is not a sound business strategy. I'm sure the regulators would agree, as well.

Addressing IoT's Problems and Fulfilling Its Potential

Let me be clear about what I am *not* saying: I am not advocating that businesses and public organizations pump the brakes on IoT solutions development and deployment. Far, far from it. I am so excited about the potential for IoT to enhance our lives, our businesses, our institutions, and our society that I want to see research, development, manufacturing, marketing, and sales proceed as quickly as possible in order to meet consumer and business demand.

In order to do that, those of you reading this chapter—and in fact, this entire book—should keep a few principles in mind about IoT risk management, remediation, and security best practices. It also is important for business and public sector leaders to consider the broader implications of where IoT is going in the future, as it relates to societal and cultural trends.

These suggestions are intended for the entire IoT ecosystem, from technology creators and enterprises integrating IoT into products and services, to governments, regulators, and "fixers."

- **Security should be designed into IoT solutions from the start, not after a breach.** I know, it sounds easy, right?

But in our euphoria over discovering the ability to connect everything to anything, we must not lose track of the increased risk profile our businesses, government institutions, and citizens can face. Fixing security breaches after the fact is very costly and inefficient. In fact, looking at how regulators are clamping down on organizations that suffer a security breach, no matter how well-intended everyone may have been, it's vital for security in IoT systems to become an essential feature, just as important as what a connected device can do. Some of you may balk at the idea of doing early-stage security integration into inexpensive electronic devices because of the perceived costs and potential impact in time to market. But I can assure you that costs and time to market will be much worse if and when you suffer a breach. Get it done right from the initial design phase.

- **Don't throw a broad, one-size-fits-all security blanket over your IoT innovations.** As big an advocate for IoT security and vulnerability defense frameworks as I am, I am completely open-eyed about the need to balance security requirements with product functionality that delivers an outstanding customer experience. The good news is that those two ends of the spectrum are not mutually exclusive—you can and should have rock-solid security on all connected devices without making businesses, consumers, or citizens jump through hoops in order to take advantage of these exciting technologies.

- **Collaboration is good for everyone.** Industry players, governments, regulators, consumer groups, standards bodies: All of these parts of the IoT ecosystem should work together to explore exciting new opportunities and to balance those opportunities with known and potential new security frameworks to protect everyone. Technology companies have often found ways around their latent competitiveness to create technology roadmaps and solutions guides that grow their market opportunity and give customers viable, productive solutions. Besides, we already know that the bad guys have put their heads together to find ways to muck things up. Don't let them get a leg up on our efforts because we are too proud or too stubborn to work together.

- **Customers are willing to make tradeoffs on things like privacy in order to use IoT for fun and profit. Don't let them go too far.** Not that long ago, Facebook members were reluctant to reveal too many personal details on their walls. Now, they promote every aspect of their lives (sometimes to their detriment) in order to enjoy the full experience of social media. This means your organizations need to be careful not to let customers' exuberance in adopting the "next new thing" put them—or your organization—in harm's way. Make sure your customers and consumers are aware of best practices and smart IoT hygiene in order to remain secure while still getting the most out of technology integrated into everyday work and home lives.

A Few Ways for Business Leaders and Board Members to Stretch Their Imaginations

Whether you're a CISO at a global financial institution, a board member of a non-profit educational foundation, or the CEO of a technology company committed to connecting every node on the global network, there are five things I recommend you do now to prepare yourself for the heady times that await us.

1. Boards should bring in a security expert—either as a member or as a consultant—so the security voice is heard loud and clear as new IoT development programs are discussed and planned.

2. Decisions about security are too often made too low in the organization, by security technicians, IT staff, or others "close to the flame." Security is a strategic initiative and needs to be treated as such by non-technical executives and business leaders.

3. Don't stifle innovation by giving in to fears about corporate-wide breaches and blaring headlines. You didn't get to this level of achievement in your careers by being timid. Be bold, but be smart. Balancing risk with reward is what leaders do.

4. If anyone answers your question about security as you roll out IoT solutions with, "That's how we've always done it," show them the door.

5. "Smart security" approaches are being implemented every day at companies such as Microsoft, the Mayo Clinic, and General Motors, to name just a few. Strive to add your organization's name to this impressive and growing list.

Conclusion

IoT isn't about to transform our society; it's already doing it. Every day, more and more applications emerge that make everyday devices smarter and more utilitarian than one could have ever imagined.

Which brings us back to one of our core themes: Imagine.

Nearly 50 years ago, John Lennon sang

about a different kind of world, one with infinite possibilities for all of us. I'm pretty sure he didn't specifically envision the role that sensors, self-driving cars, and intelligent household products would play in changing how we live, work, and play. But he did encourage us to stretch our imaginations:

"You may say I'm a dreamer
But I'm not the only one."

Unlike Lennon, I'm a business executive who loves finding the intersection between technology, customers, employees, work, and play. But just like the famous Beatle, I'm a dreamer. I can imagine the powerful and transformative role that IoT—and its eventual spin-off technologies—will play in our society.

Just don't ask me why we need a smart chip in a hairbrush.

---

[1] "Don't Give Kids Holiday Gifts That Can Spy on Them," The New York Times, December 8, 2017

5

How Data Grids Will Power the Economy and Influence Our Future

Rama Vedashree — Chief Executive Officer, Data Security Council of India

In less than two decades, since the beginning of the third millennium, digital data has transformed everything.

It started with the sheer volume of data, which became multiplied by the many digital formats and media forms. The internet and cloud have enabled digital data to become connected into a global data grid, which has enabled us to gain intricate insights into one another, as well as how our world works, plays, interacts, and governs. It has reshaped the very nature of our communities at the local, regional, and global levels—enriching our economies, enabling collaboration across the world, and allowing us to enjoy more productive lives at work and at home.

In turn, accessibility to this cyber mesh of connected and connectable data has elevated the potential for cyber risk and "digital deluge." It has created an important sense of urgency for an ecosystem of enablers—governments, enterprises, educational institutions, and advocacy groups—to work together toward the common goal of making our digital universe safer.

When I took on the role of CEO of the Data Security Council of India two years ago, I was optimistic about the commitment of interested stakeholders in ensuring that the digital economy and, in fact, our digital lives, would be safe and secure. However, a number of factors are coalescing to give us concern. The fast-paced digitization momentum across the world, rapidly growing economies like India's and China's, and the recent World Economic Forum's "Global Risks Report 2018," which cites cyber risks and data theft/fraud as global risks, are together a wake-up call for action at the global, regional, and national levels.

Still, two years later, I am even more optimistic about our ability to harness this massive wave of data, in all its many forms and connections, for the good of our global societies. Of course, I am also realistic about the need for intelligent cyber risk identification and mitigation practices in order for us to build and prosper from the "digitization of everything."

At the core of this ability to build and benefit from a cyber mesh of data are five key concepts:

1. Developing a global data grid to shape and fuel the global economy.

2. Using data as the new currency for today and, especially, the future.

3. Weighing the ramifications of Big Data in shaping the enterprise and consumer of the future.

4. Balancing our innovation ecosystem with the reality of data monopolies.

5. Enabling cybersecurity and privacy imperatives to co-exist in a data-driven world.

Where we go from here is dependent on a whole host of factors, many of which have yet to emerge and are difficult to predict with certainty. But we know this for sure: Digital data is going to change the world in even more dramatic ways than it has done since the invention of first-generation computing.

Data Grids: Powering the Global Economy

The concept of grids—interwoven, mesh-like systems and processes for a wide range of industries and applications—is well known and widely understood in our societies. Grids exist and function smoothly for such applications and sectors as power and electric, financial systems, aviation, and many others.

Now, a new type of grid has emerged—a global data grid—which merges the tremendous surge of information with all the connected points in other grids. This creates exciting, powerful business models that weren't available just a few years ago. For instance, think of how the free flow of data across physical and digital storefronts has spawned the age of multi-channel retailing that knows no geographic boundaries.

Global data grids also exist for the amazing growth in user-generated content—everything from social media platforms,

wikis, blog sites, and personal e-diaries—that encompasses everything from family genealogy and hobbies to open source software communities.

In global data grids, information will increasingly be shared from sector grid to sector grid, promoting increased collaboration that utilizes common information or generates new insights from previously unseen data. This will rapidly evolve into a global, real-time data grid, with companies, government agencies, and consumers collaborating on data creation and access.

Think about the promise offered by data-centric compliance mandates, such as the U.S. Health Insurance Portability and Accountability Act (HIPAA), which allows patients to take their personal health information with them, regardless of which doctor, medical facility, insurance company, or healthcare service they use. Now, multiply that potential exponentially across industries and around the world. We see similar global data grids being formed in areas such as higher education, tying together both physical and virtual learning centers, as well as university-sponsored research laboratories, public policy think tanks, and community development programs. Consider, for instance, the increasingly global footprint of major universities, such as Harvard, Stanford, Oxford, and Le Sorbonne—all of which have built and are leveraging their own global data grids.

That is where we are going.

Data As the Currency of the Future

A generation ago, there was a lot of talk about, "Oil as the new currency." Today, however, there is increasing evidence that data is, in fact, becoming our new currency; and that trend is likely to accelerate. Consider these data points from industry research:

- By 2020, the value of the European Union data economy is projected to hit 739 billion Euros, representing 4% of European Union gross domestic product (GDP)—more than double its portion of GDP just five years earlier.[1]

- "Digital industry"—global data-centric market segments—will increase its annual profit margin potential by more than $1.4 trillion annually by 2030.[2]

- Digital transformation will contribute more than $1 trillion to the Asia Pacific GDP by 2021, driven heavily by artificial intelligence, the Internet of Things, Big Data, and other data-driven initiatives.[3]

Of course, trying to get a handle on the financial contribution of digital data isn't new. In fact, global consulting giant McKinsey wrote about this issue as far back as 2013, when it raised the notion of separating the economic impact of digital capital from that of tangible technology assets, such as hardware, software, and IT-enabled services.

It is clear, however, that it will not be long before we no longer are writing articles or papers with the headline, "Data is the New Currency" for a very pragmatic reason: Data is rapidly establishing itself as the currency of record for all global industries. It is, in fact, becoming the "new oil." In healthcare, financial services, manufacturing supply chains, retail, utilities, government services, and in all other market sectors, data is being monetized in a wide range of applications. And we have only tapped the surface.

Perhaps typical of the impact of data on markets, industries, and economies is a recent blog post by banking industry consultant Chris Skinner, who wrote:

"If all the things we used to do (in banking) make no profit anymore, where is the money to be made in the future? And the answer is: data."

The Big Impact of Big Data Will Get Even Bigger

It is easy to be amazed at the massive growth of digital information. The much-discussed Big Data movement is now mainstream, and it has enjoyed enormous popularity as organizations learn how to harness this growing amount of data for a wide range of use cases.

But the sheer volume of data growth is not the issue. Organizations need to find new ways to efficiently access the right data from the right point in the global data grids in order to make a real difference in how we work, play, and interact. Without a strategic plan—and the right tools—for harnessing all that data, organizations will drown trying to "drink from the fire hose."

Big Data—augmented by related data-generation trends, such as mobility, wearables, virtualized infrastructure, e-commerce, IoT, distributed workforces, collaboration platforms, enterprise content management, and others—has only begun to scratch the surface of what it can do. That's due to a number of factors, such as the formative stages of data-mining tools and the early development of powerful, secure algorithms that turn raw data into actionable insights. Big data's growth, as impressive as it is, also has been limited by enterprises' desire to keep capital expenses as low as possible, which is problematic for Big Data use cases that require more compute power, more storage capacity, more network bandwidth, and more data centers.

But as prices on IT infrastructure continue to fall, and as cloud service providers become the new data centers for large and small enterprises alike, Big Data will accelerate its ability to capture, store, manage, analyze, and share data from a wider and more diverse set of inputs.

Take healthcare as an example. To say that data is exploding in the healthcare space is stating the obvious. One recent study said healthcare data is growing faster than ever—nearly 50% annually.[4] That is due to a variety of factors, including regulatory mandates, digitization of healthcare business processes and workflows, the rise of applications such as telemedicine, and the insistence of healthcare practitioners on using their own personal devices to create and share information about their patients and their practices.

Healthcare is just one prime example of an enormous opportunity for improvements, touching on both patient benefits (in the form of improved medical outcomes and better long-term health) and commercial success for hospitals, practitioners, and insurers. Public health, for instance, is a fast-growing specialty that relies heavily on data from across the healthcare data grid, as are other exciting use cases, such as global telehealth practices and infectious disease control. And applications around medical imaging, such as PACS and DICOM, are in the early stages of both commercial opportunity and dramatic improvements in patient care. Managing radiology images and other unstructured data in a global healthcare grid is literally a life-saving development and helps realize the vision of universal healthcare.

Whether it's healthcare data, information about banking transactions, up-to-the-minute feeds on traffic congestion, or real-time insights into the health of common household appliances, Big Data is going to reshape the very nature of how organizations in all industries do business

and serve their commercial and consumer customers. For example:

- Analytics engines are going to become considerably more powerful, more affordable, and easier to use, often integrating with analytics engines of social media feeds and other consumer platforms.

- Consumers will make real-time decisions based on multiple data feeds shaped by independent—yet connected—analytics engines. This will expose them to more new products, services, suppliers, and relationships than ever—and they will not have to invest a dime of their own money to take advantage of those analytics engines.

- Delivering services to commercial and consumer clients will become faster and more personalized than ever, improving the user experience and driving enhanced customer satisfaction—leading to even more consumption.

As that happens, the Big Data trend we're currently experiencing will not seem so big after all, compared to what we will experience in just 5 to 10 years from now.

How big could it be? Consider the fact that the worldwide population stands at about 7.5 billion people in 2018. Now, how many "things" do each of us use every day that could have important information that we access or share? 10? 50? More?

Are Data Monopolies and Innovation Mutually Exclusive?

With so much attention and energy stemming from important developments, such as the internet, social media, and cloud computing, it should come as no surprise that "data monopolies" have emerged—disproportionately large collections of data held and managed by a handful of innovative, ambitious, and powerful enterprises.

The commercial success of companies like Facebook, Google, Twitter, Amazon Web Services, Alibaba, Tencent, and other industry titans are remarkable examples of the combination of smart business decisions, commitment to innovation and research, bold bets on new technologies, and a little bit of good luck. The fact that these and a relatively small number of other organizations collect, hold, and leverage massive amounts of data is not, by definition, something to fear. It is, of course, something to acknowledge; we must understand its implications.

After all, the broad collection of personal data undoubtedly sparks concern over privacy rights and confidentiality. That was a big driver behind the European Union's landmark General Data Protection Regulation (GDPR), which may influence and shape data privacy regulations in other regions of the world.

And, if data is the new global currency, it's not surprising that some people are raising concerns about "whoever controls the data has the power." But there is an important balance that needs to be struck between preserving the privacy of individual data and allowing businesses and governments to use data in a responsible, innovative way to better serve their constituents.

This is not a black-or-white issue. It's highly nuanced, with the need for a delicate balance to ensure that protecting data doesn't lock out innovation, or that harvesting data to create new goods and services doesn't imperil our individual identities and rights.

The tension among companies, governments, regulators, and consumers is inevitable, with each group trying to promote its own interests. But we need to keep in mind that this doesn't need to be an "I-win-you-lose" scenario.

We also need to understand the appropriate role of government in protecting individual rights and avoiding the deleterious effect of data monopolies. Our governmental agencies and regulators should avoid going down the path of heavy penalties and overly regulated data access and usage, opting instead for collaboration among all stakeholders to strike that delicate balance between commercial innovation and individual privacy of personal data.

In fact, I believe industry players will increasingly band together to collaborate on smarter, more efficient compliance protocols, and will team with government agencies, regulators, privacy advocates, and standards bodies to do so. While this may seem like an unusual alliance, I believe it is a more efficient and effective way to ensure responsible compliance measures without stifling innovation.

Protecting Our World and Our Data Against Digital Threats

As excited as I am about the possibilities of using all this data for the common good of our societies, I am also realistic about the growing footprint of cyber threats. Every year, the incidence, impact, and innovation of cyberattacks increase, and there's no reason to think they will abate in the coming years.

Again, data—and proper access to it—is key to ensuring that applications, services, and entire economies are safe and secure. If that sounds like "data that protects data," you are right. In order to protect our most important data—personally identifiable information, financial records, medical records, intellectual property, and more—we will need to develop new tools and services to discover and remediate data vulnerabilities.

Yes, threat intelligence and other subscription-based services help to identify threats and promote joint problem solving. But we need to do more. Too often, we have incident feeds that are limited in their impact or ability to promote remediation because they lack access to critical data about threat sources, points of attack, weak points at the network's edge, indicators of compromise, and more.

Again, the notion of balancing security needs with privacy expectations is relevant here. But it goes even farther. After all, there's nothing preventing us from locking down everything tighter and tighter—servers, mobile devices, applications, cloud services, and more. Doing so, however, seriously degrades the user experience and stifles innovation in data-driven goods and services.

Data must continue to flow, reliably and securely, through networks that are increasingly global and susceptible to the efforts of bad actors. Restricting data traffic to the point of choking it impacts our data economy locally, regionally, and globally. That's why the European Union is working on regulations to unlock the data held by European institutions, and the U.S. federal government has an open data initiative.

This concept is evident in the rise of data marketplaces, or data supermarkets, which enable new companies to build markets where public data is available. In these scenarios, specific users can easily combine that data with other, free data sets for improved insights and unearthing new business opportunities and societal value.

Ensuring this cross-border data flow is going to require a more collaborative effort among commercial, governmental, regulatory, and consumer bodies. In fact, to promote best practices in cybersecurity and to protect individuals, businesses, and governments, we must find ways to promote more data sharing and greater collaboration. Take terrorism, for example. Fighting both physical and digital terrorism requires cooperation among a vast network of agencies, organizations, and data sources, all around the world. We must continue to push for ways in which governments, particularly in areas of law enforcement and national defense, work together.

We should also strive to step up deliberations and consensus building around the application of international law and governing states in cyberspace, at both the UNGGE (UN Group of Governmental Experts) and bilateral levels. The recently mooted "Digital Geneva Convention" and other proposals need attention to ensure that states do not violate established norms in cyberspace. This is necessary, not only to identify and weed out cyber criminals, but also to protect and preserve individual liberties, particularly as many governments have built offensive cyber capabilities.

In an era of digital economies and digital lifestyles, we need to treat security as a core feature and requirement in all products and services, from the onset of the design phase. Our communities, economies, and constituents demand it, and it will be on our hands if we don't deliver it.

Conclusion

Our societies and our lives have been dramatically impacted by developments as basic as the discovery of fire, as well as simple and complex inventions such as the wheel and hydroelectric power. But I believe there is no development with greater long-term implications for our world as new applications for digital data.

Data is more than seemingly random collections of ones and zeros. It is information, currency, social fabric, safety, knowl edge, confidence, and innovation. When created, shared, and managed for the good of our communities, our families, and our industries, it acts as an exhilarating source of hope for a better world. And when combined with smart, collaboratively developed security safeguards, it gives our best and our brightest the opportunity to continue to use data in heretofore unimaginable ways for the common good.

Technological advancements may allow us to connect more things to each other, but the real power and beauty of a connected society is its ability to use grids of data to bring us closer together as people, as communities, and as nations.

---

[1]   "Building a European Data Economy," Digital Single Market, 2017

[2]   "Digital Industry: The True Value of Industry 4.0," Oliver Wyman and Marsh & McLennan, 2016

[3]   "Digital Transformation to Contribute More Than US$1 Trillion to Asia Pacific GDP By 2021," Microsoft and IDC, 2018

[4]   "Report: Healthcare Data is Growing Exponentially, Needs Protection," Healthcare Informatics, 2014

6

The Future of Cloud

Ann Johnson — Corporate Vice President, Cybersecurity Solutions, Microsoft

When I think of the future of cloud computing, I automatically think of my teenager. Then I smile. Broadly.

Cloud and my teenager have a lot in common, especially as they continue to grow in size and capabilities. The rate of their physical advancement is nothing short of astonishing, and every time you look around, they are doing amazing things that seemed inconceivable just a short time ago.

Just as I marvel at my teenager's rapid physical and intellectual development, the skyrocketing adoption rates and widespread embrace of cloud for mission-critical applications are nothing short of inspirational.

Of course, my teenager doesn't improve organizational agility, scale exponentially to keep up with new workloads, or come with a predictable subscription-pricing model. And as much as I hope and plan for a smooth transition to a lifetime of health, happiness, and a solid career path for my child, I truly don't have a clue what the future holds.

Not so for the cloud, however.

I don't need a crystal ball to predict what the future holds for the cloud. Oh, I may not be able to see around the corner for every technical nuance that will add more value to the cloud or to pinpoint the economic value of the cloud economy.

But I have seen the future of cloud, and it is bright. (Yes, even accounting for the harsh reality of cyber threats. I'll explain why in a bit.)

Good News for Business Leaders: Cloud Will Transform Your Organization

My vision of the cloud's future starts in the past—when enterprises began experimenting with cloud-based services, such as SaaS, or when employees began deploying early versions of shadow IT by storing work data on cloud-based file-sync-and-share sites. Organizations soon realized that the cloud was a good resource for doing things like application testing and development, or promoting cross-group collaboration without having to deploy dedicated infrastructure.

In this phase, I thought of the cloud as *helpful.* It was an interesting and opportunistic tactical resource that allowed organizations to reduce the cost and speed the time of delivering IT resources. It helped us keep a handle on FTEs that would otherwise need to be allocated to support new digital initiatives.

Our positive experiences in using the cloud gave us confidence that we could start using it for more important services and applications that were at the very heart of our day-to-day business activities. Soon, our most important applications were migrated to the cloud—building on the tactical benefits of first-generation cloud, becoming a strategic asset in increasing IT and organizational agility, and instantly scaling resources in reaction to new business opportunities or challenges.

Today, cloud has morphed from helpful to *important,* a strategic way to not only let us do more with less, but to ensure we can utilize our people for the things that make a difference.

In the future, however, cloud will take the next step. In fact, the cloud's utility, capability, and resilience are rapidly accelerating—due in no small part to a few key technologies I'll introduce shortly. Five or 10 years from now, we will look at the things that make us excited about cloud today as quaint. That's how much things will change.

In short, the future of cloud will complete its revolution from helpful and important to a difference-maker. The cloud of the near future will be *transformational.* It will open up all kinds of possibilities in the era of digital transformation that will not only improve IT and business efficiency, but will also change the way we work, live, and play.

The cloud of the future will make our organizations and our communities more connected, more useful, more agile, and, yes, more secure. It won't be easy, of course. It will take a continued commitment to experimentation, investment of time, money, and people; a willingness to change decades-long organizational and personal behavior; and an ability to create a vision based on what you can't yet see, but you can begin to imagine.

Brad Smith, Microsoft's President, has put the cloud's future into a framework that is aspirational, inspirational, and yet practical. In "A Cloud for Global Good," he talks in very pragmatic terms about the intersection of the cloud, emerging technologies, and all stakeholders in creating a society that benefits more people in new, transformative ways.

This vision will be supported by the integration of such technical trends as artificial intelligence (AI), machine learning, quantum computing, and mixed reality. Already, these factors are changing the very nature of the cloud, with bigger and better changes to come.

The Symbiosis of Cloud and AI

Not surprisingly, the global push for deeper insights into all that data flooding our networks and the cloud has driven organizations to turn to artificial intelligence. AI, as well as machine learning and other derivatives, is transforming what we can do with data, enabling us to make better decisions, with bigger impact, faster, and more reliably. And we have only scratched the surface.

In many ways, cloud is the ultimate sandbox for AI-enabled workloads and AI application development. The ability to handle massive and rapidly growing amounts of rich data makes the cloud an ideal laboratory for AI solutions.

Consider just a handful of possibilities still emerging or soon to take shape, thanks to the marriage of AI and the cloud:

- **Healthcare:** Hospitals, practitioners, and related organizations need to solve the interoperability problem that is still hampering the delivery of coordinated care. In the face of EMR mandates, a growing regulatory footprint, and the drive for essential applications like telemedicine and population health, healthcare organizations will turn more to the cloud and AI to use that mountain of data more efficiently. Or, just consider the possibility of predicting and preventing future pandemics before they take their devastating toll on our societies and our planet.

- **Retail:** Brick-and-mortar retailers and online sellers want to sharply reduce, or even eliminate, merchandise theft, fraud, and shrinkage—a $100 billion-a-year problem for physical stores and potentially much larger in the era of an increased swing toward e-commerce and omnichannel retail. More robust and turbo-charged analytics will allow them to link inputs from IP surveillance, inventory management systems, item-level RFID, and anti-theft packaging—all in the cloud.

- **Government:** Municipalities all around the world are striving to re-engineer how they deliver social services, such as identifying and remediating sources of domestic abuse. The marriage of the cloud's infinite computing horsepower and AI's deep insights into cascades of seemingly disconnected data makes that not only possible, but highly likely.

- **Financial services:** Can the industry eradicate insurance fraud and securities trading violations, absent mountains of paperwork or without trampling on individual privacy rights? The combination of cloud and AI will make it happen, all without necessitating tons of CapEx and on-premises systems development.

- **Education:** While there is no question that infusing technology into educational curricula and arming our teachers, staff, and students with technology have helped to bridge the much-discussed digital divide, more work needs to be done. The cloud is going to be the linchpin in bringing new educational opportunities to students in rural communities with historically limited access to transformative technologies, due to factors such as location, culture, or budget.

- **Transportation:** Airlines spend billions of dollars annually simply due to an inability to keep operations intact—and revenue flowing—during bad weather. Using an AI-hypercharged cloud will give them instantaneous knowledge about rapidly changing weather conditions, which will enable them to be more predictive in scheduling and routing, with less inconvenience and danger to passengers and work crews.

At the same time, AI is turning the cloud into a richer, more functional, more efficient environment for knowledge creation, collaboration, and utility. Over the next few years, cloud service providers and private cloud developers will benefit from AI in eye-popping ways.

For instance, AI will make cloud adoption and utilization more appropriate and efficient for regulated environments, particularly for demonstrating compliance and for spotting potential anomalies before they become regulatory headaches. Audit trails will become cleaner, more precise, and more efficient in the cloud through the use of AI and machine learning engines.

This is heady stuff—a true symbiosis. Not only will AI, machine learning, natural language processing, and cognitive computing advance rapidly because of the cloud, but the cloud will become richer, more robust, and more useful as its ecosystem is embedded with AI-related technology. It will be the ultimate win-win scenario.

Turbo-Charging the Cloud of the Future With Quantum Computing

Remember how excited we used to get when a new family of microprocessors came out, allowing us to have faster PCs and take advantage of new software functionality? We have Moore's Law to thank for much of that, as well as the very smart engineers at chip-maker and software companies.

Now, get ready for a quantum leap—pun intended—in power. Quantum computing is going to transform the cloud of the future with an infrastructure overhaul we've never seen before.

I won't get into the physics of qubits or what quantum computing will mean for your data center operations. What you need to know, however, is that the cloud is about to become even faster and more useful for applications that will be developed, deployed, and run in the cloud.

For instance, consider research laboratories looking for new ways to calculate nuclear binding energy. If you don't know anything about nuclear binding energy, you're not alone. But what you can probably surmise is that this is an application that is fed by massive amounts of data, and also needs more horsepower than ever to execute and turn that data into something actionable. Enter quantum computing. Already, researchers at Oak Ridge National Laboratory are using cloud-based quantum computers to conduct simulations and calculations that would otherwise have required untold investments in hardware, software, and FTEs, just in the experimental stage.

Of course, quantum computing has yet to become commercialized, but that's not far off. So, when the technology becomes mainstream, quantum-driven applications will find their home in the world's biggest data center—the cloud.

And you can only imagine what kind of mind-blowing advancements we'll see in cloud computing's performance and scalability when we introduce quantum computing into the cloud's infrastructure.

Consider the opportunities a quantum-spiked cloud environment can support:

- Development of new clean energy sources that are more cost-efficient and that produce better yields than current generations of wind and solar energy.

- Research into new food production processes that will literally wipe out global famines.

- Uncovering exciting new ways to predict, prevent, and treat potential health problems years before they surface.

- Delivering personalized, customized, affordable one-on-one education that is motivating to students and invigorating to teachers.

Quantum computing is going to be the new physical engine of the cloud. And the cloud will never be the same.

Securing the Cloud of the Future

I worry about security. A lot. And not just because "security" is in my job title. Because when I think of security, I again think of my teenager.

Parents are hardwired to worry about their children's security. Our worries evolve, become more complex and closer to the surface as the kids get older. Not surprisingly, I have broken out in a cold sweat more than once when I think about my teenager's security.

Yes, I worry all the time about my teenager's physical and emotional security. But I also have a measured sense of optimism and confidence about the future of digital security. And that's because I'm incredibly upbeat about what the cloud community of suppliers, agents, and users has been able to do with security, and what we are all likely to do as we move into the transformative future of the cloud.

Let's be clear: I'm no Pollyanna when it comes to the target-rich environment that the cloud has become and what it will be in the future.

Those of us who have studied technology are very familiar with Metcalfe's Law, which posits that the value of a network increases exponentially in relationship to the number of people attached to it. Think about the hundreds of millions of people using the cloud every day. Now, multiply that by whatever number you like. Five? Twenty? One hundred? Think about a much, much larger cloud community, measured not only in the number of users but also, more importantly, in the number and diversity of "things" connected to the cloud. The potential threat vectors presented by hackers, organized cyber-criminal gangs, and bad state actors over the next several years are breathtaking. Not breathtaking as in surveying the Alps, trekking through the rain forest, or roaming the American heartland. I mean breathtaking as in "gulp."

So, it's important for all of us to know what we'll be up against as we necessarily and deliberately rely and depend on the cloud.

With more and more data—and with more of that data deemed mission critical—created, stored, and managed in the cloud, bad actors will naturally take aim. Developments like the Internet of Things are a great example of why: The fact that the IoT represents a multi-trillion-dollar target makes it a gigantic target for the bad guys. This is becoming even more an issue as "smart things" are connected to the cloud without sufficient integrated security or as users fail to adopt proper security hygiene.

With such a broad attack surface, in an always-on environment, fraudsters have already exfiltrated data and caused cyber mischief. So it's up to us to do more. A lot more.

Already, some things are happening. One of the best is the imminent demise of passwords. Whether you store your dozens or hundreds of passwords in a spreadsheet, on sticky notes, or in a digital wallet, passwords no longer are sufficient cybersecurity defenses.

So passwords are giving way to biometrics and other steps in multi-factor authentication, making it harder for bad guys to penetrate our firewalls and grab our personally identifiable information, intellectual property, and digital assets of every format. Still, we cannot underestimate the intelligence, creativity, and determination of hackers, whether they are lone wolves (which they rarely are), part of digital crime syndicates, or state-sponsored bad actors.

They are coming after us in the cloud, and they will amp up their efforts in the cloud of the future. There's good news, however: We're all ramping up and fortifying our cloud security frameworks in anticipation of more penetration attempts.

First, a fundamental truism is that AI will be a big-step change for cloud security, which we desperately need.

Already, cloud environments are being fortified with machine language engines to analyze global data points in the hundreds of billions of cloud-based transactions. AI and machine learning normalize the data (remember, it's all unstructured, from spreadsheets and email to cat videos on Facebook) and push out attack indicators that are more meaningful, timely, and accurate. This will make our detection efforts far better—an order of magnitude better, in fact.

Using AI on top of those machine language engines will speed scenario modeling, giving already-stretched security analysts the ability to spot trends faster and make better decisions.

Then, you'll be able to take virtual reality technology and let your security experts—and your business users, too—visualize the threats in a consumer-friendly manner.

And none of that happens without a global cloud operating at hyper-scale speed.

Security is one area that really benefits from a large, wide, and deep cloud environment, because with the right analytics tools and enough processing power, global decision-making becomes easier and more accurate.

Cloud security also will become much more automated; again, machine language tools will drive huge process improvements in developing and deploying automated defenses. This will take considerable pressure off overworked security administrators and security operations centers to manually detect and thwart attempted intrusions as simple as garden-variety viruses or as insidious as malevolent ransomware.

In short, the cloud of the future is going to be a digital fortress, more robust and resilient than ever. Cloud security will be more intelligent, more automated, and more discerning, driven by advances in AI, machine learning, quantum computing, and other transformative technologies. Cloud security also will be designed and implemented with more of an eye toward a positive user experience, making security steps less obtrusive to the user and less likely to impact our business productivity or our personal enjoyment.

I'm not predicting that we'll never have breaches or that we won't have blaring headlines about loss of personally identifiable information. But I have seen the future of cloud, and it is secure.

Now, if I could only feel more confident about my teenager's security when I'm not there, too.

Conclusion

After my child was born, I was overwhelmed with a sense of amazement for that tiny life-form. But I was so consumed by my new child's everyday needs—eating, changing, bonding, sleeping—that I rarely allowed myself the luxury of dreaming about the future.

But as my child entered the exciting world of teenage-dom, I began to focus on what the future held and how my teenager would make a mark on the world.

I feel the same about cloud. In its formative years, I was thrilled by the many benefits of cloud computing to extend the resources of traditional IT organizations, to let business users take charge of their digital destinies, and to let billions of people connect, collaborate, and build global communities. In those days, that was enough to keep most of us really busy.

Now, as the cloud has evolved from a helpful business tool to an important resource, to the point where it is now transforming so much of our work and personal lives, I am exhilarated when I allow my imagination to run free and envision what the cloud of the future looks and feels like.

Maybe my teenager will even help shape the cloud of the future in some meaningful way. But I know one thing for sure: The cloud will change the world much, much more profoundly in the coming years than it already has changed mine.

Why and How We Must Change
Our Roles and Behaviors

7

Understanding the Exciting, Exponential, and Terrifying Future of Cybersecurity

Marc Goodman — Author and Global Security Advisor

I used to be a cop. It was a great job, and I loved it. Then one day, my policing career changed drastically—all because I knew how to use the spell-check feature in WordPerfect.

Yes, that impressive demonstration of technical acumen put me among the "digital elite" in policing back in the day, and it became the catalyst for a highly enjoyable and challenging career in cyber criminology. Now, as I spend my time researching and consulting about next-generation cybersecurity threats in the real world, I have to admit: I'm profoundly concerned. Concerned about the seemingly limitless ways we are dependent on technology and the equal number of ways it can all go wrong.

However, despite these worries, I remain optimistic about the future and our ability to make significant strides in the battle against cybercrime. In order to get there, a few things need to happen, which we'll cover in this chapter:

First, you must **understand the enemy**—specifically, the threats, the vulnerabilities, and the criminals.

Next, you must **acknowledge and evaluate the traditional, tried-and-not-so-true reactions** of executives and boards of directors to cyberattacks.

Finally, you need to find and exploit the secrets that will help you **change the balance of power** between the good guys (you) and the bad guys (the ones robbing you) by throwing out the old playbook on cybersecurity and beginning anew.

The Power of Exponentials

Learning about the power of exponentials can change your view of the threats, your responsibilities, and most importantly your cybersecurity strategies for the future.

What do I mean by exponentials? Exponential technologies—computers, robotics, AI, synthetic biology—all obey Moore's Law and thus double in their capabilities every year or so. To conceptualize what these rapid changes look like, business leaders have devised a number of terms to describe the phenomenon, including non-linear thinking, inflection points, hockey-stick curves, or force multipliers.

Conversely, linear point-to-point advancement of actions and developments is comforting to us. It's reassuring to believe that we have some knowledge—or perhaps even some control—of where we are headed. Linear expectations and predictions are comforting, but they are dead wrong when applied to technology, a serious mistake that has direct implications on how we approach cyber risk.

Understand Your Enemies: They're Different Than You Think

Most organizations look at recent attacks on their information assets and usually think linearly. "Yes, DDoS attacks are increasing, and so are phishing attempts," the CISO may tell the CEO or the board. "But we're on top of it, and here's what we're doing." In other words, most organizations see the problem as having a linear path, requiring a linear approach to solutions. Spend slightly more money on malware prevention, conduct more training on security hygiene practices, have users change their passwords more often. Last year the problem was this, now it's that, so let's plot our defenses based on the fact that threats are increasing in an orderly linear fashion.

Wrong. Linear thinking about threats and enemies must give way to exponential thinking, because the pace of everything is accelerating, and it's doing so way, way faster than we had imagined. Linear thinkers believe autonomous vehicles are pure hype and will never take off. Exponential thinkers know they are already here.

When it comes to the bad guys, there's a big problem. They are thinking and acting exponentially, while we're defending ourselves linearly. Moore's Law means nothing to them. They're Moore's Outlaws.

The second thing to keep in mind about the impact of exponentials on cyber risk is the rate at which automation is taking place. You want to talk about a force multiplier? Automation in its many forms—algorithms, scripts, machine learning, and natural language systems—is creating cyber crime at scale. They're using our smart tools against us in order to scale their malevolence at a rate far greater than we could have imagined. Well, start imagining.

There is a ton of software out there to automate cyberattacks. Distributed denial-of-service (DDoS) is a great example: It's automated mischief. They've even weaponized the cloud—*our cloud*—to execute DDoS attacks and other digital warfare.

The automation of cyberattacks represents a disturbing and highly problematic development, adding mightily to the arsenal of cyber criminals, enabling bad actors to fully automate even the most complicated of crimes, such as hijacking and ransom offenses, combined with great effect the explosion of ransomware attacks in recent years.

Holding someone or something hostage for money has been around for millennia, but the analog version of ransom-based crimes took a lot of work. You needed to identify the target and study their movements, then hire some guys with guns, stalk and grab the victim, stow them away, reach out to the family, warn them not to contact the police, agree on a location for the money exchange, line up a pigeon to actually pick up the money instead of you, arrange a getaway vehicle, and hope you're not caught.

Exponentials in the form of automated threats make it much, much easier. They're taking a highly complex crime and encoding it in software. It's pretty easy to do—you don't need a PhD in computer science—and it's really cost efficient. You can buy a ransomware kit on the Dark Web for about $10, and the average ransomware payout is pegged at $163,000. Now that's what I call a return on investment.

And there's no limitation on how much ransomware you can launch. Again, exponentials are at work.

Now, let's raise the stakes way, way higher—the Internet of Things. Talk about a potential bonanza for the bad guys thinking and acting exponentially. Actually, the IoT itself is a great object lesson in exponentials. Look at the exponential growth in the number and diversity of connected things; tell me that doesn't look like a classic hockey stick. And the incremental economic value of IoT is going to run into the trillions of dollars. Think that's not an inviting target?

I call this the third dimension of cyber threats. In the beginning, we had computers. They were these big, ugly, gray boxes shoved into climate-controlled data centers or parked on someone's desk. Then we got mobile—notebooks, tablets, and smartphones. And finally, we realized we could put a chip in everything. TV used to be a vacuum tube, now it's a smart, ultra-high-resolution display with more intelligence than a supercomputer.

Computing is now fully mobile and ubiquitous, and all those endpoints are vulnerable. Your kids' toys have become turned against them; chips for speech synthesis and cloud connectivity have become ways to triangulate your child's location by truly evil people. We're going to add 50 billion new devices—probably more—to the internet by 2020, and it's all being done insecurely.

Is there anything you can do about it? Read on.

Consider Your Biases and Your Actions: It's Time for a Refresh

For CISOs, C-suite executives, and board members to defeat an increasingly sophisticated and determined cyber adversary, new ideas and dramatically different approaches are necessary. Forget about thinking outside the box. In fact, throw the box out. You'll need to think outside a geo-

desic dome embedded in a kaleidoscope. That's how many new angles, dimensions, and perspectives you'll need.

One thing I learned many years ago when I got into law enforcement was to try and understand the mindset of the person I was trying to catch. I was taught great lessons about profiling and getting inside the head of the bad guys, and the veterans on the force shared great knowledge with me about suspects' "tells" in their behavior and appearance.

Not surprisingly, there has been a lot of effort trying to get into the minds of cyber criminals: What makes them tick? What are their motivations? What are their fears? All great questions. Unfortunately, there aren't a lot of easy answers.

Remember the popular meme of the early days of the internet: "On the internet, no one knows you're a dog." Well, when you're being attacked, you are rarely sure who is doing the attacking, so pondering the mindset and motivation of the attacker doesn't do you a lot of good. Bits and bytes are flying at your corporate network, and you're not really sure if it's a competitor, a member of an organized cyber-crime ring, a disgruntled employee, or a state actor.

Here's where our new friends—exponentials—come into play. My experience has taught me that many business executives and boards still cling to the old stereotype of the attacker profile. They too often think it's some pimply kid in his parents' basement. He (or on rare occasions, she) is imagined as a lone wolf with social problems or feelings of inadequacy in traditional institutions such as schools or businesses. I'm here to tell you: Come to that conclusion at your own risk.

You must discard those stereotypes and adopt a new mindset of your own that is radically different from that most executives have historically used. You must consider that your latest cyber adversary is fully capable of, and committed to, taking down your organization. The sooner you accept that notion, the sooner you'll be on your way toward a more relevant and potent cybersecurity strategy.

Another example of exponential thinking you should employ in an effort to break down old biases and consider new actions is the notion of fear. (Not your fear, the cyber criminal's fear.)

Your strategies should not be built on ways to heighten their fear of being caught and prosecuted; they won't work. And the reason they won't work is devilishly simple: The criminals have nothing to lose.

There's a very pragmatic reason for that by my own estimations: The chances of a cyber criminal being arrested, prosecuted, and jailed is something along the lines of one in a million. Literally.

The chance that they're going to be caught and punished is the exception rather than the rule, due to the nature of international law. A cop in Milwaukee simply can't arrest somebody in Russia, France, or China—and all cybercriminals know this. They do not fear you, your defense strategies, your detection tools, law enforcement, or the criminal justice system.

Finally, business executives—and especially corporate boards and board members—need to adopt an exponentially different posture when it comes to taking responsibility for cybersecurity.

First, let's acknowledge that, while boards are made up of very smart and successful people, they are not digital natives, for the most part. They are probably 55 to 70 years old, on average, and have not grown up in business or in life attached to digital devices. Many of them are not up to speed on technology, so they rely on "trusted partners" to filter questions of technology for them. That might be the

CISO, CIO or a technical consultant, but the result is the same: They are counting on the tech people to ensure the organization is cybersecure.

That has to change. If board members lack the skill set to ask the right questions or to push back on issues they don't understand, they need to find a way to get those skills into the boardroom. Remember: Even if board members want to ask probing questions, the CISO has been known to push back. They may make their case before the board, but the CISO often answers board members' seemingly elementary questions with buzzwords and industry speak. And because the board members don't want to come off as uniformed, they don't probe further and assume all is well.

Instead, board members need to do more to understand their cyber risk posture and exposure. They need to educate themselves and not be intimidated by technical experts who may throw around buzzwords to block them.

Boards also should consider establishing a dedicated cybersecurity committee with a tech-savvy board member as its chair. After all, boards have committees for compensation, governance, and audit. Isn't cybersecurity just as essential a board responsibility?

Another idea—and this one is radical, not because it's so strange but because it's so rarely used—is the notion that boards and senior executives need to practice their responses and reactions to data breaches. All companies have been hit with data breaches; some know about it, some don't. But boards must lead the way in preparing for that eventuality so they can limit the financial, operational, legal, and brand damage that often occurs.

I don't mean having a cybersecurity response playbook or a disaster recovery protocol that gets dusted off and updated once a year. I'm talking about digital war games.

As we all know, these are routinely done in other industries, markets, and walks of life. Law enforcement and the military practice them all the time, often with terrifyingly real approaches that often make it nearly impossible to tell if the scenario is real or simulated. Of course, the airline industry does this routinely. Do you think an airline pilot suddenly asks himself after 10 years of flying, "Hmmm … I wonder what would happen if an engine were to go out at 35,000 feet over the Pacific?" Of course not—they practice for this event all the time.

Organizations need to run exercises that include members of the board, CEO, CISO, general counsel, heads of marketing and sales, CFO, and investor relations team. The board should actually run the exercise and take it very seriously. Actions should be monitored, recorded, evaluated, and shared with team members, and corrective measures should be taken to address inadequacies.

Reasons for Some Optimisim

I've talked a lot about threats, challenges, roadblocks, and hurdles. Many of these have been magnified and spiked in urgency, frequency, and impact as a result of the concept of exponentials. And you'll remember early on in this chapter that I expressed my deep concern over what's happening. I think you'll agree I have good reason to think this way when it comes to cyber threats.

But remember: I'm also very optimistic about what the future holds, especially to all the positive benefits technologies will undoubtedly yield to the world of medicine, education and the global economy. While I have highlighted many of the threats from cyber threat actors, there is also room for hope, given the tremendous amount of attention these threats are receiving. I am heartened by the increasing understanding I am seeing and hearing from many executives, board members, and technical experts about addressing the issue of cybersecurity.

In particular:

1. The questions I'm being asked by executives and CISOs are much smarter, more focused, and more results-oriented. Many of you reading this chapter have come to grips with the understanding that legacy approaches bring legacy results—and that the bad guys are playing with algorithms while too many cybersecurity defenses were designed in an era of mainframe computers.

2. There is a heightened sense of urgency on nearly everyone's part. Some of it is motivated by a desire to avoid banner headlines in *The Wall Street Journal* or having executives paraded in yellow jumpsuits out of federal courthouses. But whatever the motivation, everyone is taking this very, very seriously and has a wide-open appreciation of the heightened stakes.

3. Organizations are starting to come around to the sophistication, intelligence, creativity, and determination of cyberattackers. Stereotypes about attackers' mindsets and motivations, so deeply rooted in digital folklore and some really bad movies, are finally melting away.

4. There is a growing understanding and acknowledgement that being cyber-secure isn't about having the best technology—as important as that is—but it's more about exponentially changing the way we think and behave collectively.

A Few New Rules for Changing the Rules

One of the biggest areas of concern among both technical and business leaders is the startling, yawning chasm between the number of cybersecurity professionals needed today and over the coming years and the actual number of digital experts available to fill those positions. Some estimates put this gap at 1 million people by 2020, while others think it may be several times higher. I encourage you to plan for the high end of that shortfall range—and then increase it.

We also know, from the basic economic theorem of supply and demand, that salaries of cybersecurity professionals are rising much faster than IT industry norms. That means that even the people you have on staff—men and women you've already invested in heavily—are being approached and poached by headhunters as you read this. That also means that even if you are fortunate to hire good people, chances are you will not be able to keep them too long.

Organizations therefore need to take dramatic steps to ensure they have a pipeline of talent constantly coming to their firms to fill these positions. I'm not just talking about upping your college graduate recruiting budget for computer security majors (although you should certainly do that).

Re-evaluate how you identify candidates. I'm talking about rethinking the profile of the kinds of people you hire and train for those roles. For instance, think about the kinds of people who succeed in any organization: What qualities do they possess? Intelligence. Work ethic. Communications skills. A willingness to ask "dumb" questions. An ability to learn from mistakes.

These and other qualities are not necessarily limited to computer science grads from MIT or Berkeley. Think about recruiting people with these demonstrated skills from non-traditional corners of your organization. People like field service engineers or accounts payable clerks. Or truck drivers and copywriters. There are tons of people in your organizations with the requisite personal attributes and mindsets—if not necessarily the deep technical expertise—that can be harnessed to fill that growing gap. Don't worry. I'm sure you'll have a ton of great security engineers who will be at the top of their field when it comes to knowledge about tunneling or reverse malware engineering. But you're going to need a lot more assets and greater diversity of those assets. So think exponentially.

Focus on the user experience of security. Another part of cybersecurity that needs an exponential shift in mindset is the cybersecurity user experience and design. This is an area that is ripe for innovation, if for no other reason than so much of what has passed for security alert software has been woefully inadequate.

How many times do your employees get some pop-up message on their screens while they're looking on the internet or working on email, and what they see is ugly and confusing? The design of security warnings is abysmal and painful. Users too often default out of the windows because the warnings get in the way of them doing their work, and they don't see why it's a big deal to let the warning slide.

It's not enough that our security protocols work in theory—they have to work where the rubber meets the road at the end of a keyboard used by somebody in your company in sector 4G. And that requires a good understanding of human behavior, something infrequently accounted for in organizational cybersecurity strategies. Setting a policy is only the first step. Making sure it is reasonable, understood, and followed is a whole different ball of wax.

Rethink and re-architect the organizational chart. Lastly, rethink your organizational approach to cybersecurity by getting rid of whatever you call the cybersecurity department on your organizational chart. When you put a nice, neat box around cybersecurity, you're sending a message: These are the ninjas of cybersecurity. They have the magic potion, the elixir that will defeat the cyber thieves. It's their concern, not yours.

Throughout this chapter, I have argued that we need a much broader and more radical way of thinking about your cyber defense team, one that takes into account the exponential nature of our world.

Cybersecurity needs to be crowdsourced to include all hands on deck. It's not just the responsibility of a few dozen or even a few hundred technical experts locked up in your IT organization.

Cybersecurity is not just "their" problem. It's an "everybody" problem. It's not a department; it's an attitude. If you don't expand your idea of how to solve the problem by ensuring that everyone has skin in the game, you are on your way to losing the game. And the stakes of losing, already quite high, are about to become astronomical.

The good news is, there is much we can do to protect ourselves and our organizations from digital threats. The first, and perhaps most important, step is to begin to think exponentially—because in the age of Moore's Law, every minute counts.

8

Dealing With the Evolving Adversary Mindset

James C. Trainor — Senior Vice President, Cyber Solutions Group, Aon

The views presented in this chapter are my own and not those of the Federal Bureau of Investigation.

Incident #1: On Nov. 24, 2014, employees at Sony Pictures opened their computers to the sound of gunfire, scrolling threats, and a skeletal image now commonly referred to as the "Screen of Death." By the time the cyberattack was over, more than 3,200 computers and 830 servers were destroyed, highly confidential files were released worldwide, and 47,000 Social Security numbers were compromised.[1]

Incident #2: In 2010, the FBI announced that hackers were using passwords and other security measures to illegally transfer thousands of dollars at a time, from bank account to bank account. The attack, known as GameOver Zeus, affected hundreds of thousands of computers to the tune of more than $100 million.[2]

Incident #3: In the Fall of 2015, a hacker impersonating a phone company employee gained access to the private email account of John O. Brennan. At the time, Brennan happened to be the director of the U.S. Central Intelligence Agency.[3]

Incident #4: In January 2018, a former U.S. National Security Agency contractor, named Hal Martin, pleaded guilty to stealing a massive amount of confidential security information, including NSA cyber-hacking tools. While there are ongoing questions about the plea agreement, there is no question that the stolen tools were used in the devastating WannaCry ransomware attack in May of 2017.[4]

Incident #5: In September 2016, a Kosovo citizen named Ardit Ferizi was sentenced to 20 years in a U.S. prison. He pled guilty to accessing a protected computer without authorization to steal personal identifiable information from approximately 1,300 individuals, including members of the military and government personnel. Ferizi stole the information with the goal of handing it over to ISIS.[5]

What these five incidents have in common is that they caused extensive financial and reputational damage and/or had the potential to significantly compromise a country's national security.

Different Types of Attacks

Here's what they *don't* have in common: the motivation and mindset of the perpetrators. Each of these incidents represents a different category of cyberattack that businesses, governments, and law enforcement agencies must be prepared to prevent and address. These are:

1. **Nation-State:** North Korea targeted Sony Pictures because of the pending release of a comedy called *The Interview.*

2. **Criminal:** GameOver Zeus was one of many criminal attacks that earned the alleged mastermind, Evgeniy M. Bogachev, a $3 million bounty from the FBI for his capture.

3. **Hacktivist:** The Brennan attack was the work of an organization called Crackas with Attitude (CWA). The five alleged perpetrators ranged in age from 15 to 24.

4. **Insider:** The Hal Martin attack is viewed by many in law enforcement as a potential catastrophic event because it makes all potential adversaries more dangerous.

5. **Terrorist:** Ferizi was captured after posting a tweet that stated, "We are extracting confidential data and passing on your personal information to the soldiers of the khilafah, who soon with the permission of Allah will strike at your necks in your own lands!"

Understanding the Evolving Adversary Mindset

I spent more than 20 years at the U.S. Federal Bureau of Investigation, and in my last role as Assistant Director of the Cyber Division in Washington, D.C., I led the team that developed and implemented the FBI's national strategy to combat cybercrime. One of the cases I worked on was the Sony attack, which was historic for many reasons.

For one, it involved a wide range of malicious acts against Sony, including intrusion, destruction, and threats to employees and the public. The government was able to respond quickly. Within days, the FBI identified the perpetrators and, within six weeks, President Obama signed an executive order issuing sanctions against three North Korean organizations and 10 individuals.

Responding to this type of breach required an understanding of the legal and regulatory environment, the technical environment, privacy issues, media-related issues, and more. Preventing a breach of this size and scope is just as challenging, if not more so. It has been difficult enough to understand the mindsets of each of the individual types of adversaries. It becomes even harder when these adversaries have multiple motivating factors and sponsors, such as government-backed attacks for both profit and geo-political warfare.

Another reason I consider the Sony attack to be historic is because it portends what we can expect in the future, where there is a blending of mindsets, behaviors, motivations, and techniques from all types of adversarial actors. We are already seeing examples across the globe from various nation-state actors—principally from North Korea, but also from Russia and China.

At the same time, those who would do harm for profit, politics, or principle are becoming more sophisticated all the time, with easier and cheaper access to tools and technologies. We are even seeing the emergence of cybercrime-as-a-service. And we are giving our adversaries a larger potential attack surface, with innovations such as the Internet of Things (IoT), the growth of big data analytics, and our exponential use of massive social media platforms.

Responding to the Evolving Environment

As the threat landscape evolves, and as it becomes harder to distinguish between a threat from a nation-state and a threat from a criminal enterprise, the onus is on all of us to be better prepared so we can prevent attacks and respond quickly and appropriately when there is a breach. Of course, that is much easier said than done.

In my experience, many company executives feel that cybersecurity is too broad and all-encompassing, and that it can be overwhelming. They don't know where to start; they have a hard time measuring the return on investment for cybersecurity; and they are concerned about escalating costs. An exception to this is companies that have experienced a cyberattack. Those are the companies that have a sense of great urgency and purpose.

All of us reading this book, all of us who are passionate about protecting our future and making it safe to navigate the Digital Age—we all need to adopt a similar sense of urgency. Our adversaries are getting bolder and more sophisticated. We have gone from Sony, where there was an attack on freedom of expression and business operations, to attacks on democratic processes and elections. It won't stop there. We are seeing an increase in ransomware, extortion and, eventually, we can expect to see more attacks that threaten the loss of human life.

Given the changes in the mindsets, motivations, tools, technologies, and behaviors of our adversaries, how do we respond? What are the steps we can take now to be better prepared, to be true to the exciting promise of the Digital Age, while recognizing and fighting back against the inherent dangers of an evolving adversary mindset?

I suggest we start by focusing on these key areas:

Connectivity: As we expand our connectivity, we also expand our attack surfaces. Adversaries can harness IoT devices as botnets, causing heightened concern over a potential distributed denial-of-service (DDoS) attack on critical infrastructure. One company has warned about a massive botnet that is recruiting IoT devices to create a cyber storm that could take down the internet.[6] This is not to say we shouldn't move forward with IoT innovation. But we must be aware of increased vulnerabilities. Securing IoT devices is different from securing traditional PCs, laptops, and smartphones. We must quickly get smart about how we use these devices and how we secure them. Do we really want to create an army of toasters that our adversaries can use to attack us?

Regulatory/Legal: The risk of fines, negative publicity, and other penalties tends to be a fairly strong motivator for organizations to focus on cybersecurity with a greater degree of urgency. In Europe, we are seeing that compliance with General Data Protection Regulation (GDPR) is forcing organizations to do a full assessment of their security profiles to ensure a variety of protections. These include providing data breach notifications, anonymizing data to protect privacy, safely handling the transfer of data across borders, and others. It is important to recognize that while GDPR is a product of and requirement within the European Union, it impacts any company around the world that possesses the personal data of EU residents. This is a good thing. In the U.S., questions are being raised whether any regulations—and what kind of regulations— could have been used to either prevent or mitigate the massive Equifax cyberattack that affected more than 140 million Americans. It is the hope of many that Equifax turns out to be a cautionary tale of what can happen when there is a lack of government oversight.[7]

Vulnerability awareness: Ransomware attacks are continuing to grow, with many instances still going unreported or underreported. We are also seeing that spear phishing and social engineering tactics are getting more crafty, more targeted, and more advanced. In 2017, attackers deployed new spear phishing tactics against organizations across all sectors, including major technology companies and government agencies. Hackers tricked employees at international energy companies into opening documents to harvest usernames and passwords, granting access to power switches and computer networks. Fraudsters targeted UK students with an email scam to steal personal and banking details. At the same time, the spread of misinformation continues, and data integrity attacks are on the rise—impacting the market value of companies and our ability to respond to natural disasters, and influencing public opinion.

Disrupting the Attack Lifecycle

This is also an important time to invest in cybersecurity education, awareness, and training. The more we understand about how attacks work, the better job we can do at lessening their impact—regardless of the motivation and mindset of the adversary, and regardless of our roles and responsibilities within our organizations. The way attackers work is to follow a series of six stages that comprise what we refer to as the "attack lifecycle."[8] These are:

1. **Reconnaissance:** This is the planning stage, during which attackers research, identify, and select targets.

2. **Weaponization and delivery:** Attackers determine which methods to use to deliver malicious payloads, such as automated tools, exploit kits, and spear phishing attacks with malicious links or attachments.

3. **Exploitation:** Attackers deploy an exploit against a vulnerable application or system, typically using an exploit kit or weaponized document. This allows the attack to gain an initial entry point.

4. **Installation:** Once they've established a foothold, attackers install malware to conduct further operations, such as maintaining access, persistence, and escalating privileges.

5. **Command and control:** With malware installed, attackers then actively control the system, instructing the next stages of the attack. They establish a command channel to communicate and pass data between infected devices and their own infrastructures.

6. **Actions on the objective:** With control, persistence, and ongoing communication, adversaries can act upon their motivations. This could be data exfiltration, destruction of critical infrastructure, theft, extortion, criminal mischief, or some combination of all the above.

Being able to leverage knowledge about the attack process provides an advantage for defenders because attackers must be successful at each step to succeed. The defender only has to "see and stop" the adversary at any stage to cause the adversary to fail. To be able to do this successfully, an organization needs to have a holistic approach to addressing cyber risks. In general terms, this includes:

- **Increase visibility.**

- **Reduce the attack surface.**

- **Prevent known threats.**

- **Discover and prevent unknown threats.**

- **Quantify risk.**

- **Transfer risk.**

When discussing cybersecurity, I often compare it to healthcare. If I eat well, exercise, don't smoke, and see the doctor regularly, I reduce the likelihood of getting sick. But we all get sick, and that's when health insurance comes in to cover the costs associated with an illness. The same thing applies in cyber. If an organization performs the first four steps successfully, then a safety net of cyber insurance can help mitigate catastrophic financial consequences.

How do you accomplish these objectives? Disrupting the attack lifecycle and reducing risk relies on a combination of technology, people, and processes.

- **The technology** must be highly automated and integrated across all network environments, including fixed, mobile, physical, on-premises, and cloud, from the perimeter to data centers, branches, endpoints, and IoT devices.

- **The people** must receive ongoing security-awareness training and be educated in best practices to minimize the likelihood of an attack progressing past the first stage.

- **The processes** and policies must be in place and enforced for rapid remediation should an attacker successfully progress through the entire attack lifecycle.

Preparing for the Future

One of the ideas that recurs throughout this book is the maxim that cybersecurity is everyone's responsibility, as discussed in chapter 10. Investing in cybersecurity education, training, and awareness is a necessary step in that direction. But there is more work to be done.

As participants in a global economy, as nations, as individual companies, and even as individuals, we can all create an atmosphere of cybersecurity cooperation and collaboration. A model for the future, at the policy level, is the U.S.-China cybersecurity agreement, which was signed in 2015 and renewed in 2017. Under terms of that pact, the countries have agreed to refrain from state-sponsored cyberattacks on one another's private-sector companies.

As organizations and institutions—companies, academia, government agencies—we can all be more proactive in sharing threat intelligence so we can prevent attacks and react in real time to minimize the damage of successful attacks. As individuals, we can take advantage of cybersecurity education and training to ensure that we are following best practices, based on our roles, responsibilities, and vulnerabilities within our organizations.

For example, I strongly encourage board members to be aware of and adhere to the five principles of cyber-risk oversight developed by the National Association of Corporate Directors in the U.S. These are:

1. Directors need to understand and approach cybersecurity as an enterprise-wide risk management issue, not just an IT issue.

2. Directors should understand the legal implications of cyber risks as they relate to their company's specific circumstances.

3. Boards should have access to cybersecurity expertise, and discussions about cyber-risk management should be given regular and adequate time on board meeting agendas.

4. Directors should set the expectation that management will establish an enterprise-wide cyber-risk management framework with adequate staffing and budget.

5. Board-management discussions about cyber risk should include identification of which risks to avoid, which to accept, and which to mitigate or transfer through insurance, as well as specific plans associated with each approach.

Conclusion

We live in interesting times. Each day, it seems, brings headlines of a new cyber-attack or threat (see graphic on page 57). In 2016 alone, the FBI's Internet Crime Complaint Center (IC3) received nearly 300,000 complaints.[9] In February 2018, the Center for Strategic and International Studies estimated that global losses of cybercrime in 2016 were approximately $600 billion. This is an increase from $445 billion in 2015.[10]

Exacerbating the challenge is the reality that the mindsets of our adversaries are a moving target. While adversarial motivations and intentions may have been identifiable in the past, we are now dealing with an environment where there is a melding of the mindsets. What may seem like a cybercrime for profit, or a hacktivist attack, may in reality turn out to be a state-sponsored event or an attack initiated by a company insider.

Recognizing that the motivations of our adversaries are evolving is an important step in the right direction. It helps us all to be more aware. This awareness should also translate into a professional and personal responsibility to take action: Whether that is to undertake cybersecurity training, to hire experts for board meetings, or even just to make sure we are using two-factor authentication.

We can't always predict criminal behavior. But we can be educated, aware, and proactive in making sure that we are doing everything we can to mitigate and minimize risk. As we look to the future of cybersecurity in the Digital Age, that should be our mindset.

---

1 "The Attack on Sony," 60 Minutes, April 12, 2015

2 "GameOver Zeus Botnet Disrupted," FBI.gov, June 2, 2014

3 "Student pleads guilty in hacking ring that targeted CIA Director John Brennan," Politico.com, Jan. 6, 2017

4 "A Stolen NSA Tool Is Being Used in a Global Cyberattack," The Atlantic, May 12, 2017

5 "ISIL-linked Hacker Sentenced to 20 Years in Prison," The United States Attorney's Office, Eastern District of Virginia, Sept. 23, 2016

6 "New botnet could take down the Internet in 'cyberstorm,'" says Checkpoint, Internet of Business, Oct. 23, 2017

7 "Equifax Breach Puts Credit Bureaus' Oversight in Question," NPR, Sept. 21, 2017

8 Lockheed Martin has registered the term: Cyber Kill Chain®, which describes a similar framework in seven phases: Reconnaissance, Weaponization, Delivery, Exploitation, Installation, Command and Control, Actions on Objectives

9 "2016 Internet Crime Report," FBI Internet Crime Complaint Center (IC3), June 2016

10 "Economic Impact of Cybercrime: At $600 Billion and Counting—No Slowing Down," Center for Strategic and International Studies, Feb. 21, 2018

TYPES OF ATTACKS AND DATA

Types of Data

- Customer Information
- Intellectual Property
- Legal Information
- Merger & Acquisition
- Military Technology
- PII, PCI, PHI
- Policy Information
- Trade Secrets

Types of Attacks

- Business Email Compromise (BEC)
- DDoS
- Destructive Attacks
- Doxing
- Espionage
- Extortion
- Ransomware
- Theft of Data
- Website Defacements

9

The Evolving Role of the CISO: From Risk Manager to Business Enabler

Justin Somaini — Chief Security Officer, SAP

One of the first things I do in my role as Chief Security Officer is reach out to the heads of other departments to find out how I can integrate myself into their operations. In one more extreme instance, I asked if I could join the sales department on a part-time basis. Not as a salesman, thank goodness, but in my role as CSO. The head of sales was a bit perplexed, but agreed. For a year I participated in sales meetings and even went on sales calls.

I learned about conversion rates and vicariously experienced the unimaginable thrill of closing a big sale and the crushing pain of losing one. By the time the year was up, I had a solid understanding of how our sales organization worked and, perhaps even more importantly, I had developed close working relationships with a number of key people in the department.

You may be thinking: You're a chief security officer. Why would you spend a year in the sales department, even part time, when your job is to protect the company from security breaches and ensure that it remains compliant?

I would answer that merely protecting the company from security breaches and ensuring compliance is actually not a very good description of my job, nor the job of my peers and colleagues around the globe. Not in 2017, not in 2018, and certainly not in the years ahead.

The role of the CSO, or as many prefer, the chief information security officer (CISO), has come a long way in the 20-plus years since the CISO title was first created. Today it is evolving at a faster pace than ever before. The CISO now must identify himself or herself as a business enabler and, just as critically, he or she must be recognized in the same way by others—from the boardroom to the executive suite to the various lines of business and departments that keep the organization focused, functioning, and moving forward on a day-to-day basis.

How could I enable sales if I didn't understand sales? Or marketing, human resources, finance? How can I enable the business if I don't have a firm understanding of how the business works, what motivates the teams, what the corporate culture feels like in the trenches?

These may seem like fairly obvious questions, but they are not necessarily the questions most CISOs have asked in the past. Looking to the future, I believe these are the kinds of questions that will increasingly define how CISOs operate. They will also be a factor in who fills those key roles and how security practitioners interact and collaborate within their departments and across the organizations at large. If the CISO is empowered to enable the business, he or she must speak the language of business and be conversant with the basic activities and values of the business.

The Transition to Business Enabler

The CSO is a continuously evolving role that drives a continuously evolving skill set. In order to be successful, practitioners need to be proactive in maturing the role as well as themselves. Twenty years ago, the job was basically to manage the firewall and secure the perimeter. You didn't have to know much about what you were protecting, as long as you knew which technology solutions would do the best job of keeping the bad guys at bay.

The world today is much different. Digital technologies and connectivity have infused every aspect of the business. This elevates risk, but it also elevates the value and importance of the cybersecurity function. The CISO increasingly has a seat in the executive suite because security is no longer just about risk; it's also about competitive differentiation.

The most fundamental way in which security can act as a differentiator is by removing hurdles to enable and empower the sale of products and services to the customer. When I think of my objective at SAP, it is to have a secure company and a secure customer. It's pretty straightforward, yes. But making it happen is anything but simple.

For example, security should be able to empower faster, more agile and more reliable product development. That is one

reason organizations are more inclined to include security early on in development processes and why we are seeing the rise of SecDevOps. In addition, security must support business and technology innovation—think Big Data analytics, the Internet of Things, social networking, and machine learning, to name a few—to enable true competitive differentiation and potential market disruption.

There are other ways to drive business enablement. If we build better, more reliable security protections into solutions than our competitors do, we can build customer loyalty and help retain existing customers. If we can create security solutions that are seamlessly aligned with the company's direction, we can create differentiated products, services, and potential revenue streams. For example, the company comes out with a new service that offers advanced security monitoring and alerts for an additional $10 a month. If we can drive operational efficiencies and effectiveness, we can help the organization accelerate speed to market and reduce overall costs.

The Evolution of the CISO

How do we get there from here? What are the skill sets that will differentiate the best CISOs from the rest? What do business leaders and board members expect from their CISOs, now and in the future? How can we ensure that we are truly enabling the business, while still performing our fundamental responsibility of having a secure company and a secure customer?

I suggest we start by focusing on three specific areas:

1. **Ensuring that we are extremely disciplined in the things that are known:** This should encapsu-

late the basic tasks of the cybersecurity domain—controls, vulnerability scanning, patch management, application security, and more. We need to be absolute professionals in these tasks and functions. If you can't deliver on the basics, you can't deliver, period.

2. **Becoming proficient in addressing today's more expansive expectations:** For example, we can talk about risk management, but we need to actually define it and articulate it for our organizations, so decision-makers understand what they are investing in, and why. We must be proficient in empowering specific initiatives that are impelling our organizations forward, such as cloud computing, modernizing legacy applications or enabling secure mobility, digital transformation, and other organizational imperatives.

3. **Analyzing, predicting, and preparing for the future:** Technology is moving at a rapid pace, to be sure, but there are certain things we can predict about the future with pretty clear certainty. We know that the Internet of Things is something we must make secure. We know that IT consumerization will continue to redefine customer expectations. We know that jurisdictional fiefdoms are continuing to impact how we think about security. We know that technologies such as artificial intelligence and machine learning will help drive innovation, within our own organizations and among our adversaries.

We must be thoughtful and proactive in advancing security into these domains before they become a problem. Business enablement is more than merely being aware of these responsibilities and challenges; it also requires that we become excellent and proficient in communicating, collaborating, interacting, and managing our inter-relationships within the organization.

Clearing the Lines of Communication

It is not simple to evolve from the kind of cloistered, poorly communicative security department that has characterized many organizations into an operation that is fully engaged and adapted. You need to have the buy-in, support, and prioritization of the security function across the organization, whether that is sales, marketing, development, customer support, or any other business function or department.

The only way to get that buy-in is through translating and communicating the language of security so that business people understand it. CISOs have to step outside of the security domain and see what value they can add throughout the organization. In my experience, there are four fundamental objectives the CISO must be thinking of when communicating within the organization:

1. How can cybersecurity help generate, protect, and ensure revenue?

2. How can cybersecurity help retain existing customers?

3. How can cybersecurity help differentiate against competitors?

4. How can cybersecurity drive operational efficiencies and effectiveness?

To do this, you need a security team that is transparent, forward-leaning in engagement with the organization and, perhaps most important, deeply knowledgeable about how the business is run and what the various departments truly do.

How can the CISO expect the company to understand the risks, if we can't transparently explain what the reality is? We need the rest of the organization to see the world through our eyes.

CISO: The Next Generation

Every business and every culture is different. A for-profit organization is not going to have the same goals and objectives as a non-profit. A company with a global customer base is going to operate differently than a company whose customers are regionally located.

One of the many things I learned in my year with the sales organization was that our sales teams in South America had much different motivations and ways of operating than our sales teams in North America. Would I have been able to truly understand this if I hadn't taken the time—and had the interest—to learn in great detail how the organization worked?

Tomorrow's CISOs will have to be on intimate terms with every aspect of the organization. I think it is wise for security professionals to follow the intent of an MBA rotation program and spend a quarter inside the marketing organization, a quarter inside sales, a quarter inside finance, a quarter inside HR or manufacturing, or some other department central to the overall operations of the business. You get a basic, simple education over time. It's not academic. It's real. You get to watch the everyday lives of your constituents. It helps you change your security model and mindset.

People often ask what characteristics to look for in potential CISOs. The first thing I look for is someone with a strong moral compass. I look for people who will do things beyond their responsibilities. If she sees something wrong, she fixes it, without looking for credit. I look for people who have a basic curiosity. We are a horizontal function across the business. I want someone who wants to ask: How does the business operate? How does it grow? And I certainly want someone who is curious about security technology. If you're not curious about new technology, you're not going to take the time to explore new ways of doing things. In cybersecurity, we always have to be willing to adopt new technologies and new solutions to solve new problems.

If I have to go around telling people what they should be doing, I am not doing my job very well. I want people to be unsatisfied with what they have, who are waiting for me to move on so they can step into my role. You can't teach someone to be a CISO; they have to be able to do the job, to learn, and to adapt, and they have to be forced to grow. They have to be self-critical and very open mentally. Curiosity is amazingly important. In order for you to convince the rest of the business to take security seriously, you must understand what motivates them and how you can better influence them. In order to do that, you've got to get to know them.

Steps to Take Now

How does any executive get defined as being successful? You have to make your number, whatever it is. In security, because we don't generate revenue, we're often measured in terms of risk mitigation, not necessarily business enablement. If you are successful, you may have no incidents. If you have no incidents, people will think there's no need to invest in security. So you have to communicate: Let us show you how we are being attacked and how we are blocking these attacks.

Once you really understand the business, you can talk the talk much more effectively in the language of business enablement. For example, many companies are looking to drive business in China. Security needs to be part of that discussion. We have the power and potential to help the company overcome hurdles, and if we can overcome those hurdles, we can help the company acquire new customers and open up new revenue streams. That is how you win the hearts and minds of executives and that is how you motivate them to give you a seat at the table.

Here's one more measure of success that may not be obvious to CISOs who are not yet focused on business enablement: Do your peers in the organization include you in relevant discussions? Do they like you or hate you? Do they see you as obstructionist or do they see you as part of the culture of change? If people don't want to include you, you are not going to be able to help them. It puts the onus on CISOs and their teams to be more engaging, open, and inclusive.

The path to business enablement is a journey. There are simple steps we can each take immediately, and it doesn't necessarily mean spending a year in the sales department, although, if you haven't done it, I highly recommend it. The things security professionals can do now to be more proactive in supporting business enablement include:

- Send an email to the heads of sales and marketing, and tell them you want to learn. Ask if you can sit in on weekly sales calls. That one step will go a long way. They will understand who you are and what you do. Right now, they probably have no concept. Identify people in the organization with whom you need to build relationships, and ask them what you can do to help.

- If you don't already do this, read the company's financial reports religiously. They will give you valuable information about your business that you won't always be aware of during the normal course of day-to-day activities.

- Reach out to your peers and build some kind of "state of the union" report, or annual cybersecurity report, or a compelling infographic. Give them something that is interesting and informative, so that people with either little time or lack of interest will spend some time with it and learn something from it. We must be looking at how we change our language so that it resonates with non-security people. Develop a cadence of different deliverables and materials, using all of your resources, including online. Then track what works best in your organization, both with your peers and with the executive board.

- Look at your team and your culture. Are you open about the problems of cybersecurity? If necessary, have a cybersecurity town hall meeting. Keep open office hours for everyone to come by and air grievances or simply communicate about real issues and opportunities. Your team will see the change in tone and direction, and they will naturally follow suit.

- Take a hard look at yourself. Do you love what you do? What really motivates you? Are you curious about the overall business? Where do you spend your time on a monthly basis? Most of us avoid the things we hate and go to the things we like. Are you self-critical? What do you resist, what do you find to be stressful, do you avoid having critical conversations with your boss or peers?

Conclusion

This is a great time to be a cybersecurity professional. Our role in our organizations, and the world, is becoming more critical and more highly valued. It also means we take on more pressure and have more responsibility. Doing things the way we've done them in the past just won't cut it in today's environment.

To prepare ourselves and our organizations for the future, we must understand and speak the language of business enablement. We must be curious about how the business works, and we must be articulate in explaining how we can help. We must evolve and we must do it quickly. The Digital Age isn't waiting for anyone.

10

Cybersecurity and the Board:
Where Do We Go From Here?

Mario Chiock — Schlumberger Fellow and CISO Emeritus, Schlumberger

"Everyone is responsible for cybersecurity."

Perhaps more than any other phrase, this may turn out to be the defining axiom for the next phase of the Digital Age. As we become more dependent on digital connectivity, we concurrently become exposed to additional risk. No one can afford to be the weakest link. Each organization must ensure that each of its people, whether employees, contractors, or anyone else affiliated with the business, understands what he or she must do to protect the organization and its digital assets.

It starts right at the top, with the board. Board members, perhaps more than anyone else, can set the cybersecurity agenda and tone for the entire organization. Not only can they set the agenda, I would argue that they *must* set the agenda and risk tolerance. They represent a critical line of defense within the organization's overall cybersecurity posture. Beyond that, board members are increasingly vulnerable targets of cyberattacks. The actions they take can have a huge impact on the organization, both practically and symbolically.

The challenge, however, is that boards of directors are typically not selected because of their deep expertise in cyber-

security. So how do board members gain knowledge and insight so they can have a positive impact on the organization? How do they adjust to a rapidly changing world, where innovations such as artificial intelligence and the IoT are making cybersecurity a constantly moving target?

And, perhaps most importantly, how do board members define the role they take—now and in the future—so they are not just a *part* of the "everyone is responsible for cybersecurity" paradigm, but they are actually *leaders* in defining and executing it?

The Evolving Role of the Board

The onus on boards to get smart about cybersecurity is a relatively recent phenomenon. In the past, boards looked at guiding a company from a business perspective when it came to risk management. As an example, perhaps an organization had specific intellectual property that was highly valuable and at risk for theft. This would have been of concern to the board and, as part of their oversight responsibilities, they would have insisted that management have a plan to ensure its protection.

But cybersecurity is a different world. Risk comes in various forms, flavors, and factors. We are now dealing with ransomware, data breaches, and DDoS attacks, among others. We are dealing with potential attacks that can cripple our operations, expose us to lawsuits and regulatory fines, destroy our reputations, irreparably damage customer goodwill, and prevent us from going forward on our journey toward digital transformation.

We are also in a world where it becomes increasingly important to quantify risk and to determine where we are vulnerable. It's not just our employees, for example, to whom we have to extend protections. Hal Martin was an outside contractor when he stole the NSA tools that were used in the WannaCry ransomware attack in May 2017.[1] The Lockheed-Martin attack in 2011 was linked to a third-party vendor.[2] In a similar way the attackers of the Target breach first got an ID from an HVAC contractor.[3] We are now seeing attackers breaching our resources, such as high-performance supercomputers or cloud resources, to use them for nefarious purposes such as theft of cryptocurrency.

In this new world, attacks can come from anywhere, at any time, and without any warning. Our cyber world is drastically different than it was five years ago—just as it will be drastically different five years from now when we will have, literally, billions more connected sensors and devices.

Plus, we will have had five years' worth of advances in artificial intelligence, machine learning, robotics, and other "exponential" technologies, as discussed in Chapters 3 and 11. It's not just a question of what *we* can accomplish with those technology innovations, it's also a question of what *our adversaries* will be able to accomplish with those innovations.

Getting Smart About Cybersecurity

In this new world, in this ever-changing environment, if you sit on a board, you and your fellow board members must get smart about cybersecurity.

You can't exercise oversight if you don't know what questions to ask, or even worse, if you choose to put your collective heads in the sand and pray that corporate management knows what it's doing when it comes to cybersecurity. In today's cybersecurity environment, and tomorrow's, boards must be proactive, not reactive.

Step 1: Understand and Define the Board's Role

The first step in getting smart is to understand and define the board's role. The board's primary responsibility is oversight. Boards do not have to enact cybersecurity policies, but they have to understand which policies are in place, if they are being monitored, and how they are being enforced.

If the organization is not doing enough to protect vital assets or to ensure regulatory compliance, boards have a fiduciary responsibility to at least ask questions and, if they are not satisfied with the answers, then to take action. In the typical governance responsibilities for cybersecurity, the board is the second line of defense, as follows:

LINES OF DEFENSE

FIRST LINE	SECOND LINE	THIRD LINE
• Internal Controls • Line Management	• Risk & Compliance • Board of Directors Oversight	• External Consultants • Cybersecurity Advisors

Step 2: Get the Right Advice

Recognizing that the chief responsibility is oversight, the next step is for the board to become educated about cybersecurity. Collectively, the board must have the knowledge, awareness, and insight to ask the right questions. Then, the board should be able to interpret the answers and put them into the context of the organization's overall risk profile when it comes to cybersecurity.

How does the board attain that knowledge and insight? Relying on reports and briefings from executive management is essential, but may not be enough. Some boards may seek to use their own expert, not just to interpret what management is saying and doing, but also to understand which questions to ask management—and when.

This is not a totally foreign concept for boards, but it is perhaps new when it comes to the world of cybersecurity. Boards have traditionally hired third-party companies to conduct financial audits to assure that there is no fraud or other breaches of fiduciary responsibility by management.

So why should cyber risk be managed any differently? I see many boards trying to oversee cybersecurity from the perspective of a financial audit. This provides a limited view. Auditing is about compliance: Being compliant doesn't make you secure, and being secure doesn't make you compliant.

The organization's overall cybersecurity profile should be considered, and as such, some boards opt to hire outside experts, as they're perceived to have unbiased views. This should include an analysis of the people, processes, and technology. It should also include regular meetings with the full board and/or board committees, as well as ongoing engagement with executive management.

Step 3: Personalize Cybersecurity

Board members need to be aware that they are valuable targets for adversaries, and they must be role models for others in the organization when it comes to following best practices in cybersecurity.

If you are on the board of an organization, you have access to vital data that could be of extreme value to adversaries. You also likely have a wide range of permissions to access even more data. Finally, adversaries may assume that board members are more "old school" and perhaps less "cyber-aware" or sophisticated, so they may target them for attacks. Remember the axiom, "Everyone is responsible for cybersecurity," which means everyone should take the proper precautions.

Your devices, personal emails, and social media accounts are all areas where you can be compromised. And you must always be cognizant of the risks. For example, traveling to certain countries can expose your organization to significant risk. When traveling, be careful with your IT assets. It may be worth leaving unnecessary data or equipment at home. You should also take special care with mobile devices and network connections. Big Brother may be watching.

Establish the Necessary Checks, Balances, and Processes

Getting smart and staying smart about cybersecurity are not one-time activities. Rather, they are ongoing processes that require constant care and upkeep.

Boards are generally good at making long-term decisions. They may have an annual meeting with an annual budget and a full year to react to changes. In the case of cybersecurity, that does not work. The landscape is much too dynamic. Taking a year to react to anything is not reacting at all. It's more like falling asleep at the wheel when the bus is going 110 miles an hour. So, boards need to be agile; they also need to be proactive and, when necessary, reactive to current trends and events.

Another challenge for boards is in speaking the right language. Frankly, this is less of a board problem and more of a problem for CISOs and other security professionals. Board members don't want to talk in jargon. They don't want to hear about code or patches. If the conversation gets too geeky, they tune out. While it's up to board members to be up to speed on the important trends and issues regarding cybersecurity, it is not their responsibility to know every product name and specification.

Board members don't care how many servers have been patched, they care about risk. The language should be more along the lines of, "This will happen if we don't stay up to date on patching, i.e., the business may shut down for an hour or a day or a week, which will cost us X amount of dollars." The language must shift from security and technology babble to business terms that board members speak and understand. We shouldn't need translators sitting in on board meetings.

Board members also need to understand that you do not become more secure simply by spending more money. IT and security managers may want to hire more people and deploy the latest and greatest advanced technologies. In certain circumstances, that may, indeed, be appropriate. But the people directly responsible for cybersecurity within the organization must be smart about it. I am a big believer that 80% of risk can be eliminated through basic cybersecurity hygiene (see related story: The Basics of Cybersecurity Hygiene).

When it does come to technology, however, the board should listen for specific language coming from their teams.

Words like "automation" and "efficiency" are essential in today's cybersecurity world. I often advise that the days of doing manual security are over. If we do things manually, the bad guys are going to beat us every time. Security in the 21st century has to be automated and boards need to understand that.

Another important point: We have to be smart about our technology investments. When we buy or build something new, we must get rid of the older technology. Your organization does not need to compile technology. In fact, when it comes to cybersecurity, that approach will actually work against you.

Finally, it is important for boards to have a sense of history. In order for companies to enable their people, processes, and technologies to evolve for the future, it is quite beneficial to understand where they've come from and what trends may be driving future changes. For example, antivirus was a big part of cybersecurity 25 years ago. Modern CISOs should be talking about endpoint protections rather than antivirus.

Prepare for the Future

Cybersecurity is about preparation. As mentioned, 80% of risk can be eliminated through basic cybersecurity hygiene. But how can we prepare for the future when we can't always predict what the future will bring?

We know that the Internet of Things is growing exponentially, that technologies such as machine learning and artificial intelligence are becoming more mainstream. We know that our adversaries are becoming bolder and more aggressive, not merely motivated by the opportunity to make money, but also spurred by issues such as geopolitical disruption. We know that the models we've traditionally applied to cybersecurity must be adapted and modernized to address a new risk environment that is constantly and dynamically changing.

From the vantage point of the board, what can we do, how can we ensure that we as individuals and as leaders of organizations can be better prepared? Here are some suggestions:

- **Focus on risk mitigation.** If you can identify risks, you can take steps to quantify them. There are certain flex points when risk is heightened—during a merger or acquisition, for example. Be aware of these flex points and take the proper steps to mitigate risk when appropriate and necessary. Every company has a different view of the types of risks they are willing to take. It is critical, as a board member, to understand and help define the company's overall risk acceptance.

- **Invest in education, training, and awareness.** Just as everyone is responsible for cybersecurity, so should everyone participate in education, training, and awareness programs. These programs need to expand beyond employees and contractors. Remember, it can take just one person failing for a breach to succeed.

- **Measure, monitor, and mitigate risk.** CISOs and CEOs need to be able to develop measurements so that board members can monitor progress and ensure that the organization is moving in the right direction when it comes to cybersecurity.

- **Develop high-level framing.** Board members need a high-level framing of risks and opportunities to be educated regularly on the fundamentals of cyber-

security. They also need to be educated on some of the new technologies, as well as the importance of automation.

- **Prepare for the worst.** Crisis management, incident response drills, and cyber-incident simulations are needed at all levels, including the board. Start small and simple, and then increase the severity and sophistication to bridge the gap between technology and response.

- **Translate security into business language.** Organizations should have a business-oriented equivalent of a cybersecurity framework for board members. This would spell out the organization's security model in a non-technical manner that focuses on risk, using business terms that board members can easily relate to and understand.

I would like to stress two additional points that are important for board members:

1. **Public-private partnerships can be extremely valuable.** Our government and law enforcement agencies, as well as our regulatory bodies, have access to information and resources that can help every organization be better prepared to prevent and/or respond to attacks. I encourage every board member to be an advocate for public-private partnerships. Sharing information within an industry and with the government can help reduce the mitigation burden on any one entity.

2. **You don't always need a very large security team.** As we keep hammering home in this chapter: Everyone is responsible for cybersecurity. If you get enough people buying in to that concept, you can create great virtual security teams that can work together

to mitigate risk. This approach is especially valuable at a time when nearly every organization is facing a shortage of experienced security personnel. This approach can also help develop cybersecurity expertise for the future.

Conclusion

There is another way to communicate the concept that everyone is responsible for cybersecurity. We can be more direct about it and say: *You* are responsible for cybersecurity. It doesn't matter to whom you say it; it applies. In fact, when applied to board members, it seems to take on a deeper meaning, doesn't it? It states the reality that as a board member, you have a certain responsibility, not just for your own personal cybersecurity protections, but also to the organization as a whole (see graphic on page 71).

It's a difficult challenge, to be sure, especially in this fast-changing world. But it's a challenge every board member should be ready to take on with passion, enthusiasm, and commitment. The future of the Digital Age is in our hands. Let's make sure we are prepared.

---

[1] "A Stolen NSA Tool is Being Used in a Global Cyberattack," The Atlantic, May 12, 2017

[2] "Lockheed attack should put U.S. on high alert," InfoWorld, June 6, 2011

[3] "Target attack shows danger of remotely accessible HVAC systems," Computerworld, Feb. 7, 2014

THE BASICS OF CYBERSECURITY HYGIENE

Organizations can significantly reduce risk by focusing on cybersecurity hygiene. Board members can help protect themselves and their organizations by being aware of the basics, which are:

- Keep operating systems patched and current; make sure each OS (operating system) is a supported version.

- Keep third-party programs patched and in their current versions.

- Remove unused programs and sample code from production servers.

- Don't leave default configurations intact—especially default passwords.

- Back up all data and configuration files.

- Install protection software and anti-malware, keep an application whitelist, and perform integrity checks.

- Deploy encryption in transit and at rest.

- Use secure passwords (do not embed in code / do not store unprotected).

- Proactively manage and monitor access privileges.

CYBERSECURITY MUST BE ON EVERYONE'S AGENDA

Board
CEO
CFO
Executives

What is the potential
impact of a cyber breach?

Mitigate risk

$

**Information
Technology**

We manage the
IT infrastructure
& software

We need to protect IT

**All
Employees &
Third Parties**

Business

We need to
use the data

We need to use
the technology

We need to
protect the data
and technology

CIO
Business Systems
Helpdesk
Data Centers
IT Security
IT Operations
• Networks
• Servers
• Desktops

Operations
Marketing
HR
Legal
HSE
Supply Chain
Operational
Technology

How Work Requirements and Ethical Responsibilities Come Together

11

Cybersecurity and the Future of Work

Gary A. Bolles — Chair, Future of Work at Singularity University; Co-founder, eParachute.com; Partner, Charrette; Speaker and Writer

Throughout human history, technology has transformed work. From the wheel to the internal combustion engine, technological advances have repeatedly changed how, when, and where we work. But the pace of technology-infused work is dramatically accelerating. From consumer-driven mobile phones to blockchain-enabled contracts, technology is an increasingly critical part of work, redefining a wide range of work-related processes.

The transition from an agricultural to an industrial economy meant a dramatic transformation in the very nature of work. But this transition took nearly a century. We are today transitioning to a digital work economy, and in a blindingly short period of time. As technology increasingly infuses, enhances, and—in many cases, replaces—human work, business and technology leaders need to anticipate, understand, and ultimately leverage the macro changes affecting the world of work.

For example, the increasing number of remote workers and non-traditional work arrangements means that the binary status of an employee or non-employee dissipates, requiring new approaches to everything, from identity to payment of compensation. And the fundamental risks associated with worker backgrounds and capabilities require a new way of thinking about skills and capabilities that can be supported by next-generation technology infrastructure.

What will it mean in the near future, when machines that use artificial intelligence act more like humans, and blockchain-enabled payments mean organizations may not even know who—or what—is performing specific functions? How will changes in how we perceive digital identity and trust inform the way we manage, compensate, and, perhaps most importantly, secure our workers and workplaces?

Today's reality is that exponential technologies are dramatically transforming the world of work, requiring an entirely new cybersecurity mindset. Decision-makers, ranging from enterprises to governments, need to understand the fundamental dynamics of this rapid shift in the world of work and the inevitable impact on cybersecurity. They must also determine the kinds of strategies they can follow to not only mitigate those risks, but also to effectively prepare themselves to leverage a more dynamic and adaptive workforce.

The Basic Building Blocks of Work

To truly understand these changes, it is helpful to think of work as a set of building blocks. Work is fundamentally three things: human skills performing tasks to solve problems.

Whether the problem is a dirty floor or an enterprise requiring a new market strategy, our role as workers in any environment is to solve problems. Humans are trial-and-error machines, and the reason we are paid as workers is to use our skills to solve a broad range of problems.

Yet many of the tasks we perform in our work are repetitive, requiring minimal creativity. Such mundane work uses little of what makes us unique as humans, and, in fact, technologies such as software and robotics can often perform these tasks with better accuracy and precision. Many of these repetitive tasks are also more easily outsourced, performed by workers in other geographies who often accept lower pay for the same activities.

The combination of automation and globalization operates hand-in-hand to allow work to be "unbundled"—split into separate tasks and spread among a combination of remote workers and distributed technologies.

The Impact of Exponential Technologies

All of these fast-paced changes in the world of work would be seismic enough on their own. But they are fueled by the rapid rise of "exponential" technologies.

Inventor and futurist Ray Kurzweil was fascinated by the growth curve of Moore's Law, the observation by Intel co-founder Gordon Moore that microprocessor price/performance was doubling every 18 to 24 months. Kurzweil realized that this dramatic sequence of the increase in value was actually logarithmic, starting out linearly, but turning into a "hockey stick" of growth over time.

Kurzweil applied this analysis to a range of technologies and found they often progressed along the same kind of exponential curve. In fact, the interaction of these exponential technologies accelerated their individual development even more rapidly. For example, technologies, such as machine learning (often called artificial intelligence, or AI), robotics, high-performance computing, and LIDAR (laser-based radar), all combined to enable a science-fiction-class product known as the self-driving car.

The rapid development and adoption of connected digital technologies has had a seismic impact on a range of industries, in which market leaders had traditionally maintained dominance due to their "bundled" business models—an idea originally suggested by John Hagel, now at Deloitte's Center for the Edge. For example, leaders in the newspaper industry integrated functions like a physical plant, content creation, content curation, distribution, and ad sales, and that vertically integrated combination provided huge market advantage. Along came the internet, and those formerly integrated components were unbundled, allowing new market players like Google and Facebook to quickly gain tremendous market power through new business models. Media industries became "re-bundled" around online ad marketplaces, leaving only small pieces of the reshaped market pie for incumbents.

In the same way, exponential technologies will continue to unbundle work, breaking apart the traditional construct of a job, and allowing tasks to be performed by constantly changing combinations of local and distributed workers, technology-infused work, and often, work performed by technology. Today, humans drive for Uber, and tomorrow autonomous vehicles will obviate the need for traditional drivers.

As work itself becomes unbundled, the same kinds of mechanisms apply to the re-bundling of work. New kinds of value are being created in the digital work economy, allowing the enterprise to solve external and internal problems in ways that were never before possible. These technology-infused processes provide a broad range of exciting new ways to perform work and to enable dynamic new strategies for channeling human energy.

The Rise of Alternative Work Relationships

For example, unbundled work enables a broad range of work contexts, each of which can bring unique advantages to the enterprise.

In the past, the traditional "one person, one job" approach meant that the enterprise workforce often wasn't optimized. Workers with a broad range of skills and capabilities were often restricted to performing a limited set of tasks that employed only a subset of their capabilities. A tremendous range of human potential has for a long time been left unrealized, locked into an inflexible, industrial-era model of work, often characterized by repetitive and uncreative tasks.

With this poorly optimized model, enterprises took on substantial costs. Tasks performed by each worker weren't always distributed efficiently. Even with an increasingly mobile workforce, workers were less likely to be located where new work was needed. And coordination between workers remained far less efficient than it could have been.

Think of this as a huge amount of capability in the enterprise left on the shelf: an unrealized set of assets that rarely reached its potential. Yet, in a world of unbundled work, enterprises are able to distribute work when, where, and how it is most

effectively performed—and, most especially, by whom.

This flexibility gives rise to a range of "direct" alternative work arrangements, including part-time temporary, full-time temporary, part-time permanent, piece work, team-allocated work, and gig work. And it allows a range of indirect worker relationships as well, such as problems solved by workers through crowdsourcing, "cloud work," and prize platforms. These kinds of arrangements serve to "soften the walls" of organizations, allowing a wide variety of workers and business partners to dynamically bind around the problems defined by the enterprise and its customers.

The Blockchain-Enabled Workforce

Suppose a manager determines that her team won't be able to make a critical customer deadline to deliver new designs for a website. She works with the team to quickly define a set of success characteristics for the project, and posts it to a work marketplace.

A response immediately comes back from the marketplace, from a worksource with a high trust rating. The manager is able to see the worksource's trust rating sources, and finds that other managers in her company have used this worksource before. The worksource response includes a series of questions about the deliverables. The manager answers these questions, defines a set of preferred project milestones, and offers several payment options. Because the project involves a new product offering, one of these options is an independent coin offering (ICO) that allows the worksource to participate in future income from the product.

Satisfied with the dynamic work agreement, the manager finalizes the contract, which is immediately placed into an open distributed ledger. The manager is able to see all of her existing work contracts, including those of her current team, and to manage the deliverables of the project and compensation for the worksource. And she may not ever know if the worksource is a person, a team, or a piece of software.

That's the world of work on blockchain technology. Now, imagine an entire organization based on these kinds of digital agreements, built on distributed ledgers. Since an organization is already a set of agreements between employer and worker, these "distributed autonomous organizations"—which exist today—provide new ways to incorporate workers into the problem-solving processes of an enterprise.

A Brave New World of Digital Identity

Technologies, such as smart worker contracts, also represent an opportunity to incorporate new identity models.

Open distributed ledgers simultaneously support anonymity, verification, responsibility, and value transfer. Anonymity allows workers to perform work without necessarily becoming deeply integrated into an organization's enterprise systems. Verification allows the enterprise to confirm the worker's capabilities and portfolio, and lets the worker confirm that the enterprise is a trustable entity. Responsibility means that the contract has built-in confirmation that the worker has performed the required work and that the enterprise will provide compensation as agreed. Value transfer means that the actual work product is given to the enterprise and the worker gets paid.

The ways in which value is transferred blurs the lines between IT and operations, creating both new headaches and new opportunities for the enterprise. Today, most value transfer is calculated and performed on the basis of country-based currencies. But the rise of ICOs built on blockchain-based open ledgers, such as Bitcoin and Ethereum, means that new business relationships—from paying a worker for an hour's work to buying another company—will be performed using a complex web of digital currencies. Business and IT decision-makers will need to experiment with these value transfer mechanisms to continually determine how they can best meet the needs of the enterprise.

Machine Learning / AI Transforms Work

As we've seen, AI and robots don't take jobs, per se: They perform tasks. But those tasks can add up. As an increasing amount of formerly human tasks are performed by technology, decision-makers—from workgroup managers to chief human resource officers—will need to determine whether the relationship between humans and technology is complementary or competitive. In other words: Is technology an enhancer of human work or a work replacer (see page 82)?

Much of innovation today is focused on automating human work, because the processes and costs associated with existing work are reasonably well known. Whether we're trying to reduce the costs of a waitress or a warehouse worker, we can currently see the tasks they perform and understand the costs of paying them for those tasks. Automating such tasks with software or robots therefore has the potential to reduce known costs and increase efficiency.

Yet this approach potentially creates a zero-sum mentality, reducing human labor to a set of easily replaced processes. Instead, we have the opportunity to turn the same amount of innovative energy to enhancing human work.

In fact, productivity software is already doing this. There are few accountants today, for example, who can craft a pivot table by hand. That's what Microsoft Excel is for. Picture an architect using augmented reality glasses that overlay a building with the schematic of its internal infrastructure. Or imagine having an AI learning partner that continually gives you advice on new skills you can develop, and helps you find the right learning opportunities to rapidly hone those capabilities. By focusing on technologies and strategies that enhance human workers, the enterprise workforce gains superpowers that can bring tremendous competitive advantage.

Machine Learning / AI Becomes Work

Inevitably, however, the lines between technology and humans will continue to blur. Beyond the strategic issues for humans and work, enterprise strategists will increasingly have to contend with software performing a range of new tasks and increasingly appearing like humans. In our blockchain-enabled work process, the remote worker is assumed to be a human. But what if it isn't?

Today these are often called bots; tomorrow they may be AI companions, and the next day they will be AI workers. Software's ability to emulate the activities and interactions of humans will mean that traditional processes for validating an actor's humanness—from simple mechanisms like captchas, to complex challenge-response sequences—will become less secure. In some cases, these new software actors will be welcomed and intentionally integrated into workflows. But in other cases, they will be autonomous systems intent on compromising the security of the enterprise. Identifying which is which will become a core enterprise skillset.

In fact, these technology components— from AI applications to robots—will increasingly be seen as having "identity," with a set of known capabilities and a capacity to make decisions. They will function as part of the "stack" of enterprise technologies, operating with increasing autonomy, and creating greater complexity as the interactions between independent programs generate unpredictable interactions. Enterprises that can anticipate such complexity and create flexible strategies, allowing them to leverage software that becomes increasingly "smarter," will gain competitive advantage.

Rethinking Hierarchy As the Organization Becomes Unbundled

Our current approach to managing large organizations of workers through a pyramid-based hierarchy actually comes from the Prussian Army, when "moving men and machines" required strict adherence to orders handed down through the ranks. In a time when the leading communications technology was a carrier pigeon, the only way to ensure that messages were accurately transmitted was to demand obedience to a hierarchical command structure.

Yet in an era of ubiquitous communications technologies that instantly span the globe and software that increasingly infuses a range of business processes, organizational hierarchies no longer ensure the greatest use of enterprise resources. Instead, flexible workgroups that dynamically bind around external and internal problems are the greatest human assets the organization can have. Rather than thinking of such a self-organizing enterprise as a hierarchy, picture it instead as a network of networks, with Venn diagrams of workgroups overlapping with each other as they perform the work of the enterprise. In the digital work economy, even the organization itself is becoming unbundled.

Security Ramifications of the Digital Work Economy

In the brave new world of unbundled work, with technology infusing an increasing amount of human activity, a huge mindshift is needed.

The fundamental underpinning of human-based security, digital identity, has a range of new ramifications in the digital work economy. Even though the traditional context of the employee involved a variety of roles in the organization—and therefore a variety of security models—the new range of alternative work relationships means the enterprise security fabric needs better flexibility and greater comprehensiveness than ever before.

What are the range of activities and roles that workers will perform, and how will their access permissions be determined? Who decides when and how a new worker becomes integrated into the enterprise's information fabric? How will enterprise decision-makers determine the aggregation of access rights across multiple projects and geographies? How will permissions held by workers in flexible arrangements be automatically aged and removed? How will organizations determine whether a worksource, human or otherwise, can be trusted?

These are just a few of the security questions raised by the new world of work. Enterprises that invest in strategies to incorporate these dynamically changing issues will be far better prepared to understand and leverage new work-related technologies.

For example, as dynamic work contracts are built on blockchains, enterprise security strategists need to stay deeply informed about the ways in which digital trust is being transformed. At their best, agreement processes that support the rapid, new creation of solutions and friction-free transfer of payments will provide new opportunities to compete in new markets while maintaining high levels of trust and tracking. At their most challenging, though, blockchain-based work processes will create entirely new risks, opening security holes through which sensitive information and other digital assets can be rapidly compromised.

In fact, these new technologies will fundamentally reshape the enterprise's understanding of trust, down to a completely granular level. Whether the relationship is as simple as confirming that an email message was truly sent by a particular person, or as involved as a set of complex payment transfers using digital coins, exponential technologies will drive an entirely new approach to trust in the world of work. Enterprise IT and business decision-makers will need to develop a comprehensive understanding of all the contexts of trust that matter, from physical security to digital data access, and for a range of potential stakeholders far broader than ever before.

Strategies for Security in the Digital Work Economy

Solving the security challenges of the digital work economy with dynamic processes and policies means the enterprise can be agile and adaptive. Ignoring them will mean, at best, an inability to integrate problem-solvers into the organization's process of delivering value to customers, putting the enterprise at a tremendous competitive disadvantage. At worst, it will mean creating a widely expanded attack surface that will add exponential risk to any organization.

Critical capabilities will include:

- **A fluid infrastructure for identity:** Enterprise identity data models must continually allow for new players and roles to be rapidly defined, provisioned, and distributed. But these roles must also be dynamically managed, with automated oversight and aging.

- **A comprehensive infrastructure for defining and managing data:** The rate of compound annual data growth is projected to be 40% for the foreseeable future. Data management policies must grow and adapt as enterprise data assets reach breathtaking scale and become increasingly distributed globally. Enterprise security policies must also incorporate the likelihood of changing laws and regulations around the world, as well as the need to manage, secure, and remove data as required.

- **A bigger, more comprehensive and strategic role for trust management:** Trust management will increasingly become its own arena. The dynamic management of trust and value transfer through open ledger platforms, such as blockchain, will become commonplace. The ability to understand, design, and implement complex trust interactions between enterprises will be a core enterprise skillset.

- **Tight, seamless integration between cybersecurity and business operations:** As the ways in which value is transferred blurs the lines between IT and operations, decision-makers within technology, cybersecurity, and business will need to work in concert to manage the organization's digital value assets. Experiment with paying for and selling products and services through micro-ICOs to practice with new forms of value transfer. This will empower the enterprise to become adept at managing a portfolio of digital assets.

Conclusion

The transition to a digital work economy is not only inevitable, it's already here. The urgency is real. Enterprise IT and business leaders must understand the dramatic shift in the very nature of the workforce, or face inevitable disruption. Those who ignore it will find themselves left behind in the race to leverage new technologies transforming where, when, and how we work.

Yet, in this transition, enterprise decision-makers are being offered a set of opportunities that can create a broad range of competitive advantage. As the world of work changes dramatically, enterprise leaders will find that managing a dynamic, fluid, and all-encompassing security function can unleash a huge amount of economic value, giving the enterprise the ability to rapidly take advantage of new business opportunities fueled by exponential technologies.

WORK IS CHANNELLING HUMAN ENERGY

One caution to enterprise decision-makers: The transition to a digital work economy brings with it an important responsibility. At its most fundamental, work is the channelling of human energy. Yet as technology has the capability of automating an increasing percentage of human work tasks, enterprise decision-makers intent on reducing labor costs have a critical decision to make. This conundrum is reflected in a simple question:

If you could automate every single task in the enterprise and replace every single human, would you?

This is not an idle question. Much of the public concern about the future of work focuses on the potential for robots and software to replace a huge percentage of tasks formerly performed by humans. Yet thinking only in terms of reducing the costs of human labor fundamentally misses the point.

Rather than thinking of work as a cost center, enterprise leaders need to see the incredible opportunities that can be created for workers who are freed from mundane tasks to pursue new ways to create value for the enterprise and its customers. Unlocking opportunities for expanding the human potential to solve problems will be a critical skillset for the dynamic enterprise.

12

The Ethics of Technology and the Future of Humanity

Gerd Leonhard — Author; Executive "Future Trainer;" Strategist; Chief Executive Officer, The Futures Agency

The Next 20 Years Will Bring More Change Than the Previous 300

If this statement sounds somewhat preposterous, please keep in mind that we are now crossing a crucial threshold that was previously unthinkable. Technology is no longer simply changing our environment, i.e., what is *around or outside us,* or what hardware we use. No more is it just a tool. Technology is well on its way to becoming a creative force—and a thinking machine, as well.

Technology is now gearing up to go *inside us,* thereby changing who we are and rapidly redefining what it means to be human. All this, as some of my fellow futurists are fond of saying, to allow us to "transcend the limitations of humanity."

If intelligent machines are to perform our routine work for us, we will have to train them, teach them, connect them to us—in effect making digital copies of ourselves, cloning our knowledge (and possibly some of our unique human intelligences) in the cloud. This will alter us; and it will alter our view of what we are and what we could be, as well as what the machines are. And this is only the first step. Try to imagine:

- Nanobots in your bloodstream monitoring and even regulating cholesterol levels.

- Augmented virtual or mixed reality devices that look like regular eyeglasses or even contact lenses, giving you ready access to the world's knowledge, at the blink of an eye.

- The ability to connect your neocortex directly to the internet and transform thoughts into action or record what you think.

- Developing a relationship with your digital assistant or robot because it seems so real, so very human.

None of this is as far away as you may think, and the societal, cultural, human, and ethical implications will be mind-boggling. Clearly we must prepare for this challenge today, or we will find ourselves ill-equipped to handle these new realities. If we are not able to clearly define and articulate an agreed upon set of Digital Age ethics, we run the risk that unfettered technology expansion will not only be dangerous, it will also cause us to question the very nature of our existence: What is it that makes us human?

Defining Ethics

Before we venture further into why ethics in technology is critical to our future, first let us attempt to define what ethics is. Riffing off the late U.S. Supreme Court judge Potter Stewart, I propose this as a working definition:

Ethics is knowing the difference between what you have a right or the power to do and what is the right thing to do.

If we accept this definition and apply it to what is coming in the next 10 years, we can quickly see a serious challenge emerging.

The Future Is Exponential, Convergent, and Combinatorial—and So Are the Resulting Ethical Challenges

Right now, we are at the take-off point of exponential progress. Henceforth, change is no longer gradual but sudden, in almost all scientific and technological progress—such as quantum/3D computing, nanotechnology, biotechnology, cloud computing, hyper-connectivity and the Internet of Things (IoT), AI, geoengineering, solar energy, 3D printing, autonomous vehicles, and pretty much everything else.

What's more, most of these exponential technologies are dual-use—meaning they can be harnessed for incredible, positive innovations as well as for evil purposes. As William Gibson, the science fiction writer widely credited with pioneering cyberpunk, likes to say, "Technology is morally neutral until we apply it."

Let's imagine the world a mere 10 years from now—some 50 to 100 times more advanced—a world where most science fiction has become science fact. It is likely to be a world where literally everyone and every*thing* around us is connected, observed, recorded, measured, and tracked. I estimate there will be some-thing like one trillion devices on the IoT by then, where IA (intelligence augmentation) has truly become AI (artificial intelligence), and where at least 80 percent of the 10 billion earthlings are connected at high speeds, on cheap devices, wearables, and via digital assistants and robots that we can communicate with, as if we are speaking to a good friend. Add genetic engineering and the rapid convergence of technology and biology to this equation, and the sky is the limit—literally—in terms of possibilities (see page 89).

Exponential thinking, therefore, becomes mission-critical, both to realize opportunities and to foresee and address the consequential ethical challenges and moral quandaries.

A Perfect Storm of Combinatorial Forces

Even more important, the true challenge to humanity lies in the fact that while all these technologies are unfolding exponentially, they are also causing traditionally unrelated industries (and the sciences underneath them) to converge. These so-called megashifts, such as datafication, cognification, automation, and virtualization (see megashifts.com) are already combining with each other to create entirely new possibilities and challenges.

These convergent and combinatorial forces will soon create a perfect storm of immense progress and enormous challenges that transcend the realms of technology and business by impacting society, culture, and humanity as a whole.

Get Ready for the Next Generation of Unicorns

Looking back at the warp-drive success of the unicorns of the past seven years (i.e., those companies that were or are privately valued at over $1 billion, pre-IPO, such as Uber, Xiaomi, Palantir, Airbnb, and Spotify), we can already see examples of the exponential-combinatorial-convergent story. And this is just the beginning.

For instance, Spotify's business model became feasible only because of exponential and combinatorial technological change: Streaming 20 million songs to 150 million users is now doable, thanks to the fact that we finally have cheap yet powerful smartphones connected to fast mobile networks. In addition, we now have new ways of paying online, AI/algorithms that create playlists, and last but not least, sufficient market pressure on the record companies to provide the licenses. It is quite revealing to note in this context that Spotify is no longer really in the business of "selling music." Rather, it sells convenience, intelligence, interface, and curation—the result of a convergent and exponential outlook on the future, something that apparently is always reserved for industry outsiders.

Airbnb makes for another great example. It boasts a vast, global database of users' short-term rental listings, with mobile devices as the primary use case. It employs intelligent rating and pricing technology (AI once more, if you will), has social media built in to the system, offers digital payment options, and has been propelled by the rise of the sharing economy. Put all this together, and you have warp-drive growth.

While these tech innovations are all mostly positive developments that often enrich our lives, we must brace ourselves for what is about to come: new superstar, exponential, unicorn organizations that combine AI and biotechnology—thus achieving the complete convergence of technology and biology—or fuse AI, nanotechnology, and the material sciences.

Understanding the Urgency to Construct Ethical Frameworks

However, the prospect of such exponential growth puts us on the horns of another dilemma. We must now urgently construct ethical frameworks that will keep up with this furious pace. Without these ethical frameworks in place, unfettered and thereby socially destructive growth will become increasingly toxic and disastrous.

Clearly we must prepare for this challenge today, or we will find ourselves ill-equipped to handle these new realities. Business ought to take a lead on this, and so must savvy politicians and public officials. Whoever is the thought leader in these thorny issues will be more influential than Warren Buffett has been in matters of investing.

Donald Ripley in the 1995 movie Powder: *"It has become appallingly clear that our* **technology** *has surpassed our* **humanity.**"

Every Extension Is Also an Amputation—but What Should We *Not* Amputate?

Marshall McLuhan talked about this in his landmark 2001 book *Understanding Media,* and it rings even more true in the present day: Every technological extension of ourselves is also an amputation of another part of us (or another extension).

If we continue to have closer relationships with our screens than we have with other people, if we will indeed "transcend human limitations" by spending our lives in augmented or virtual spaces, or if we are to connect our neural networks directly with an AI in the cloud, then we will certainly lose—i.e., *amputate*—many things that make us human. I firmly believe this is a consequence we must reckon with.

We stand to lose human elements, such as emotions (which can be emu-

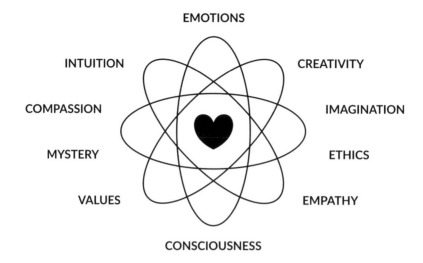

EMOTIONS

INTUITION

CREATIVITY

COMPASSION

IMAGINATION

MYSTERY

ETHICS

VALUES

EMPATHY

CONSCIOUSNESS

lated by but are fundamentally incomprehensible to computers); imperfections (smart machines won't tolerate errors); surprises and serendipity (machines don't enjoy them), and mysteries (machines hate them).

Generally, it would become nearly impossible to retain what I call "the androrithms," all the things that actually make us human. We might end up extended in many different ways, but also our basic human expressions could end up amputated. We'd be extremely intelligent, but totally dehumanized. That strikes me as a bad idea.

Who will decide what we can safely amputate—such as, maybe, the ability to read maps or drive a car ourselves? Who will define the limits of when we will no longer be human? Who is mission control for humanity?

Getting an Ethics Upgrade—From If and When to *Why* and Who

The bottom line is that we are now moving to an entirely different era as far as technology is concerned. Sometime in the next

five to 10 years, it will no longer be about *if* we can do something, i.e., technical feasibility, cost or time, can something be done, will it actually work, how expensive will it be, and how will it make money? Rather, it will be about *why* we are doing it (context, purpose, values, goals) and *who* is doing it (control, security, governance, power). In other words, it will be about ethics, ultimately. This is a crucial shift in society, brought about by exponential, convergent, and combinatorial change.

Are you ready to shift from an emphasis on science and technical feasibility to an emphasis on meaning, purpose, and human governance?

What Does Digital Ethics Have to Do With Security? The Digital Ethics Moonshot

In my opinion, technological security can only be as good as the moral, ethical, and political frameworks that surround and define it. The most advanced security technology will be useless if those who hold the key and those who use it, act unethically, with evil intent, or with great negligence. In fact, the very same technology that is employed to protect consumers and users can be used to spy on them. Some of the most potentially beneficial technologies, such as the IoT, can be used to form the biggest and most powerful Panopticon ever constructed.

It will therefore not be enough to simply improve technological firepower as the world gears up for exponential technological growth; we must also redesign and embolden our ethical frameworks. We have to reach a global agreement on what is good for humanity, at large, and what is clearly not—and, also, how we would enforce such tenets.

In many ways, this task might even be harder than the technological challenges ahead of us. In any case, I would propose to add this "ethical moonshot" to the cybersecurity moonshot that Mark McLaughlin talks about in his chapter.

Ethics in Technology, aka Digital Ethics, Will Very Quickly Become the No. 1 Issue in This Industry

Defining ethical standards on a global scale is not easy. It may even be impossible *if* we attempt to address very detailed convictions, i.e., values and beliefs that are particular to specific societies, countries, regions, or religions. But if we stay at the very top level, on a global scale, I believe we can indeed define some crucial ethical standards for humans. The key will be to focus on HUMANITY, and to act with what ancient Greeks called *phronesis* (practical wisdom) in order to ensure that all technological progress results in collective human flourishing—which is the underlying paradigm we need to adopt.

On the topic of religion and ethics, Albert Einstein (a big source of inspiration for me) repeatedly set forth that morality does not require a divine source. Rather, morality (yet another term to describe something like ethics) is a purely natural and human creation; it is simply a part of being human. The Dalai Lama wrote an entire book on his belief that ethics is more important than religion. Take note.

Meta-level ethics would, for example, assume that pretty much everybody wants to remain human, retain human qualities, and enjoy basic human rights, such as the right to free will, free decision-making, and choice (notwithstanding the few but also very noisy transhumanists and extreme singularitarians who seem overly keen on becoming cyborgs or robots as soon as possible).

Who would enjoy having their digital (or real) identity stolen, or their DNA used to program a super-soldier halfway around the world? Does anybody want his or her data and information out in the public sphere? Everybody enjoys the ability to have mystery, secrets, mistakes, and privacy in their lives.

For Your Consideration: An Ethics Framework for the Digital Age

These are the kinds of general digital ethics principles that could be the framework for a global "ethics in technology" manifesto—a kind of digital human rights declaration. In fact, I suggest five core human rights that could form the basis of a future digital ethics manifesto:

1. **The right to remain natural, i.e., biological.** We need to retain the right to be employed, use public services, buy things, and function in society without a requirement to deploy technology on or inside our bodies.

2. **The right to be inefficient if and where it defines our basic humanness.** We must have the choice to be slower than technology and not make efficiency more important than humanity.

3. **The right to disconnect.** We must retain the right to switch off connectivity, go dark on the network, and pause communications, tracking, and monitoring.

4. **The right to be anonymous.** In our coming hyperconnected world, we should still have the option of not being identified and tracked, such as when using a digital application or platform, when it doesn't pose a risk to or impose upon others.

5. **The right to employ or involve people instead of machines.** We should not allow companies or employers to be disadvantaged if they choose to use people instead of machines—even if it's more expensive and less efficient.

Conclusion

What are we without ethics? Can we still assert and own our humanity, particularly as we barrel headlong toward a future in which technology will give us the ability to blur the lines between what is human and what is machine? Just because we *can* do it, *should* we do it? And if we do, how will we define what is the *right* way to do it?

I believe we urgently need to tackle this challenge because the future could be heaven, or it could be hell (I call this 'HellVen'), depending on the decisions we make today. Technology does not have ethics, but societies depend on them. Let us remind ourselves that civilizations are driven by their technologies and defined by their humanity. Technology is not *what* we seek, but *how* we seek.

2020: The world is becoming hyperconnected, automated, and uber-smart—and everyone benefits. Six billion people are "always on," around the planet, each of us seeing different information and content all the time. We interact with platforms via augmented reality, virtual reality, holographic screens, or via intelligent digital assistants (IDAs).

2022: Our own digital egos have moved to the cloud and are developing a life of their own. Swarms of IDAs and software bots live in the cloud and take care of routine tasks. No more searching for restaurants or hotels; no more updating the doctor on what's wrong. Our bots know us and our desires, and they communicate infinitely better than we can by typing questions into a computer.

2024: Goodbye privacy and anonymity. We are constantly connected to machines, and they are getting better and better at reading our minds. Technology has become so fast, powerful, and pervasive that we cannot avoid being tracked, observed, recorded, and monitored—ever.

2026: Automation is widespread, and social norms are being rewritten. Gone are the days when routine tasks—whether blue collar, white collar, manual, or cognitive—are done by humans. Machines have learned how to understand language, images, emotions, and beliefs. Machines can also speak, write, draw, and simulate human emotions. Machines cannot *be*, but they can *think*.

2028: Free will and free choice are only for the privileged. Our lives have become tracked, guided, and curated. Because everything we do, say, see—and increasingly, feel and think—can be tracked and measured, we see a waning in the importance of free will. We can no longer easily divert from what the system thinks is best for us, because everything is observed. This makes for healthier and more responsible lives, lowers the costs of medical care, and makes near-perfect security possible. Yet, many of us are unsure whether this is heaven or hell.

2030: 90 is the new 60. Because we have analyzed the DNA of billions of connected humans via cloud biology and quantum computing, we can now determine with great certainty which exact gene is responsible for triggering which exact disease. In another five years or so, we will be able to prevent cancer. Longevity has exploded, completely changing our social systems, as well.

PART 2
Lessons From Today's World

Part 2 — Introductions

13

If You're Not Collaborating With Colleagues and Competitors on Cyber Threat Intelligence, Beware: The Bad Guys Are Way Ahead of You

Sherri Ramsay — Cybersecurity Consultant; Former Director of the U.S. National Security Agency / Central Security Service Threat Operations Center

I worked at the U.S. National Security Agency for 33 years, during the time when we first saw just how big a target the Department of Defense and the rest of the federal government was for hackers and bad actors all over the world. During those years, I learned firsthand about many of the problems those in private-sector leadership are now struggling with in their attempts to protect their digital domains.

And I learned about the value of sharing threat intelligence information when it came to protecting our networks and our data.

The other lesson I learned is one I want to emphasize throughout this chapter—an organization's success in cybersecurity depends as much on leadership as it does on technology. Maybe more.

Specifically, I learned that cybersecurity requires leadership—whether you're a CIO in a three-letter government agency or a CEO of a global conglomerate. And this leadership means having the confidence, the boldness, and, sometimes, the sheer

audacity to share! Sharing tips, vulnerabilities, mitigations, and winning strategies with those outside your organization. Even with your competitors.

Why? Because it's what the bad guys are doing to us, every minute of every hour of every day.

Every day, our computers and networks are being attacked. It takes attackers only minutes to compromise a system, and most of the time, they are able to exfiltrate our data within days, sometimes hours. And when we realize what has happened, often much later and sometimes only when notified by an external party, such as law enforcement, we wonder what went wrong, whether it will happen to us again, and how we could have prevented it. We operate in independent stovepipes, defending ourselves as if each of us was on our own island. The bad guys, the attackers, watch us as we struggle to understand and characterize the attacks.

They watch us. And then they come at us again.

The attackers meet in the dark corners of the internet to share exploits, vulnerabilities, exploitation infrastructure, and whatever other information might be helpful to those looking to attack our networks for nefarious purposes. To date, we have talked about information sharing, but we have not yet done nearly enough to dramatically move the needle in our favor.

If the bad guys are collaborating, why aren't the good guys? Why do we continue to live with this disadvantage? Are we waiting for a solution to fall in our laps?

How and Why Bad Actors Are Sharing Insights About Your Security

The harsh reality is that there is extensive collaboration among the cyber bad guys; there are few lone wolves. This extends across the entire spectrum of bad actors—nation-states, criminals, hacktivists, and terrorists. Even a single hacker is not really alone.

Why do they collaborate? Why do they share? The answer is simple. It saves them time and it saves them money. According to Etay Moor, Senior Strategist at IBM, "Information sharing is a given on the dark side of the net." That's a big reason the average cost of conducting an attack is decreasing and attacks are spreading across networks at a faster pace, year after year.

Much of the information the bad guys share is easily accessed without them doing anything special. For example, they simply use a search engine to locate spreadsheets with the word "password" in them to get the default password lists for numerous devices of interest.

Bad guys also exploit one of our biggest weaknesses: human error. Information is available on the internet that may have been posted by mistake or by someone who had no idea that the information would be useful for a nefarious purpose. And there is also a significant amount of information that has been stolen or compromised and then posted on legitimate websites, which often are created for the sole purpose of sharing stolen information with others.

There are forums created and used by the bad guys. Some have benign names like "security research forum." They promote these forums as legitimate entities, even displaying ads to cover costs or to actually make money. These forums are used to share all kinds of information that is helpful to the bad guys. They also provide anonymity for their users. This is teamwork.

The Dark Web, by design, provides anonymity for users and is facilitating a thriving underground for the bad guys. Here, everything that a person needs to break in to your networks is available for an astonishingly low cost. How low? Worms can be purchased as cheaply as $10, key loggers for $20, known ransomware for $30–$50. Furthermore, the entire exploitation/attack can now be easily outsourced, from the development of the malware to its distribution and even the conduct of the operations.

And these bad guys are coming after your networks and your data.

Why Organizations Don't Share This Information—and How It Impacts Cybersecurity

Throughout history, we have used strategic alliances to defeat our enemies and to solve our most pressing problems, from minimizing geopolitical conflict to stabilizing financial markets and tackling world hunger. Some say that the true measure of a great civilization is its ability to work together to solve difficult, seemingly intractable problems. Certainly, cybersecurity appears to meet this criterion.

But allying with others is in depressingly sharp contrast with how we are addressing cybersecurity today. Information about "near-misses" and successful attacks are closely guarded secrets. Organizations rarely share this critical information, collaborate on damage control, or provide early warning to other organizations that may be at risk. It's a losing strategy.

Why do we continue to live with this disadvantage? There are three reasons organizations have been hesitant to participate in meaningful information-sharing initiatives.

- Many of the sharing mechanisms today are associated with federal or state government, and enterprises are concerned that sharing information with the government will lead to increased regulation and oversight. Companies are concerned about the perception of being "in bed" with the government, which might affect their global market opportunities.

- In the private-sector, corporations feel that disclosure may prompt criminal or civil lawsuits. Remember all the legal brouhaha over the Y2K threat and companies' worries over legal exposure?

- Maybe the most important reason for not sharing is concern over market and reputational risk. Even a problem caused by a technical glitch or human error implies data or IT infrastructure problems or poor management. An actual attack just creates additional uncertainty.

Unfortunately, we are failing. Every new cybersecurity headline serves as a warning that no organization is immune from these attacks. Each new breach seems worse than the last. Everything, from our business communications to medical equipment to the cars we drive, is vulnerable. Fighting against network intrusions in disconnected silos and relying upon traditional enterprise security technologies and techniques has gone as far as it can go, and it is not good enough.

Breaking this cycle will require a fundamental shift in thinking. It will require leadership. Just as we evolved from the early days of perimeter defense to today's focus on intelligence, detection, and response, we must move from an individualistic model to one of collaborative "connective defense." We can only make true progress once we share our relevant information, pool our expertise, and connect our responses.

Or we'd better get ready to suffer the consequences.

Getting in Front of the Problem With a "Crowdsourced" Mindset

In building a collaborative connective-defense cybersecurity model, we can take a lesson from the concept of crowdsourcing.

Crowdsourcing, according to *Merriam-Webster,* is the practice of obtaining needed services, ideas, or content by soliciting contributions from a large group of people, especially from the online community. Crowdsourcing has certainly enhanced our travel by car. Not too long ago, we followed the directions provided to us by our GPS devices, unaware of road hazards, accidents, etc., along our routes. Now with crowdsourced information input into our GPS applications in real time, we are aware of these incidents and can take action to avoid them. In fact, the applications provide an alternative route. We are empowered as drivers because we have useful information and mitigations in real time.

Adopting a crowdsourced mindset is a great strategy for fortifying our collective cybersecurity defenses. Because cybersecurity is now everyone's problem, everyone can become part of the solution. We will need strong leadership to move in the direction of sharing relevant information and sharing it quickly.

With its long history as a prime target for cyber criminals and threats, the U.S. government recognized early on that collaboration and information sharing can make a difference in cybersecurity.

In 1998 the federal government asked each critical infrastructure sector to establish an Information Sharing and Analysis Center (ISAC). These groups were created to help critical infrastructure owners and operators protect their facilities, personnel, and customers from cyber and physical security threats and other hazards. ISACs provide a central resource for gathering and sharing information on cyber threats and network defense best practices. They are a starting point for crowdsourcing a connective defense.

The Comprehensive National Cybersecurity Initiative (CNCI) was initiated in January 2008 by President George W. Bush, and was a significant policy development, especially for its time and the current understanding of the cybersecurity environment. CNCI proposed to establish a frontline of defense against immediate cyber threats by creating and enhancing shared situational awareness of network vulnerabilities, threats, and events. CNCI advocated for making cybersecurity more collaborative and efficient within the federal government; it did so by establishing more empowered cyber centers and extending that expertise to the entire governmental sector by enabling teamwork across state, local, and tribal governments. The initiative remains one of the strongest examples of dedicated government leadership achieving a whole-of-nation approach to tackling shared cybersecurity challenges.

A potentially big roadblock to promoting collaboration in the private sector—fear of running afoul of federal laws and regulations—was mitigated by the passage of The Cybersecurity Act of 2015. This important legislation encourages private organizations to voluntarily share cyber threat indicators and defensive measures without fear of legal liability, public exposure, or antitrust complications. The act not only provides protection for companies that share information with the federal government, but also for companies that exchange cyber incident information with each other, whether or not the government is involved. For CEOs and CISOs, the most significant benefit of this law is that it empowers members of the private sector to begin collaborating with each other on cyber incidents. The private sector can take advantage of this opportunity, redefine information sharing, and create a framework for collaboration that serves its needs.

There are many powerful examples of this new spirit of openness and sharing in the private sector. One demonstration of this is the Columbus Collaboratory, an Ohio-centered consortium of private-sector companies across different industries—from healthcare and financial services to energy and consumer goods. Columbus Collaboratory is committed to using sophisticated analytics, artificial intelligence, and machine learning on a collaborative basis to identify and overcome cybersecurity threats.

Another illustration of how bold leaders have put aside the emotional turmoil of working with competitors is the Cyber Threat Alliance. Look at their roster, and you'll immediately see the participants are often direct competitors. But however fiercely they may compete in the market, all their CEOs ultimately understand the value in jointly being part of the solution.

TruSTAR, the organization where I act as an advisor, is another great example of how adopting a collaborative, crowd-sourced model really pays dividends. At TruSTAR, a threat intelligence platform helps organizations—many of which are direct competitors—share information about threats and solutions in order to overcome the organized malevolence promoted by cybercriminals.

I believe it is this crowdsourcing approach to cybersecurity that is a model not only of what can work, but also of what has to happen with far more frequency if we are to beat the bad guys and keep our networks secure and our data safe. And that will take the leadership, confidence, and boldness of those business executives and board members reading this book.

We cannot afford to do any less.

Building a Connective Defense to Share Cybersecurity Information

These efforts demonstrate the benefits of working as a team to defend ourselves against the growing number of attacks against both government and the private sector. This cannot be a feel-good exercise to make us feel warm and fuzzy about teamwork. This is a pragmatic, hard-headed, enlightened approach, accomplished by pooling resources and getting better insight into threats and defenses.

If we don't do this, adversaries will always have the upper hand, and we will continue to endlessly spend money, but never be able to win the battle.

Unfortunately, mention the word "sharing" when it comes to cybersecurity, and many corporate leaders start twitching. But we must take the emotion out of this issue by appreciating the many benefits of crowdsourcing to create a "connective defense."

What are the requirements of connective defense?

- **It must preserve privacy.** Collaboration on cybersecurity should not cost participants the trust of their clients.

- **Participation in it must deliver real value to the individual contributors.** It is not sufficient to create an exchange where sharing is one-directional. Members must be incentivized to participate in a timely exchange of actionable data.

- **The member connections must be fluid.** We cannot limit ourselves by allowing existing personal or industry relationships to define our sharing paradigm. We need to have dynamic connections, driven by the targets of an attack campaign and composed of those in the network who want to contribute to timely active defense.

- **The system has to be transparent and trustworthy.** There cannot be any doubt about the motivations of contributors or the operators of the system itself. There must be transparency around how members are vetted and admitted and how the data is used and protected.

Keep in mind another important issue: What information is being shared? When we talk about sharing intelligence, some ill-informed people may reflexively interpret that as proprietary and private information. But the information that needs to be shared isn't personally identifiable information, health insurance data, context-specific content, or intellectual property. It is information that will identify an attacker in the network and mitigate the attack.

This connective defense by enterprises working together will help all of us detect, investigate, and mitigate emerging threats far more quickly than we ever could working alone.

In doing so, we are taking a page—in fact, the most strategic page—of the cyber attackers' go-to-market plan. We can finally close the gap with our adversaries and change the discussion from embarrassing failures to inspiring successes.

Isn't it about time?

Summary

Let me be very clear about this: The old model for cybersecurity no longer works. It's broken, and it can't be fixed. We must work together like the bad guys do—only better.

Keeping an incident quiet or sharing only among a few friends potentially exposes others to the same attack, which is a fundamental breach of fiduciary responsibility, whether you're a CEO, board member, CISO, or government official. A true exchange—a connective defense—will give our organizations the best opportunity not only to defend our digital infrastructure against attacks, but it also will enable others to understand the threat landscape and help all of us.

Sharing is best if it is voluntary, not under a government-reporting requirement. An exchange will add value and will enable real-time correlation and mitigation to all participants. Let's learn from government agencies' experience in plotting our paths; those of us who worked in the government's cyber centers know that this collaboration model can and does work.

The technology is advancing, the legal climate is changing, and the opportunity for us, the good guys, to gain the higher ground is here. The lack of effective collaboration among organizations in both the public and private sectors is our Achilles' heel. The bad guys will continue to exploit it as long as we let them.

Let's fix this problem!

14

Compliance Is Not a Cybersecurity Strategy

Ryan Gillis — Vice President for Cybersecurity Strategy and Global Policy, Palo Alto Networks

Mark Gosling — Vice President, Internal Audit, Palo Alto Networks

In many boardrooms around the world, members are receiving serious presentations from their chief information security officers about the status of their efforts against a whole host of security and privacy regulatory mandates that have increasingly significant potential fines. Board members are undoubtedly taking their governance responsibilities seriously and are likely asking tough questions to determine how big of a regulatory risk their organizations may be facing and if they are on track to demonstrate compliance.

But while compliance is important, it should not overshadow the board's focus on the greater issue of managing cybersecurity risk.

Clearly, this is not an either/or scenario between risk and compliance. Organizations and their boards need to pay strict attention to both issues. The most successful organizations are the ones that understand the tight relationship between the two, even in the face of mounting cyber threats, and act accordingly regarding budgets, manpower, and executive focus.

Compliance and security are not mutually exclusive; far from it, in fact. Ideally, compliance can document and provide metrics that reflect an organization's cybersecurity risk management approach. If you take the necessary steps to safeguard your most critical data across your networks, cloud environment(s), and endpoints, and regularly train your employees to practice good security hygiene, your organization will be well-positioned for compliance.

That's why it's important to remember that, in an ideal scenario, compliance is a **floor** for your organization's cybersecurity efforts, not a **ceiling.**

As important as it is for organizations to demonstrate compliance with regulatory mandates, it's not the be-all and end-all for executives. And board members should not become distracted by the latest new thing in the regulatory game—nor should they view cybersecurity risk as an unsurmountable threat fueled by the latest breach headlines.

Instead, board members should help their organizations focus on the big picture of cybersecurity—reducing risk, increasing business opportunity, and using precious resources wisely and strategically.

Cyber risk discussions now take up more time, energy, and attention for board members. And, with a deluge of information about cyber risk and regulatory demands out there, it can be hard to make sense of it all. However, the common goal and focus for all board members, organizations, employees, customers, partners, government agencies, and regulatory bodies should be straightforward: Reduce cyber risk. Reducing cyber risk is too often rooted in either the anecdotal lessons from public breaches or the penalties associated with compliance and legal issues. A sound approach is more about ensuring the long-term vitality, competitiveness, and solid financial footing of the organization—and perhaps using your organization's security as a competitive differentiator and a mechanism to ensure the trust of your customers.

In an Era of Hyper Compliance, Don't Get Distracted From the Real Goal

Around the globe, new regulations designed to address digital challenges—from protecting private information to ensuring that critical infrastructure is not compromised—are consuming an increasing amount of attention. Business and technical decision makers, with the support and guidance of their boards, have devoted significant financial and personnel resources to shape these policies, avoid unintended consequences, and demonstrate compliance.

But organizations that focus myopically on regulations, rather than on the bigger issue of cyber risk reduction, are going to be hard-pressed to align their security practices with their core business priorities.

While no one wants to be hit with fines or have to spend hours explaining and negotiating with regulators after a data breach, it is essential for organizations to remain true to their business priorities first. And that's a critical role played by board members.

Instead of asking, "Did we pass that PCI DSS audit?", board members should ask questions that emphasize whether critical business goals could be impacted by security problems.

- What types of data exfiltration could include our latest intellectual property?

- How are we ensuring that customer records are not stolen, tampered with, or erased?

- Can we be certain that our email messages with that potential acquisition partner do not appear on the screens of our top competitor?

Let's also keep in mind that even the best-intentioned compliance mandates can have very real, and very unattractive, consequences if not enveloped by a broader cyber risk reduction framework.

New regulations have the potential to result in confusion, conflict, and inefficiencies that actually may increase cyber risk, not reduce it, by diverting valuable resources from threat detection and prevention toward reporting and accounting. Take, for example, the lessons learned from the implementation of the original U.S. Federal Information Security Management Act of 2002. This regulation required U.S. federal agencies to produce hard-copy binders on the status of the security of their networks, essentially diverting scarce IT and security personnel and resources away from actually securing those networks, in favor of recordkeeping. This is really more of a "checkbox" regulation, rather than a way for organizations' networks to be truly secure—another example of being compliant, but not necessarily secure.

This is a vital lesson learned for more effectively identifying and implementing common goals in cyber risk reduction and threat prevention among all parties—

boards, executives, customers, trading partners, industry groups, regulators, and governments. Because being "secure" is not a static end-state that lends itself to inflexible compliance checklists. It requires a constant evaluation of risk, relative to a rapidly evolving cyber threat landscape.

As you read Part 2 of *Navigating the Digital Age,* we encourage you to pay attention to the words of Verisign Executive Vice President Danny McPherson. Danny has done a great job of putting an exclamation point on this issue:

> *"…compliance is not—repeat, not— your goal. Or, at least it should not be the key focus of your cybersecurity program. And let me tell you why:*
>
> *Being compliant is not the same as being secure. "*

Major Board Implications

Certainly, board members must continue to ask tough questions of all their senior executives, including but not exclusively, their CISO and CIO. Specifically, board members' questions on cybersecurity must rapidly swing from, "Are we compliant?" to "What is our risk profile?"

This means that board members need to move from a somewhat passive, detached approach to security oversight to one that is more proactive. Take the results from a recent study conducted by the National Association of Corporate Directors (NACD) about cyber risk. Following were the top four answers board members gave to the question, "Which of the following cyber risk oversight practices has the board performed over the last 12 months?"

- Reviewed the company's current approach to protecting its most critical data assets (82%)

- Reviewed the technology infrastructure used to protect the company's most critical data assets (74%)

- Communicated with management about the types of cyber risk information the board requires (70%)

- Reviewed the company's response plan in the case of a breach (61%)

"Review" and "communicate," as important as they are, do not go far enough to identify and act on the best ways to reduce cyber risk, especially with a prevention-first strategy. Instead, boards need to become both more intimately knowledgeable in how executives charged with reducing cyber risk are identifying threats before they do damage and in becoming true partners in helping those executives fortify their defense plans.

This also means that board members need to accelerate their own education on cyber risks—both in general and as it specifically pertains to their organization. For instance, in the NACD survey of directors, 73% of respondents said their boards had "some knowledge" of cyber security risks. Clearly, in order to fulfill both their fiduciary responsibility as directors and to make good on their requirement to understand and support their executives' risk prevention, they need to become even more conversant on cyber risks and in identifying the right solution specifically tailored for the unique requirements of their organization.

Whether that means utilizing outside cyber security consultants as board advisors, putting a cyber risk specialist on the board, or taking some other steps, is obviously the board's call. But it's a call that needs to be made. After all, a study conducted by NASDAQ pointed out that 91% of board members are unable to interpret a cybersecurity report.[1]

And that is a big problem.

Board Oversight Questions

To facilitate a more robust and effective strategic plan for reducing cyber risk, board members need to ask a new set of questions designed to provide a deeper understanding of current and potential risk levels and a stronger basis for taking action to protect against current and emerging threats.

- **Which people, processes, and technologies are currently being used to defend your network?** Your CIO and CISO also must be able to tell you what your organization is already doing about spotting risks before they are weaponized, and where they believe the next attacks are likely to occur. This information needs to be aligned with a thoughtful, open discussion on how, where, and when resources are being deployed against the threat identification and protection processes.

- **What additional resources are needed in people, processes, and technologies in order to limit risk?** Of course, no one is going to give the CISO a blank check, so ask tough questions to determine where the greatest financial efficiencies can be gained by making smarter—and not necessarily bigger—investments.

- **Which threat intelligence services is the organization using, and how are they performing?** It's vitally important to know what demonstrable impact those services are making to help the organization spot risks and protect against them before they pierce its defenses.

- **How do our organization's security training programs need to change to reflect the new realities of cyber risk?** Should existing education programs for users, partners, and even customers be modernized, overhauled, or scrapped entirely in favor of approaches that better reflect the coming threats?

- **Can your legal and compliance officers identify all existing regulations that apply to cyber and information security, and do they understand which new mandates are under consideration or in development?** How will those emerging requirements impact your organization's threat profile? And, should your representatives become more involved in the process of framing those mandates in order to ensure that they really do help reduce risk and not become just another checkmark on the compliance "to do" list?

- **Are representatives from the security team included in every business planning meeting that's being held?** This is an extremely important mindset shift for organizations: Boards need to be in front of this transformation and move from "security as an afterthought" to "secure by design." This means everything from new product development and supply chain management to marketing programs and customer retention—not just compliance or data governance.

- **What is your plan to keep up with the pace of change?** Ultimately this is one of the most important questions. By anticipating change, you will be better prepared to understand the impact on your organization, infrastructure, and the associated risks, which will directly affect your ability to safely and quickly adapt to change.

Conclusion

One of the biggest things board members can do to ensure that their organizations' cybersecurity resources are deployed in the most effective and efficient manner is to remember that unyielding, relentless attention to aligning cyber risk reduction with business priorities will go a long way toward achieving compliance goals.

Board members who help their executives focus on reducing vulnerabilities and properly balancing risk with opportunity will have the biggest impact on their organizations' successes—but only if they remember that compliance is a byproduct of that effort, not the ultimate goal.

This chapter was adapted from "How Can Board Members Help Turn Cyber Risk Reduction from a Goal into a Reality," published in January 2018 in NACD Directorship, the official publication of the National Association of Corporate Directors.

---

[1] "Grading global boards of directors on cybersecurity," Harvard Law School Forum on Corporate Governance and Financial Regulation, 2016

Cybersecurity Awareness, Understanding, and Leadership

15

Security Transformation As a Business Imperative

John Scimone — Senior Vice President and Chief Security Officer, Dell

Despite everyone's best intentions and significant investments in budget, manpower, and corporate attention, organizations in every industry and geographical location are falling behind in the all-out-fight to protect their digital assets against cyber threats.

Why? While reasons vary for each organization, a few truths have quickly become self-evident. For instance:

- It takes much, much longer to detect sophisticated intrusions than it does for bad actors to carry them out.

- Hackers can try an indefinite number of times and only need to succeed once; defenders must be successful every hour of every day.

- The sheer volume of detected IT vulnerabilities is multiplying faster than ever—and those are just the ones we can actually detect.

- Businesses are rapidly digitizing their operations, building increased dependence on the same infrastructure that is becoming increasingly vulnerable.

- Hacking tools are more sophisticated and easier to access, and the financial barrier to "market entry" for hackers is dropping.

- The ability to confidently attribute cyberattacks remains elusive, creating an environment where criminality can exist without accountability.

The result: Cyberattacks may be the most prominent "low-risk / high-reward" enterprise in the history of humankind.

Get Ready for Security Transformation

This narrative represents a grave risk to modern businesses and demands aggressive management. Clearly, whatever our organizations are doing is not enough. Not nearly enough. Traditional approaches are not even slowing the advance of cybercrime, never mind actually defeating it. No board member, CEO, or CISO should be willing to accept this status quo.

Instead, business leaders—not just the CISO and CIO—must enter a new era of security transformation. A radical rethinking of security—yes, a transformation—is essential. This approach, by the way, is not overly dependent on cutting-edge security tools, serious financial investments, or recruitment of experienced professionals—although all of those are certainly necessary.

Perhaps what is needed most is for board members and business executives—including CISOs and CIOs, by the way—to move beyond traditional approaches to cybersecurity threats. We must all enthusiastically embrace security transformation rooted in a realistic recognition that cyber threat actors can hit a business with devastating consequence at any moment, 24/7/365, and that this is no longer a black swan risk in terms of likelihood. This compels a level of aggression in attitude and activity that is currently missing from the dialogue.

Security Transformed—Resilience on an Equal Footing With Defense

As much as we are seeking to prevent a cyberattack, we are also preparing for a cyberattack. As you can imagine, there's a world of difference between the two approaches. A key element in preparing for a cyberattack is the notion of resilience. Of course, every business leader and board member understands that systems, applications, and technology investments don't deliver any value if they are not available or if the data they contain cannot be trusted. In fact, when systems are down or data integrity is in question, it's even worse: We lose economic value and business competitiveness because we're chasing our tails fixing problems, rather than creating value for our customers.

That said, CISOs have historically been charged with ensuring resilience primarily for regulatory compliance and to avoid lawsuits regarding service interruptions. But resilience is much more than simply passing audits or avoiding fines and contract claims for failing to demonstrate compliance. As business leaders, you want your security forces to be fixated with laser-sharp focus on ensuring availability of essential resources in order to avoid problems and assure business success—not simply on "being compliant."

When considering cyber risk management, we can break it down into three component parts:

1. Threat management
2. Vulnerability management
3. Consequence management

Unfortunately, there really is painfully little we can do on the threat management front. Unless you are part of a law enforcement or related government organization with investigatory and arrest powers, one's ability to impact the threats on the other end of the keyboard remains limited.

From a vulnerability management perspective, our adoption of pervasive mobility, cloud computing, personal applications, and the exciting world of the Internet of Things all increase our cyberattack surface and associated risk profile. As a result, the number of publicly reported vulnerabilities more than doubled in 2017.[1] Now, these are risks well worth taking for most businesses—in fact, the decision to not digitally transform would be a death knell for most businesses today—but we also need to acknowledge that with this shifting business technology footprint comes substantially increased cyber risk.

As a result, the CISO spends much of his or her day focused on vulnerabilities—fixing them, mitigating them, and devising ways to avoid them in the first place. Not surprisingly, this has left scant resources for consequence management.

That's where a commitment to resilience becomes essential. Recognizing that in the current environment where threat actors and vulnerabilities remain pervasive and uninhibited and are likely to remain so for the foreseeable future, a greater focus and priority must be placed on how to manage the consequences that come during and after an attack. Organizations need to focus on developing the capability to effectively fight through what is increasingly becoming the inevitability of an attack. In order to do this, businesses must focus as much on security-minded business process improvements and continuity planning as on the deployment of additional security tools.

Security Transformed—Custom-Tailored, Risk-Aligned Programs and Investments

Transforming the way security is planned, deployed, and managed must change with the reality that business conditions are constantly evolving, operational initiatives are always in flux, and—especially—the bad guys are forever evolving their own tactics.

Traditional approaches no longer work in an era marked by heavy reliance on digital assets that range from monolithic data centers and traditional applications to the "connected enterprise." For instance, the legacy approach—which does not necessarily mean it's been in place for decades, but more refers to an outdated approach—to security has mostly been binary: Either your organization is secure, or it's not.

But the lessons of past breaches have taught us that security is best measured as a scale of risk. Remember what I said earlier: We're not trying to completely prevent breaches, but rather anticipate and respond to them so we can effectively reduce their impact to an acceptable level. Since you can't stop everything in today's vastly complex and vulnerable technology landscape, you need to establish a clear sense of priorities and invest most meaningfully in both defending and preparing a resilient posture for those areas.

Another transformative way of looking at security is the shift away from standard "best practices." As comforting as it is for business executives to hear from their CISOs that they have aligned with well-established best practices on security, the harsh reality is that best practices are not actually effective in meeting the risk expectations of most modern enterprises. (If they were, we wouldn't be reading about the latest breach at a premier corporate brand so frequently.) In addition, the notion of best practices can also obscure the reality that security no longer can be a one-size-fits-all paradigm. CISOs have recognized that security strategy must look and behave differently for every organization, based on its business strategy, risk tolerance, and perceived value of the protected business assets.

Security Transformed—Structure Matters

Business leaders also should evolve their most basic assumptions about how structured security responsibility within the organization must change. Historically, the CISO most often has reported to the CIO or some other senior technical officer. That organizational structure makes sense if you assume that security is a corporate technology initiative rather than a business risk management function. However, remember what IT organizations are going through these days, with practices such as shadow IT, tech-savvy end users firing up their own virtual machines, affordable public cloud services used for business applications, and oceans of unmanaged endpoints, ranging from smartphones to wearable computers. In security transformation, the CISO is best able to defend the organization when he or she is positioned to look across all cyber risk, not just the risks created by the corporate IT organization. Further, beyond simply reactive risk management, CISOs should be leaning forward to focus on digital opportunities, a role best enabled when the CISO is positioned to have visibility across all of an organization's digital activities and in tight and direct alignment with other business executives.

Security Transformed—Perimeterless Security

Finally, security transformation mandates that cybersecurity defense go far beyond the traditional emphasis on keeping bad guys off the network and away from valuable data. Instead, a more enlightened, business-centric approach to cybersecurity should embrace and account for new digital models, including widespread mobility, cloud platforms, and increased third-party risk factors. This shifts the emphasis away from devices and platforms, and toward the protection and defense of digital identities and the data that is most important to the business.

Some examples of how organizations are embracing security transformation include: the idea that security is not a binary concept and should be measured on a scale of risk; or why security programs should not be driven primarily or exclusively by compliance mandates, but instead should be tailored based on business priorities, such as operational efficiency, brand reputation, or market competitiveness. We should begin to think of cybersecurity not as a component of IT risk, but rather, as a business function that addresses business risk across the entire enterprise. And we should ensure that our cybersecurity programs are following the data and identities that are so key to protect, regardless of where the evolving technology and third-party landscape takes them. In whole though, the most essential aspect of security transformation is fundamentally understanding and accepting that the current approach—level of attention, investment, tools, skills, business process tradeoffs—is woefully inadequate to effectively manage cyber risk, and then having the fortitude and commitment to implement the changes necessary to address this disparity.

Putting It Into Action: Questions Board Members and C-Level Executives Should Ask Their CISOs

If you're a CEO, COO, CFO, or board member, you need to be proactive and talk with your CISO about what they are doing to transform security protocols and processes. And that does not mean asking which new intrusion detection tool they've bought or which advanced persistent threat remediation program they've implemented. Instead, your conversations need to focus on ways to turn security transformation from a technical discussion to a business one, and you should seek to understand if the appropriate level of boldness and urgency is present in every aspect of the program.

I encourage you to ask your CISO such questions as:

- What is the likelihood that the breach that just hit Company Y will happen to us?

- If it does happen to us, what is our legal, operational, brand, and compliance exposure?

- How have you transformed our security protocols and practices to move beyond what isn't working at other peer companies like Y?

- Are you confident our overall business risk tolerance is clearly defined, and is our cybersecurity then properly aligned to it? If not, what do we need to do to achieve that definition and alignment?

- What is the most glaring vulnerability in our cyber defenses today, and what is it likely to be three years from now? What plans are in place to address both of these and against what timeline?

- Does a risk-governance structure exist that clearly defines corporate roles and responsibilities relating to cybersecurity-risk identification and management? Do your business stakeholders understand their roles, and have they effectively operationalized them? Is accountability being introduced where dependent stakeholders are not meeting expectations?

Hopefully, this discussion will demonstrate to you that your CISO understands and is committed to a transformed approach that is appropriate and necessary to support your business.

And, if you don't like the answers they give you, you should encourage them to reconsider their strategy—radically, if necessary. After all, if they are investing in legacy best practices that are benchmarks in most companies in your industry, your organization is just as likely to be the next victim of a major attack. That's because the status quo, for most organizations today, is an ineffective posture, as evidenced by the constant stream of public breach notifications. And for a modern business to survive and thrive, it must transform its security posture alongside the broader business and digital transformations that are already underway.

---

[1] CVSS Severity Distribution Over Time, National Vulnerability Database, NIST

16

The Importance of Cybersecurity Preparation and Leadership

Stephen Moore — Vice President and Chief Security Strategist, Exabeam

If your organization is like most, you probably have an incident response plan designed to help your teams work their way through a cybersecurity attack. It covers the technical and nontechnical steps the organization must take to respond. It has passed the muster of auditors and been reviewed countless times for the purpose of fulfilling regulatory compliance requirements. All in all, you are proud of this document and can point to it and say, "Yes, we are prepared."

And then a breach happens.

Guess what? You're not prepared. No matter how much time and effort your teams have put into their incident response plan, there is no way they could possibly foresee and prepare for the massive toll a major data breach will inflict upon your organization and your people.

Through my experiences, I've learned what to do if your organization has been breached, and what not to do. I've learned about the steps organizations can take to ensure they are better prepared to handle a breach, including some ideas I will share here. Most of all, I've done my best to learn what it takes to be a leader and what it takes to inspire confidence and comfort in times of crisis.

On the Frontlines

There's no way to synthesize everything that happens during a breach, the gravity of it. You might be a mid-level manager and all of a sudden find you are thrust into technical response, and also asked to communicate with senior-level executives, customers, and with people across the entire organization responsible for responding to the breach. Very few are prepared for this drastic change in pressures and responsibilities.

I must make the point that nothing can prepare you for what it is like to be in the vortex of a data breach, especially those of great depth and breadth. I'll give you one example: Time. Talk to people who've never been through a breach, and they'll tell you that the impact and implications will probably be mostly over in a matter of months. All I can say is, "No way." It is going to take years for the company to recover; and even then, there are likely to be lingering issues.

A breach will affect every aspect of your business: the retention and attraction of new clients; your personnel and corporate culture; whether people will even want to work at the company; your reputation.

You will likely be dealing with multiple investigations, audits, regulatory groups, the press, and a retooling of your technology infrastructure. Not to mention litigation. All of this will go on for years and will be a huge and constant drain on resources. Going forward, every aspect of the business will be shaped by the breach.

The Human Impact

The toll this will take on your people is something that you can't measure, anticipate, or really appreciate until you're actually going through it. The pressure on your people is immense. Most organizations don't have the depth of management, the training, and the people with the right skill sets to adequately deal with a major breach—both immediately and over the vast span of time the circumstances require.

Even if you have adequate response and communication plans, you need people to execute them. In a breach, a communications funnel gets created and most of the information is communicated through a small group of people leading the investigation. It is up to those people to synthesize the information for the appropriate individuals—whether board members, senior-level executives, auditors, clients, the media, partners, or any other effected parties.

There is an art to this, and most people forced into these roles are not prepared to do them well. They must learn, and learn fast.

Steps to Being Better Prepared

Given the immense challenges and dramatic impact that a cybersecurity event will impose on your organization and its people, how do you prepare for something that is probably beyond any preconceived expectations you may have established? It sounds like an unsolvable riddle, but can you prepare for something that can't be prepared for?

Actually, you can. I've developed several ideas that I believe will help individuals and organizations do a better job of preparing their people to deal with the ramifications of a cyber breach, without forcing them to constantly strive to do hero work.

No. 1: Write Your Breach Notification Letter Before You Suffer a Breach

Lacking experience, organizations need to work backward, starting with the breach notification letter. Sit down at the highest levels possible within the organization—senior management, CISO, perhaps even including board members—and write the breach notification letter, under the direction of counsel and as a draft "working" document. Interestingly enough, doing this will uncover many of the key challenges you will face. This is the finest executive tabletop exercise known to me, due to the questions and outcomes. When you sit down and write a notification letter that the world may one day see, you're going to have to start asking the right questions:

- Who writes the letter?

- What is the tone?

- Whose names are on it? The CIO? CEO? CISO?

- Who will answer questions from the media?

- What are the ingredients that go into the letter?

- There are the staple talking points, such as "we've retained outside experts and contacted law enforcement." But do we have a pre-existing relationship with them? Shouldn't we?

- How well-prepared are the people inside the organization to do the work that will be required? Are they trained for this?

- What will it cost to pay an outside organization for public relations? What type of executive coaching do they provide?

- How do we securely share information and communicate if breached?

- Who meets with the press? Who coaches these people prior to meeting with the press?

- How do we contact clients? By letters? Phone calls? Email? Via the web site?

- Where do we host our breach information website? What happens if our site is part of the breach?

- Are we going to do credit monitoring? What does that cost? Is it worth it?

- Most importantly, who is the source of truth for investigative answers? Won't they already be a little busy? How often do we update these talking points? Are we able to answer these in-house today, or do we lack this ability?

I could go on with more questions, but I'm sure you get the point. These are typically not questions that organizations raise until they've suffered a breach, and at that point, it is too late. You've already gone from the frying pan into the fire.

No. 2: Conduct a Field Trip to the Source of Truth—The Security Operations Center (SOC)

If you have a breach, who would you call internally? Who would that person call next? Who would prepare executives for difficult interviews and questions from clients?

Work your way down to the unfiltered answer: those staff members normally ignored and probably working buried within your information security team— your security operations center (SOC). Without question, the reputation of your organization and your future professional comfort is in their hands. Have you even met them? Do you understand their workday, their challenges, and their pain? How well can they articulate their investigative processes?

Their problems and observable risks must be externally supported and prioritized. Seek their counsel *before* you have no choice but to seek it. Please do not underserve your SOC.

No. 3: Build a Better Type of Response Plan and Response Action

A plan untested, unshared, or created in a vacuum of experience is only good for those who can avoid the negative effects of its failure.

When I started this chapter, I was skeptical about the standard incidence response plans that most organizations use to satisfy executive management or outside auditors. Frankly, I've never seen a good one when it comes to actually responding to a breach. These response plans typically cover technical issues, but they don't discuss things like leadership or communications. And they don't address breaches as the multi-year events that they often are in the real world.

A more effective incidence response plan will address the pertinent questions raised by the breach notification letter. Who's in charge? What's the tenor and spirit of the organization? How do you sound? How large was the breach—how many records or systems were affected? How open do you want your plan to be— do you want to be cold, verbose, and succinct, or do you want to be open and share as much as you can? Do you share early before all the details are known, or wait to run out the clock? I recommend sharing early and honestly, knowing that additional updates will be made as the investigation unfolds.

No. 4: Plan to Deal With Issues Around Response Capabilities, Technology, Infrastructure, and Physical Space

Once you've suffered a breach, your entire technology infrastructure will likely be under investigation. Your IT teams will be buying new technology while they are still cleaning up the existing environment. Plus, you will likely be bringing in outside consultants, not just on the technology side, but across the board.

Along this line of thinking, remember that your multi-year plan, pilot projects, and pending budget requests will probably be green-lit. You will need three critical technical capabilities: visibility, analytics, and automated technical response. You can ensure you have these capabilities before a breach, or acquire them quickly post-breach. I'd suggest prioritizing these capabilities before a problem occurs; it's much less expensive.

Visibility removes technical blind spots, generally through data lakes to store event data and analytics to make sense of it all and create attacker timelines. And then response is your cleanup. Remember, without complete attacker timelines, you won't have complete response.

Logistically, do you have physical space for additional hardware while you remediate and clean existing infrastructure? Do you have enough rack space, cabling, and power to deal with all of the extra equipment? Ever think about allocating this ahead of time?

You also need to think about creating a landing zone to house all of the people you are going to bring on board to help. Where is the secure command center, and is it most convenient for the staff?

No. 5: Teach Your People Well

Your people, many of them technical mid-level managers, will be thrust into public-facing activities. Are they ready for it? Have you trained them? Do you feel comfortable having them speak to your most important customers? Do you have a backup plan and a backup plan for that?

You might need 25 more spokespeople. Have they been trained to speak in public, handle an interview, an auditor, or government official? This goes beyond what your corporate communications team can manage, because many interactions need to be technically oriented. You can use outside people to help, but they are most likely going to be speaking from a script. Is that the image you want to present to your customers, partners, and the general public? Crisis tends to burn through veneer.

The responsibilities are not just outside-facing. There are internal challenges as well. Mid-level technical managers, need to be articulate and clear when speaking to everyone, especially newly acquainted executive-leadership team members.

This is one of the hidden costs of dealing with a breach. It's natural to think about lost revenue, a declining stock price, damage to the brand's reputation. But there are a lot of people-oriented costs that must be addressed as well. If you can plan for some of these in advance, and spend the time training your people to handle a variety of roles, you stand a much better chance of mitigating some of the other challenges as they arise and threaten to cripple your organization once an attack takes place.

No. 6: Build Relevance With Your Sales Teams

This is advice aimed primarily at CISOs and other security leaders. Despite what we think, the board and executive leadership are often focused on one main goal, which is the retention and acquisition of customers. Everything else flows from that, beginning with the perception of the brand's reputation. In a breach, you will be asked: "Does our present situation put any pending deals on the bubble?" and "Who might leave?"

Clients and prospects will have a ton of questions, and how you answer them will be critical. Again, it is essential that you encourage comfort and confidence. When I speak to CISOs, I often ask how many have presented at their sales quarterly business reviews or even know their sales teams. Curiously, I've never had a positive acknowledgement. Let's change this.

A breach creates ongoing challenges for those who make money for the company; understand the sales pain. You will be pleased to discover that doing this opens a wonderful door of relevance for your organization and even personal brand.

You may think your job is to keep the bad guys out, but it's also to facilitate the business. I've learned to develop a strong relationship with the sales team, and it has given me an incredible amount of clout. Once I took the time to build the trust of the sales team by putting them first, my career changed. It changed who I was talking to in the organization, how I was treated, and the types of conversations I was involved in.

No. 7: Don't Rely Solely on "Hero Work"

People are not superheroes, and if your plan is to rely on herculean efforts you will probably fail. On the other hand, you want to create space for people to do hero work, which is usually the result of the type of leadership you provide and the type of culture you create.

If someone is operating in fear, he or she will not innovate, will not do hero work, will not be the brand ambassador, contributor, or thinker you need. Fear creates indifference quickly, and the level of indifference is often directly tied back to bad management. Your leaders have to take the heat, so the people on their teams can take the chances that hero work requires. You have to keep morale up and shield your people from pain or fear of failure. Hire and promote servant leadership today.

Leaders have to be leaders, and often in times of crisis, you see them slip back into the technical. This acutely means the leader doesn't trust his or her staff. Once you get into a position of leadership, you can't afford to be that technical person anymore. If you're spending your time playing around on a console, you're not a leader.

Conclusion

The skills involved in responding to a breach are much different than those involved in attempting to prevent it, particularly for most members of your technology teams. The reality, however, is that you have to rely on these people to step up their game and provide a level of leadership.

You need your leaders and spokespeople to inspire comfort and confidence in all directions. You can get ahead of the game by preparing them beforehand and being aware of which people are likely to step up and provide leadership in a time of crisis.

You can ensure that the overall organization is prepared so there is less chance that the people responsible for responding will be overwhelmed. You can ensure that there is leadership depth. You can take the time to write your breach notification letter ahead of time, answer the questions, and align resources to support those capabilities into your corporate culture. You can visit your SOC.

As an organization, you will likely be judged less on whether you suffered a cyberattack, and more on how well you responded to it. The better prepared you and your teams are, the better able you will be to respond appropriately. You won't be able to anticipate every scenario—nobody can—but strong preparation and leadership will help you deal with the unexpected.

17

Data Manipulation, Law Enforcement, and Our Future: Seeking to Build Trust in Our Digitally Connected Systems

Dr. Philipp Amann — Head of Strategy,
Europol's European Cybercrime Centre (EC3)

While we have traditionally considered data manipulation as the practice of altering documents and other information, that definition is changing. When we think about data manipulation now, the alteration of documents and information done with a criminal or harmful intent has become a major concern, but not the only one. We also think about things like fake news, social engineering through the discrete mining of social media information, and the use of data as a tool—or a weapon—to shape people's thoughts, ideas, opinions, and, ultimately, their actions.

As highlighted in Europol's Annual Internet Organised Crime Threat Assessment, data remains a key commodity for cyber criminals. However, it is no longer just procured for immediate financial gain, but it is also increasingly used, manipulated, or encrypted to further more complex fraud, for ransom, or directly for extortion. The illegal acquisition of intellectual property or its manipulation can reflect the loss of years of research and sub-

stantial investment. Data manipulation in this context can also mean using hiding techniques such as steganography to exfiltrate data or hide command-and-control commands.[1]

Data manipulation has become a moving target for those of us in the business of combating criminal activity online, building trust, and protecting our way of life in the Digital Age. Adversaries who manipulate data with malicious intent are constantly developing new tactics and attack modes, seeking any edge in a world where all of us are increasingly dependent on digital connections. This includes activities by criminals who hide their identity, mask their location, and obfuscate their financial transactions.

The Evolving Role of Law Enforcement

What can we do about data manipulation? The first focus for law enforcement is on investigating criminal behavior and prosecuting those responsible for crimes. With certain aspects of data manipulation and the often related criminal abuse of information technology, we have made significant headway in investigating and prosecuting criminals and shutting down illegal activities. A few examples:

AlphaBay and Hansa: In July 2017, authorities in Europe and the U.S., including the FBI, the U.S. Drug Enforcement Agency, and the Dutch National Police, with the support of Europol and other partner agencies, announced that they had shut down AlphaBay, at the time the largest criminal marketplace on the Dark Web, and Hansa, the third-largest criminal marketplace on the Dark Web. Both AlphaBay and Hansa were enabling massive amounts of illegal drugs, stolen and fraudulent identification documents, access devices, malware, and fraudulent services to be traded amongst cyber adversaries, which were enabling future data-manipulation crimes to be committed.[2]

Operation Power Off: In April 2018, the administrators of the distributed denial-of-service (DDoS) marketplace *webstresser.org* were arrested as a result of Operation Power Off, a complex investigation led by the Dutch police and the U.K.'s National Crime Agency, with the support of Europol and a dozen law enforcement agencies from around the world. *Webstresser.org* was considered the world's largest marketplace for DDoS services. These services enabled cyber adversaries to use data manipulation to launch approximately four million attacks measured, aimed primarily at critical online services offered by banks, government institutions, and police forces.[3]

There are many more examples of successful law enforcement efforts that we can cite, but I am pointing to these because they have specific common characteristics:

1. **They involved a coordinated effort across law enforcement agencies all over the world, along with the support of governments, regulatory bodies, and private companies.** This is an absolute necessity if we are to successfully address criminal activity online, including today's data manipulation challenges.

2. **The crimes involved activities that were clearly illegal, and thus fit into the law enforcement model for investigating and prosecuting criminal activities.** But, as cybercrime and malicious data manipulation evolve, not every instance will be clearly defined by legislation or regulation, thus making it more challenging to prevent, defend, investigate, and successfully prosecute perpetrators.

3. **In each instance, law enforcement was in a position to be more reactive than preventative.** Our ultimate goal is to be both. Law enforcement needs to successfully leverage resources from all around the world, not only to *respond* to crimes, but also to *prevent and deter* the criminal activity from happening in the first place, and ultimately to become more proactive.

These examples also highlight the high degree of professionalism, collaboration, and industrialization of the underground economy, where services and tools supporting the entire "cybercrime value chain" are readily available online and to non-tech savvy individuals.

Disrupting, Deterring, Diverting, and Defending

In dealing with malicious data manipulation and cybercrime, the expectation is that law enforcement—together with all relevant partners and in accordance with its mandate—will take on a more expansive and complementary role in defending against, disrupting, and deterring illegal activities *before* they can do harm and cause losses. This is why prevention and raising awareness are key topics, particularly in relation to addressing high-volume and low-level criminality online.

Law enforcement is in a unique position. Not only do we understand specific modi operandi and techniques when it comes to cybercrime; we are also constantly monitoring trends and threats, while analyzing the evolving motivations impelling those who would do us harm.

However, when it comes to data manipulation, even when activities are motivated by malicious intent, we are sometimes unable to contribute as effectively as we would like. One reason is that not all of the forms of data manipulation we encounter are properly defined as criminal by legislation. In other words, the intent may be malicious, but that doesn't necessarily make it a crime. There is also a lack of a harmonized common legal framework or an underuse of existing legal frameworks and provisions, meaning the same activity might be criminalized in one jurisdiction, but not in another.

Access is another issue. Not every organization involves law enforcement when it first encounters a problem. There are many possible reasons for this. However, I would ask executives to preemptively think about how they work with law enforcement— *before* they have an issue. By building a proactive partnership with law enforcement, you will be better equipped to prevent an attack and enable a stronger and more impactful response should an attack occur.

Even in instances where access is possible, we face challenges in relation to loss of data and loss of location, which create substantial obstacles for investigations. There

is also a need for standardized rules of engagement with private industry to establish a clear understanding of the extent to which private parties can engage with us and we with them.

When it comes to young people with strong information and communication technology (ICT) skills, we also support projects such as the "deterring youngsters initiative," which, together with industry and academia, aims to divert young people away from a potential pathway to cybercrime by offering positive alternatives.[4] We see this not only as an opportunity to divert such talent to positive activities, but also as a way of addressing the shortage of ICT skills.

Cooperating, Collaborating, and Connecting

If there is one thing we've learned about today's cyber environment, it is that we are all in it together. We can gather strength in numbers and in pooling our knowledge, experience, and resources. It is a truism of the Digital Age that we are all connected. Our adversaries try to take advantage of our uber-connectedness—we should do the same in fighting them.

This touches upon the question of safeguards against and regulation of data manipulation, as well as responsibilities. Should it be left to tech companies to self-regulate when it comes to issues around data mining, data privacy, and data manipulation, or should the discussion involve all stakeholders, including industry, law enforcement, and the public? I would argue for the latter approach.

Regulatory and legal frameworks are just one example. If you look across the cybersecurity spectrum, you will see that every facet involves some level of cooperation and collaboration—from technology platforms designed to work seamlessly together, to law enforcement agencies that work together to not only investigate crimes, but also to detect, deter, divert, and to help defend.

The No More Ransom initiative is a great example of a joint initiative between law enforcement and industry, aiming not only at prevention and awareness, but also victim mitigation.[5] The joint platform is currently available in more than 30 languages and supported by more than 120 partners, offering more than 50 decryption tools, free to victims of ransomware.

Building Transparency, Oversight, and Trust

In order to attain the levels of collaboration and cooperation necessary to address data manipulation, we must trust our people, processes, and technologies and build trust-based relationships between industry partners and law enforcement. This means we have to also address issues around transparency and oversight, which are becoming far more complex as technology innovation continues to accelerate and flourish.

The growth of big data analytics and automated decision-making creates new issues in terms of transparency and oversight, and therefore trust. This challenge could become exacerbated with the expansion of machine learning and artificial intelligence. When we allow automated decisions to be based on an algorithm, we may not have a clear way to determine if the data or the algorithm has been manipulated, which becomes further complicated if the algorithm has a built-in bias. This can add risk and make it difficult to audit and/or verify the outcome of such processing.

Trust is also an increasing issue in the area of fake news. It's not just that fake news is being created and real news is being manipulated; sometimes only partial information is shared, thus creating a narrative that seems plausible, but which is not based on all of the available information. It is designed to support a specific idea rather than provide an accurate depiction of events. The challenge is compounded because adversaries are not necessarily breaking the law; they are merely taking advantage of their deep knowledge of social media and search-engine algorithms to manipulate data.

Finally, trust is also a key ingredient to successful public-private partnerships.

Moving Forward

Data manipulation is on the verge of becoming one of the largest criminal industries. Today's reality is that law enforcement has a vital role to play in creating a more impactful and proactive response, not merely reacting to criminal activities. Everyone benefits from a holistic, adaptive, and complementary approach that involves all relevant partners, one where organizations can leverage the capabilities provided by law enforcement agencies. For example:

- **With prioritized and coordinated joint actions** against the key cyber threats—supported by adequate legislation—we can increase the risks for cybercriminals and impose real consequences.

- **With effective prevention and disruption activities,** we further tip the scales to the detriment of criminals by leveraging cooperation and partnerships across law enforcement, government, and private industry.

- **With advanced technologies and open platforms,** we can use shared threat intelligence, machine learning, and automated decision-making to reduce risk and improve responsiveness. This enables us to eliminate manual processes and use software to fight software while adhering to strict data protection regulations.

- **With greater collaboration and commitment to sharing,** we can band together as a community to use combined resources in the war against data manipulation. The cyber industry has made great progress in this area through the establishment of platforms such as the Cyber Threat Alliance (CTA), a not-for-profit organization that enables near real-time, high-quality cyber threat information sharing among companies and organizations in the cybersecurity field. Another great example for collaboration that includes law enforcement as a key partner is the Cyber Defence Alliance. And we have also made significant headway together with the members of our own Advisory Groups.

Looking Ahead

How do we turn this vision of cooperation and collaboration into reality? Europol and its European Cybercrime Centre (EC3) and its many different partners in law enforcement, industry, and academia are a prime example of the power of a networked response to cybercrime at scale. However, we need to continue to improve and forge new alliances, further our cooperation with other partners, and continuously adapt our response. We also need to focus on areas such as regulations and technology to clarify criminal activity, improve our preparedness, and enhance our ability to coordinate a response:

Regulations: With General Data Protection Regulation (GDPR) in Europe, we are seeing the benefits of proactive regulation with a strong cybersecurity element. GDPR forces organizations to understand what data they have, where it is stored, who works on it, who can manipulate it, and how to protect these assets. That is linked to quality and information management, with organizations defining how they run their businesses in relation to cybersecurity risk. It also promotes the idea of designing security protections into products and services.

Taking a broader perspective, GDPR is about improving business and management practices, understanding core business processes, and identifying the assets of an organization, as well as its risk posture. While GDPR is an important piece of legislation, its impact on the WHOIS database going dark after May 25, 2018, had substantial cybersecurity implications, not only for law enforcement, but also for the internet security industry as a whole. This highlights the need to strike a balance between privacy and protection of fundamental rights on the one hand, and security and safety on the other.

Technology: Cyber criminals are adopting new approaches to increase their capacity to manipulate data and commit cybercrime. We must use current and emerging technologies to prevent them. This means the use of shared threat intelligence, open platforms, AI, machine learning, and more. It also means we must explore the benefits of innovations, such as blockchain technology, to create an environment that is more transparent, trustworthy, and resilient.

Big Data analytics, machine learning, and AI can improve cybersecurity through better threat detection and prediction, intelligence collection and analysis, and faster response. With effective use of information, the deployment of scarce operational resources can be better targeted to intervene precisely where issues, crimes, and threats can be expected. However, it is important that we use such tools carefully, proportionally, and in line with relevant legislation and regulations.

An example of using technology and information collaboratively and effectively can be found in the Adversary Playbooks program that has been developed by the CTA. CTA members leverage an automated platform to share actionable intelligence to create Adversary Playbooks that provide a consistent framework to identify broad threat indicators and adversary chokepoints. These playbooks typically incorporate several core elements: technical profiles, typical plays, recommended actions, and technical indicators.

Suggestions for Business Leaders and Executives

Beyond regulations and technology, business leaders and executives have a vital role to play in addressing the evolving challenge of data manipulation. They have a responsibility to set the cybersecurity agendas for their organizations and decide on the appropriate investments in people, processes, and technologies. Suggestions on steps business leaders and board members can take:

Develop an understanding of the evolving adversarial mindset: Executives can look to sponsor initiatives that drive your organization to build a proactive trusted partnership with law enforcement agencies. In doing so, you can gain insights into the motivations, technologies, techniques, and business models of cybercriminals, which can help to define the steps your organization can take to be better enabled to prevent an attack. Also look to collaborate with organizations, such as the Cyber Security Information Sharing Part-

nership, which enable secure threat intelligence to be shared.

Require organization-wide training and education: We all must be educated about the risks of data manipulation and the need for improved cybersecurity. This often starts in the executive suite, where C-level executives must understand risks so they can make the proper investments and strategic decisions. It also extends to security personnel, who are in relatively short supply in comparison to the need. So inspire, incentivize, and reward your IT security personnel to keep vigilant and informed. And recognize that, as leaders, we must leverage education and training in our work and classroom settings so users are aware of how they can mitigate risk whenever they go online.

Insist on a holistic approach: Cybersecurity should be part of a holistic approach that should be part of all processes. Business leaders and board members need to establish a cybersecurity culture whereby everybody is aware of his or her responsibility, and security and privacy "by design" are guiding principles. Since humans are often the weakest link, ongoing training, education, and creating awareness are indispensable tools in protecting against cybercrime and data manipulation.

Conclusion

The world is changing before our very eyes. The threat to data encompasses all three principles of confidentiality, integrity, and availability. By gaining access to data and subsequently exposing such data, criminals undermine the confidentiality of information. By manipulating the data, they undermine the integrity, and by attacks such as ransomware, they make the data unavailable. While data is a commodity now, it is increasingly emerging as a cybercrime attack vector through means such as data manipulation, compromised processes, and the increased potential to shut down basic infrastructure services and other pillars of our societies.

The good news is that no one is alone. In fact, we are all connected, both literally and figuratively. Our connected networks give us the ability to coordinate and collaborate in the face of data manipulation and cybercrime. Will we be able to build the trust necessary among our people, processes, and technology to overcome these threats? We must, we can, and we will.

---

1   "Criminal Use of Information Hiding (CUIng) Initiative," http://cuing.org/

2   "Massive Blow to Criminal Dark Web Activities After Globally Coordinated Operation," Europol, July 20, 2017

3   "World's Biggest Marketplace Selling Internet Paralysing DDOS Attacks Taken Down," Europol, April 25, 2018

4   "Cyber Crime vs Cyber Security: What will you choose?," Europol, https://www.europol.europa.eu/activities-services/public-awareness-and-prevention-guides/cyber-crime-vs-cyber-security-what-will-you-choose

5   "No More Ransom project helps thousands of ransomware victims," ZDNet, July 27, 2017

The Convergence and Divergence of Compliance and Cybersecurity

18

Why Secure Availability—Not Compliance—Should Be Every Business Leader's Goal

Danny McPherson — Executive Vice President and Chief Security Officer, Verisign

Compliance takes up an inordinate amount of an organization's time, budget, and manpower, particularly when it comes to ensuring that access to IT resources and vital information are safeguarded at all times.

And I'm here to tell you that C-suite executives and board members alike—and yes, even a lot of us chief security officers—are fretting, fussing, and fidgeting over the wrong thing. That is, given that most IT security resource allocation still focuses on accommodating inherently reactive compliance objectives rather than considering overall enterprise cyber risk management, we may not be adequately protecting what we care about most!

An organization's overall *cyber risk* can be calculated [in part] by considering *threats* posed by motivated capable adversaries (to include intentional or unintentional insiders), the organization's *vulnerability* to those threats, and the immediate and residual *consequences* that result (e.g., be they impacts on confidentiality, integrity, or availability). Furthermore, enumerating what you care most about, and what enables it, is a critical first step in a comprehensive cyber-risk management program.

Let me be clear: I'm not saying that compliance isn't important. No one wants to risk fines, sanctions, or damaging publicity over regulatory violations. And no one wants to see our executives do a digital "perp walk" for the compromise of sensitive information.

That's why cybersecurity challenges have made compliance a source of anxiety and angst for C-suite executives and board members. I don't need to do a roll call of data breaches in your industry—we don't have enough hours in the day for that. Let's just all agree that those breaches, data losses, and regulatory compliance missteps are exacting huge costs on all organizations' finances, operations, legal exposure, and brand reputation, not to mention the long-term residual effects on impacted parties.

$$\text{RISK}_{cyber} = \text{Threat (Capability, Intent)} \times \text{Vulnerability} \times \text{Consequence}$$

I'm sure that just the simple thought of a banner headline with your organization's name linked to a data breach sends shivers down your spine. I know that's what it does to me.

But compliance is not—repeat, not—your goal. Or, at least, it should not be the key focus of your cybersecurity program. And let me tell you why:

Being compliant is not the same as being secure.

For that matter, being compliant does little or nothing to ensure that your critical systems are available at any point in time, which jeopardizes everything you do. That's why you need to focus on taking the right steps to enable secure availability of essential services and key resources in the face of broadening cyber threat vectors. If you do that—and only if you do that—you'll have a fighting chance to maintain operational integrity and achieve compliance in today's incredibly interconnected internet ecosystem. Let me explain why.

Why Availability Matters and Why It Must Be Secure

For as much attention, spending, and energy that goes into the process of demonstrating compliance, it's important to remember that compliance is a very limited way to look at the security of essential systems or data.

Compliance regulations tend to be inherently reactive and very targeted, either by industry, geography, or type of information that needs to be protected. These requirements often focus heavily on the confidentiality and then on the integrity of the data. Although these are certainly important issues, they do little or nothing to ensure overall resilience—that is, that mission-critical systems and data are available when employees, partners, and customers need them. Besides, demonstrating compliance is too often viewed by business leaders as an event, typically played out in this conversation:

CEO to CSO:
How did the HIPAA audit go?

CSO:
Great, we passed with flying colors.

What the CEO says:
Glad to hear it; nice work.

What the CEO thinks:
One less thing to worry about until next year.

Demonstrating compliance—either with an external regulatory body or an internal function—is usually a point-in-time status check. But no one should delude themselves into thinking that their ability to demonstrate compliance guarantees them another second of secure availability. And even a few minutes of interrupted systems availability can cost millions of dollars, compromise customer trust, and tarnish an organization's reputation.

That's because, at any point in time, a cyberattack can:

- Take down a city's water filtration system.

- Disrupt an internet service provider's wide-area network infrastructure.

- Circumvent a retailer's digital loss prevention system.

- Interrupt a manufacturing plant's robotics-based assembly line.

- Undermine a municipality's online voting system.

If any of those systems—or any other mission-critical application—is rendered literally or functionally unavailable because of cybersecurity attacks, the compliance status you proudly hail won't mean a pile of beans.

Fortunately, many executives are getting the message—a message that is often delivered by an anxious and persistent CIO or CSO, or a business leader who realizes that the organization will not demonstrate compliance unless it focuses on the bigger picture of secure availability and resilience. With increasing frequency, executives and board members are buying in to the notion that secure availability is the very foundation of compliance. As such, there are more nuanced discussions with business leaders and in boardrooms that go far beyond compliance-centric issues, such as confidentiality and data integrity.

Not surprisingly, organizations with a culture built around collaboration among business and technical leaders are demonstrating real leadership in promoting secure availability first, with compliance being one result of that focus. And those where the CEO and board see cybersecurity as a technology problem best handled by the SecOps team or solely by doubling the infosec budget … well, let's just say they are setting themselves up to be the focus of the next banner headline.

A Sobering Thought: New Business Initiatives Often Expand Your Cyber Risk Footprint and Threaten Compliance

In this book, and in many other discussions, you'll undoubtedly read and hear a lot about the exciting business opportunities made possible by the integration of technologies into everyday business processes and common "things."

Trends such as the Internet of Things, cloud computing, enterprise mobility, and digital transformation are making organizations more efficient and better positioned to bring new products and services to market faster.

They also are making organizations—and their entire business ecosystems—more vulnerable.

Take IoT, arguably one of the most exciting and promising applications of technology in decades. But when billions of everyday items are connected via the internet—not only to each other, but often also to our core business systems and IT infrastructure—we dramatically increase risks that threaten secure availability and, in turn, compliance.

Another dual-edged sword is the increased use of technology to enable customer self-service, such as online banking, omnichannel shopping, or ordering and managing municipal services from a digital consumer device or through a public cloud service. Yes, it creates a boatload of new services and improved customer engagement. And yes, it also introduces a boatload of unmanaged endpoints and easily accessible points of entry into our digital infrastructure, where systems can be disabled or rendered ineffective if availability is interrupted.

Mobility, cloud, virtualization, and other technology also are driving new workforce models, such as distributed teams, virtual collaborations, and new models for when, where, and how people work and share information. Those provide flexibility and empowerment for our employees, but they also represent big security headaches as more things that organizations care about live in more places with fewer direct capabilities to protect them.

Each and every one of these new opportunities carries a substantial risk factor that can result in regulatory or internal policy compliance challenges. However, these challenges will pale in comparison when new products and services are rendered unavailable due to security lapses or even network connectivity issues anywhere along the digital ecosystem.

Lessons Learned: Using a Three-Tiered Approach to Secure Availability

As I've stressed in this chapter, compliance is best achieved with a more strategic focus on secure availability with consideration of overall cyber risk to the enterprise. But actually achieving secure availability takes patience, practice, and a process rooted in business goals, not in technology.

Over the years, I've worked with my business colleagues to identify and overcome cybersecurity challenges—and to help ensure compliance objectives are met along the way. I've come to think of this as a framework for delivering secure availability, comprised of three major components:

- Doing what you **have** to do.

- Doing what you said you were **going to do.**

- Continuously refining and adapting to what **"good" looks like.**

Every organization is likely to develop and deploy this framework in its own unique manner, depending upon its own business goals, risk appetite, organizational strengths, and enterprise vision. But the issues within each of these three pillars are applicable to all organizations looking to ensure secure availability.

Doing what you have to do. This is where everything starts. After all, your organization must comply with the laws and regulatory obligations of the different jurisdictions where business is conducted. These include issues revolving around custodianship of information and data privacy regulations, and ensuring that you are acting responsibly with the data that others have entrusted you to safeguard. I'm sure you're thinking these are pretty fundamental, and you're right. These are table stakes, essential requirements for ensuring secure availability and meeting compliance mandates. But without meeting these baseline requirements, you might as well get ready for a regulatory assault—and a costly and damaging security incident brought on by a security breach or data loss.

Doing what you said you were going to do. This is all about a rock-solid commitment to actually following through in all ways—contractually, regulatory, internal policies, and even morally. This should be part of your organization's governance framework, jointly worked out among business leadership, IT and security teams, and legal officers. Again, the goal here is to ensure secure availability; if done right, compliance will be the byproduct. This is why your governance programs must go beyond good policies and policy management to extend to enforcement in the same way organizations enforce human resources or financial policies. Reporting must be consistent, transparent, and designed to easily flow up the organization. And, of course, policies and enforcement processes need to be communicated throughout the organization in both security awareness and targeted training programs. If you have a data loss prevention policy, but you're not educating your employees about how to label, securely share, transfer, and store data, or for how long and where, you'll run into big problems and find it extremely difficult to achieve a state of continual compliance.

Continuously refining and adapting to what "good" looks like. Fortunately, there are a number of useful and well-regarded standards for the protection of systems and digital assets, especially when it travels to and from the internet. Your CSO and IT executives undoubtedly know about the National Institute of Standards and Technology (NIST) Cyber Security Framework (CSF), a voluntary framework that provides models based on the principles of "prioritization, flexibility, and repeatability." And the Center for Internet Security publishes a list of the top 20 security controls, which presents a great opportunity to identify the best value for information security investments. Certainly, business leaders need to get behind these and other applicable frameworks that help identify key security and resilience objectives, as well as corresponding metrics their organizations should consider embracing. These can also help measure the organization's ability to ensure availability and to provide a foundation for compliance.

Until fairly recently, internet engineers tended to measure availability in terms of internet access and service level agreements (SLAs). We didn't necessarily work ourselves into a frenzy because we lost corporate or residential internet connectivity for a few hours or even a day. But we've evolved in very meaningful ways in terms of how we gauge the business impact of service availability interruptions. Today, if you can't deliver uninterrupted core services to your employees, customers, and partners, you're in deep, deep trouble. So, we can't let our organizations get to the point where systemic dependencies bring down our systems and restrict our access to critical data and services. We must collaborate in order to get a fuller and higher-definition picture of risks and their impact and longer-term consequences.

In the U.S., if an organization's security program is intelligence-driven, the Cyber Security Act of 2015 makes it much easier for them to ingest and share cybersecurity indicators without the threat of antitrust violations hanging over their heads. Because attackers exploit asymmetries in ways defenders don't have the luxury of doing, they are constantly adapting their tactics and techniques; without adequate information-sharing and community collaboration, organizations may be lured into thinking that their state of security readiness and secure availability is much higher than it really is.

Steps Business Leaders and Board Members Can Take Today

Once an organization understands that enabling secure availability—and, by extension, demonstrating compliance—is a business issue rather than a technical one, it has taken the first step toward achieving that goal. And there are efficient ways for business executives to learn from the lessons and experiences of others to support those efforts.

First, keep in mind that your organization should study high-profile and particularly relevant breaches and learn how they may relate to your own situation. What vulnerabilities did the breach expose that may be relevant to your organization and operations? How did other organizations respond to mitigate the damage, both technically and from a communications perspective? What is your plan if such an incident were to impact you? What was the impact on their business operations, and how exposed are you?

Second, you must—absolutely must—have a game plan for DDoS attacks and ransomware. This is vital, because more and more organizations are being hit with these attacks every day. Why wouldn't they be? They're cheap to implement, and the bad guys are smart enough to either extort their intended victims or ask for ransoms that are small enough to be considered "nuisances" by business leaders and boards. Furthermore, your preparedness here will also enable you to better identify, protect, detect, respond, and recover from whole classes of destructive malware and other attacks, as illustrated in Figure 1, on page 137.

But how you respond when you are hit needs to be carefully planned and meticulously carried out, and that's where the business experience and acumen of your executive leadership and board comes in very handy. They'll also engage you in some very probing question-and-answer sessions, but don't fear those—embrace them. If you've done your homework, you'll have a vital opportunity to ensure that your defense strategies are aligned with business priorities.

Third, use regulatory and governance requirements as an opportunity for more internal dialogue and game-planning. I used to cringe at the thought of quarterly disclosure filings, internal risk reporting, compliance documentation and audits, and the like. Eventually, however, I began to embrace these and other opportunities to discuss cyber risks, impending threats, impact, and preventative steps with my business colleagues and board members— from a whole of business perspective. I saw them as my chance to sound warning bells and highlight key cyber risks before something bad happened. I also saw them as a chance to provide important updates to key stakeholders about the latest changes, what we've done to ensure that our key assets remain available, and, of course, that we're still in compliance with applicable obligations.

At the end of the day, we should be worried less about passing audits and demonstrating point-in-time compliance than about the fundamentals of cybersecurity: availability, confidentiality, and integrity.

Your chief compliance officer might blanch at such heresy, but your focus on secure availability will do more than keep the regulators off your back. It will ensure you still have a business tomorrow.

Figure 1: Five phases of NIST Cyber Security Framework (CSF) 1.1
Credit: N. Hanacek/NIST

19

Enabling the Digital Revolution in Europe: Building Effective Cybersecurity Policy Through Trust and Cooperation

Michal Boni — Member, European Parliament

We are about to enter an exciting new stage of the Digital Age. 5G infrastructure will bring new opportunities; new personalized digital services will drive innovation and invention; data and information transfers will be available at the highest speeds; new business models will enable Industry 5.0; the Internet of Things will develop on an unprecedented scale, with billions of devices communicating with each other.

At the same time, we are beginning a new era of human-machine collaboration, with unlimited possibilities for data processing, thanks to the use of algorithms and artificial intelligence. Moreover, we continue to see rapid development of high-performance computing networks, as well as expansion and improvements in the underlying technologies for cloud and storage solutions.

All of this promises to unleash a huge change in how we work, communicate, spend our leisure time, and educate our children and ourselves. As leaders in our fields, whether we are in government or private industry, how do we ensure that we can make the digital world secure as we stand at the brink of this new digital transformation?

The answer is simple: Trust.

Building Trust

Building trust is perhaps the most crucial factor in enabling the digital revolution that is right before us, maybe even more important than the technology itself. Building trust requires two basic things:

1. Awareness of the need for cybersecurity and, at the same time, the need to protect personal data.

2. The development of a proper legal and institutional framework for cybersecurity and data protection.

How can we make this happen? What can we do to achieve better cybersecurity awareness? What practical measures can we take to make the digital world secure? How do we build the levels of trust required to ensure that people feel safe when they are using the advanced technologies of the Digital Age?

Three things must happen. First, we must overcome the divisions we face with regards to cybersecurity in the context of a digital single market in the European Union. Second, we must put in place enforceable cybersecurity policies that are based on risk analysis and management. Third, we must build a shared responsibility model to assess and address cybersecurity dangers.

As an EU legislator, I believe strongly that dialogue and cooperation between government policymakers and industry stakeholders are essential to addressing these challenges so we can collectively develop and execute the right policy responses that can unleash the digital revolution. I believe if we can effectively address these challenges, we can provide a path for the rest of the world.

Key Challenge: Certification

In the EU, the journey starts with establishing common, harmonized certificates, which, when accomplished, would also help facilitate the achievement of our shared global objectives. In the EU, we presently have 28 separate sets of national rules for certification, a level of fragmentation that is an enormous obstacle to improving cybersecurity.

Currently, there is a patchwork for cybersecurity certification schemes and initiatives in Europe. On the one hand, national certification initiatives are already in place or are emerging, without being mutually recognized. On the other hand, not all EU Member States are part of the main European mechanism based on mutual recognition, known as SOG-IS.

The SOG-IS Mutual Recognition Agreement of Information Technology includes 12 Member States plus Norway, and has developed a few protection profiles on digital products, such as digital signatures and smart cards. Members can participate in a mutual recognition agreement as certificate consumers and producers. While this allows companies with certification in one country to use it in all other participating countries, it is not a sustainable long-term solution.

The way toward a common, harmonized certification framework is necessary, as proposed in the draft Cybersecurity Act on which the European Parliament is currently working. Establishing this common certification framework is a process, and it must move from a voluntary model at this stage to a mandatory model after we've had some years of experience.

In establishing the Act, an open perspective is needed, using a market-led approach that does not incorporate too much administrative pressure. This kind of flexibility is crucial if we want to implement certification schemes that will correspond not only to the current threats, but also to incoming, future dangers.

The open model in the area of European certification ought to be clear, transparent, and based on this industry- and market-led approach. There are no one-size-fits-all solutions that would suit all sectors, devices, services, infrastructures, software, and hardware.

It is important to recognize that a case-by-case approach is paramount to successfully address cybersecurity issues. It is also crucial to conduct proper risk assessments and, after that, to propose a candidate certification scheme. This should depend on the results of risk analysis linked to different levels of possible assurances.

A Model for Building Certifications

The European Commission has proposed three levels of risk from which to build certifications: high, substantial, and basic. We have to consider these levels and determine whether we require strict definitions of assurance levels. Another challenge is what to do with the concept of self-assessment. Who determines risk and how will that be accomplished? What will be the driver: convenience/self-assessment or clear requirements based on the significance of cybersecurity?

The norms, standards, and technical requirements for cybersecurity certifications should be discussed by experts and industry stakeholders. This should first take place at the level of expert working groups, set up by the European Union Agency for Network and Information Security (ENISA), that would define each candidate certification scheme.

It is better to have a real platform for cooperation on merit issues related to cybersecurity needs than to have a more general advisory group. At the same time, the real work of finding optimal models of certification schemes should be done at the level of the Cybersecurity Certification Group, in which representatives of national regulatory bodies are responsible for certification.

The common, permanent work of the Cybersecurity Certification Group will enable it to harmonize the conditions for certifications. This is the only format that will facilitate the most balanced and effective approach to bringing together the two key stakeholders: Member States and the business community.

Essential for Success— Cybersecurity Awareness

Why is it so important to bring together Member States and the business community to improve cybersecurity?

First, if we want to raise awareness of cybersecurity issues, we must involve all partners and give them the appropriate roles. Every company—small, medium, big, and those with high or low levels of deployment of IT solutions—should start to analyze its cybersecurity risks. All must have competencies to manage those risks. And all sorts of industries should be open to sharing the responsibility in many areas.

In addition, we as individuals must be involved in protecting ourselves in the area of cybersecurity. Reducing risk often depends on our habits, our knowledge and understanding of cybersecurity problems, our everyday choices, and our personal cybersecurity hygiene.

Finally, it should be an imperative to provide people with the skills in this area. Cybersecurity hygiene principles should be incorporated as a critical part of all educational curricula in all European countries. Everyone should be properly trained.

No Easy Task— Cybersecurity Coordination

In the EU, cybersecurity is not necessarily centrally driven. Coordination is needed, and we must determine which institutions should coordinate the policies for cybersecurity at the European level. Perhaps by doing this successfully in Europe, we can provide a framework for achieving similar objectives worldwide.

Many of the goals and requirements for pan-EU coordination are described in the Network and Information Security (NIS) Directive, the EU's first law focused specifically on cybersecurity, which was adopted in 2016.[1] The NIS Directive comprises three parts:

1. **National capabilities:** EU Member States must have certain national cybersecurity capabilities of the individual EU countries, e.g., they must have a national Computer Security Incident Response Team (CSIRT), perform cyber exercises, etc.

2. **National supervision of critical sectors.** EU Member States have to supervise the cybersecurity of critical market operators in the country: Ex-ante supervision in critical sectors (energy, transport, water, health, and finance sector), ex-post supervision for critical digital service providers (internet exchange points, domain name systems, etc.). The legislation also stipulates that, by the end of 2018, we will have indicated in every country those operators that are responsible for security of the critical infrastructure.

3. **Cross-border collaboration:** Cross-border collaboration between EU countries, e.g., via a network of operational CSIRTs across the EU to rapidly react to cyber threats and incidents; and the strategic NIS "cooperation group" between Member States to support and facilitate strategic cooperation and the exchange of information, and to develop trust and confidence.

Thanks to this legal act, the European Union has made it clear how important it is to have cybersecurity strategies and proper division of responsibilities between government, military, and business institutions, in all EU countries.

A Complex Journey

We must acknowledge that the NIS Directive is only a first step in the complex journey of addressing the cybersecurity challenges facing the EU in the Digital Age.

At the European level, the capacity of ENISA should be adequate to tackle new measures and tasks. The EU has to support ENISA in its function to collect data on cybersecurity incidents, per the role

ENISA was given in the NIS Directive providing support to the pan-EU CSIRT network and cooperation group described above.

The purpose is clear: More cyber-threat-information sharing means more understanding of the various forms and schemes of cyberattacks, and greater recognition of attacks means more security solutions for defending our devices and systems. With its new mandate as laid out in the Cybersecurity Act, ENISA should play the key role in the European Union as the body responsible for cybersecurity issues.

It is obvious that ENISA needs to cooperate with all partners—certainly with businesses, as we have discussed throughout this chapter. ENISA should also cooperate with different EU institutions responsible for security such as Europol; with international partners such as NATO units working on cyberwar; and with experts from academia and other important institutions.

A Necessary Factor—Research for Innovative Cybersecurity

Without efforts aimed at instilling trust and cooperation between industries using common, modern, and ongoing research, we run the risk of failing in the fight against cybercrime.

We need new research projects that are innovative and focused on implementation of the rule often described as "cybersecurity by design." We need to develop a framework for using the capacity of AI to support risk analysis, the predictability of cyberattacks, and the development of new instruments in the processes of crisis management.

European Union investments should support the improvement of technological solutions crucial for cybersecurity. At the beginning of May 2018, the European Commission announced a proposed budget of €100 billion for the next EU Research and Innovation Framework Programme, called Horizon Europe (2021-2027). In parallel, these technology investments should be used to develop the cybersecurity industry in Europe. There is a huge potential among many companies to achieve global leadership in the cybersecurity area. Of course, the approach to cybersecurity should be focused not only on European goals, but also with a global perspective in mind.

Why a Cybersecurity Roadmap Is Needed

All of the issues discussed in this chapter are in some way related to the Cybersecurity Act. The Parliament wants to finalize it as quickly as possible and start the dialogue with the European Council.

But that is not the end of the work. We are still at the very beginning of addressing the very real societal and business challenges we face. It is therefore important to consider what other steps should be taken—and when—and to build a cybersecurity roadmap to ensure the involvement of all stakeholders at all levels of each of the processes. Everyone's commitment is paramount to our success.

How can we draw the institutional dimension of this solution? What kind of perspective for stronger cooperation and commitment between the EU institutions and Member States can establish a realistic path toward implementation? Which steps can each of us take to build the trust required to achieve our objectives?

In short, what can we do, individually and collectively, to build the foundation of an EU cybersecurity environment that truly addresses our combined interests? Here are some suggestions:

- Provide input to me and other MEPs, as well as the European Commission and the Council.

- Talk with your national governments.

- Determine how to engage with ENISA.

- Help guide us on what more you—as individuals and citizens—can do to improve cybersecurity.

- Help us understand what you need— whether it is education, awareness, guidance, recommendations on best practices, or anything else.

- Bring ideas from other countries, including ideas that can help foster global cooperation.

Conclusion

We have a great opportunity in the EU to secure the Digital Age. But the only way we can successfully address the cybersecurity challenges we face, here and abroad, is by cooperating and building trust.

As we stand at the dawn of this new stage of the digital revolution, we must all recognize the shared responsibility and opportunity that has been placed in our hands. Let us make sure we can overcome the divisions that pull us apart and build a path forward that binds us all together.

---

[1] NIS Directive, European Union Agency for Network and Information Security (ENISA), enisa.europa.eu

20

Beyond Compliance: The Human Element of Cyber Resilience

Ria Thomas — Partner and Global Co-Lead for Cybersecurity, Brunswick Group

Over the last several years, with the rise in massive data breaches, which lead to public outcry, governments have responded with ever-increasing regulatory requirements. The European Union's General Data Protection Regulation (GDPR), which came into enforcement on May 25, 2018, may be the most well-known of these governmental efforts.

The need for such a regulation and the complex efforts it took to address its requirements highlighted how poorly prepared companies can be when looking at the issues surrounding their obligations. And yet, GDPR only addresses one significant aspect of cyber risk to a company—the potential loss of individuals' data and its privacy, which the company has a duty to protect.

Like GDPR, most cyber regulations are created to protect society from behavior that could cause negative impacts. These regulations are likely rooted in the experience of previous attacks and may not extend to other issues until there is enough widespread acknowledgement of the need for certain practices to be modified.

As such, compliance with regulation alone cannot cover the business risks and impacts a company faces from cyberattacks.

Businesses can move beyond compliance by striving to understand the human element. By changing corporate cultures and altering behaviors, they can take proper steps to ensure they are taking the right approach to cybersecurity and, consequently, protect their valuation and hard-earned reputation.

For the leaders of any organization, whether you are part of the executive management team or the board, the path to better cybersecurity extends to the people, processes, technologies, and cultures you put in place, regardless of whether a regulation requires it.

Being prepared is not merely about achieving or even maintaining compliance; it is about adopting a cybersecurity culture that ensures the people in your organization are ready to deal with any eventuality, whenever it may occur. And that includes you. Active board and executive committee-level ownership of cybersecurity and its enterprise-wide prioritization are essential for comprehensive, company-wide cyber resilience.

Understanding the Human Element of Cyber Resilience

In today's business, cybersecurity is a combined human and systems challenge that requires the close attention and involvement of the company's senior leadership. First, it is critical to undertake the necessary technical investments, not only to protect your company, but also to be able to demonstrate that you understood the technical risks and sought to mitigate them to the extent it was feasible.

That being said, it is important to acknowledge that cyber risks are caused by humans. And cyber prevention is managed by humans. How you work to prevent a cyberattack and how you respond to one starts with understanding who is involved. There are three general categories of players to consider when we are dealing with cybersecurity. These are:

1. **The people attacking the business.** These are the people who are out to harm your organization, whether for profit, geopolitical gain, mischief, mayhem, or any other reason. As has been discussed in other chapters within this book, the nature of these attackers is changing all the time, including their motivations and attack methods. One important point to remember: Regardless of the motivation, methodology, or attack mechanism, it is human actors who are behind the attack and whose often unpredictable actions you will need to confront.

2. **The people responding within the business.** The ability to minimize the operational, financial, and reputational impacts of a cyberattack does not rest in the hands of one individual or one group within a company.

Instead, it requires both vertical and horizontal leadership and coordination.

Board members set the governance strategy and hold the keys to accountability in terms of how the company leadership prepares and responds to a cyber crisis. Executive leaders build the culture, make key investments, and ensure a crisis structure that integrates the company's information-sharing and response coordination; they also undertake critical strategic decisions during a cyber crisis. Neither the board nor the executive committee can be successful, however, without the people who work under them. These individuals are the ones on whom they need to rely to obtain an accurate, timely understanding of the technical, operational, financial, and reputational implications of the attack. They are drawn from across the business and should include cyber/IT, legal, human resources, corporate communications, government/regulatory affairs, et al.

Part of being prepared means knowing that the entire organization needs to come together, not only to create an integrated picture of the business impacts but also to coordinate a response that will minimize the potential fallout. It requires that each person understands their role, responsibilities, and what is expected of them during a cyber crisis.

3. **The people impacted by the cyberattack on the business.** A key element to maintaining resilience in the face of a cyberattack is demonstrating that senior leadership understands the human impact of the cyberattack on those to whom it has an obligation.

These are not only the people inside your organization, but outside it as well.

If an attack impacts your infrastructure, you may not be able to provide services to your customers. If you are in a critical industry, such as banking, utilities, healthcare, or transportation, the results can be devastating to individuals who rely on those services. If you are in retail or another customer-facing industry, you can lose sales and customer goodwill. If you suffer a data breach, important personal records of customers could be exposed on the Dark Web, creating risk of identity theft, financial loss, and other consequences.

It is critical to understand that you, the company leadership, are making decisions based not just on what is best for your bottom-line. Rather, you should demonstrate you are minimizing and mitigating the impacts on the people directly affected by the cyberattack; this focus will ultimately affect your bottom line.

Building a "Beyond Compliance" Corporate Cyber Culture

Adopting additional measures to ensure compliance with a regulation can be a critical turning point in how a company addresses a specific cyber risk that the regulation seeks to address.

It is imperative, however, not to assume that compliance alone will protect your business from the wide-ranging ramifications of cyberattacks. Instead, the focus should be on each aspect of the human element described above.

Given the range of evolving cyber threats and risks, the first step for company leaders, whether in the boardroom or the executive suite, is to take the time to understand the threat environment for your organization, including the potential business risk and the potential business impact.

Assessing the threat environment involves more than the technical risks. It also requires you to understand how your various strategic business decisions may be increasing your risk of a cyberattack. For example, as you enter into a new business venture, acquisition or partnership, or you move into a new international market or build critical intellectual property around a cutting-edge technology, who are the human beings interested in attacking your business? What could they be seeking to achieve? What kind of damage can they cause?

The next step is to engage with all of the key members of your organization who will need to create an integrated understanding of the impacts and who will be required to come together to help coordinate the corporate-wide response. Are they aware of leadership's expectations of them during a cyber crisis? Do they know their roles and responsibilities? Will the existing crisis structure, whether formal or informal, be able to handle a multi-faceted cyberattack?

As part of the pre-cyber crisis preparation, it is also critical that company leadership invest in raising employee awareness, not only of cyber risks but also of the behavior that may be expected of them to protect the organization from cyber threats.

The above measures will allow you to stay resilient in a cyber crisis because the human beings you need to rely on to minimize the long-term impacts, especially to your reputation, are already within your organization. Creating a corporate-wide, cyber-resilient culture requires not only their active engagement and participation, but their buy-in.

Finally, during a cyber crisis, you should take into account the spirit of most regulations: How do you ensure that your priority is understood to be the human beings who are most impacted by the attack on your business? These are not only your customers, partners, and your employees, but also the general public. What are the principles by which you lead your company through the cyber crisis? Are they protecting your business operations and valuation? Or do your actions and words convey that you have understood the weight of the trust that has been placed in your business by the human beings on the other side of the crisis?

It is possible that a cyberattack on your business and its ramifications will not fall within the confines of a particular regulation, such as GDPR, but it may still have an enormous impact on the public. How the public reacts has little to do with compliance and everything to do with perception: Did you do everything you were supposed to do? Put more succinctly: Did you do the right thing, even if you were not required by law to do so?

To accomplish this, you need to ensure that you have the right strategies and policies in place to reflect that you have planned for and thought about these things *before* the incident took place. This preparedness approach is where the right culture can leverage institutional muscle memory. You will not be able to think everything through in advance, but if your core group understands their roles and responsibilities, you are in a much better position to do the right thing and shape public perception in a positive way.

Conclusion

Compliance with regulations alone does not ensure cyber resilience. Instead, your organization's ability to overcome the myriad impacts of a cyber crisis starts with understanding your cyber risks, the potential impacts, and the measures you need to put into place in order to maintain your ability to steer through the crisis. Those efforts cannot be successful without taking into account the human beings that form the core of the threat, the response, or the impact.

IMPLEMENTING A CORPORATE-WIDE CYBER RESILIENCE APPROACH

How do you ensure that your organizational cybersecurity culture goes beyond compliance into resilience? Here are additional suggestions and questions to consider for each of these critical aspects of your cyber resilience approach:

1. **Assessing risks of a cyberattack:**
   - Do you have a comprehensive understanding of the business risks you face from the technical, operational, and strategic threats posed by a cyberattack?
   - How would you define a worst-case scenario, e.g., timeline of acceptable operational disruption; type of market impact; level of government scrutiny; public/media attention?

- Are you addressing challenges regarding a possible lack of skilled cybersecurity staff?

2. **Understanding the impacts of a cyberattack:**
    - What processes do you have in place to understand the multiple impacts of a cyberattack across corporate units or of one that is combined with physical attacks?
    - How do you prioritize or reconcile conflicting national or international regulatory requirements, such as GDPR?
    - What liabilities and obligations exist to internal and external stakeholders, including employees, customers, partners, and regulators?
    - Do you have a program in place to assess the impacts of an attack by an aggrieved employee with access to your business and customer critical data or your network?

3. **Planning and executing your cyber crisis response:**
    - Is there a corporate-wide incident management plan in place for a range of cyberattacks that accounts for your cyber risks?
    - Do senior leaders across the organization understand their roles and responsibilities? Is there a structure of support under them to ensure they have the information they need in a timely manner?
    - Is there an employee awareness program in place to increase employees' understanding of cyber threats and the need for good cybersecurity practices, including those relating to their social media activity?
    - Who are the internal and external stakeholders you need to notify and/or alert? How will you prioritize?
    - How do you deconflict information shared by your business units and coordinate how much information is being shared with whom and when?

4. **Communicating with internal and external stakeholders:**
    - Does your strategic communications plan include prescripted, pre-authorized messaging related to the cyberattack scenarios that are relevant to your cyber risks?
    - Is there a process by which you notify employees and external stakeholders, especially if key methods—phones, email—become corrupted or disrupted because of a cyberattack?
    - Who is the "face" of your company during a significant cyberattack? Have they been media-trained? Are they ready to lead by example?

21

Why Corporate Governance Matters So Much in Cybersecurity

Paul Jackson, GCFE — Managing Director, Asia-Pacific Leader, Cyber Risk, Kroll

In the high-pitched, relentless battle against cyberattacks, much of the attention and energy has been focused on technical solutions, regulatory compliance, and balancing risks with opportunities.

What about corporate governance? What role does executive and board-level oversight play in ensuring robust cybersecurity … and what role *should* it play?

When most of us think of corporate governance, we tend to associate it with such business functions as financial integrity, hiring practices, legal and regulatory assurance, and corporate strategy. But the increasingly critical and complex issues presented by cybersecurity now have risen to the point where it must be a core component of an overarching corporate governance framework.

And that is happening not a moment too soon.

For instance, there is increasing evidence that boards are playing catch-up when it comes to prioritizing cybersecurity as a vital governance issue. A 2018 global study of more than 1,000 board members conducted by McKinsey indicated that cybersecurity was a "potential business disruption" topic on the agendas of only 37%

of boards. The good news is that figure represents a nearly 50% increase in just the past two years; the bad news is that cybersecurity remains a dangerously weak area of understanding for boards in assessing its potential impact on business operations. In fact, only 9% of board-member respondents said their boards had a "very good" understanding of cybersecurity's potential for impacting business operations.[1]

Let me give you a real-world example of this disconnect. A large, Asia-based supply chain company asked our firm to do a thorough penetration test of their networks as part of what they assumed would be a routine due diligence exercise. But we discovered that an expensive monitoring solution was not achieving its intended goals and was not being properly managed. It quickly became clear that an attacker could have gained full control of the network, including full access to the CEO's system and had the potential to badly damage business partners' systems. Leadership was shocked to learn this, prompting an urgent rethinking of how to restructure cyber governance and remove reliance on the internal IT team to solve security problems.

This is why leadership, both among C-level executives and in the boardroom, has to step up in making cybersecurity a more prominent element in corporate governance. But how?

I believe there are four major areas where corporate governance needs to evolve when it comes to cybersecurity:

- Inverting the cybersecurity leadership responsibilities.

- Adopting and "living" the right cybersecurity framework.

- Addressing the organizational structure.

- Getting smarter so business leaders can ask the right questions.

Inverting the Cybersecurity Leadership Responsibilities

One of the biggest problems is that cybersecurity has traditionally been designed with a bottom-up approach. In that model, individuals tasked with securing IT systems identified technical solutions to protect the infrastructure, applications, and data. Organizations spent untold billions of dollars on technology, only to find that it wasn't enough to stem the impact of expanded threats, increased vulnerabilities, and innovative attackers.

This brings to mind a popular adage: When every problem looks like a nail, every solution must be a hammer.

This bottom-up mindset brought about cybersecurity defense, detection, and response policies that were developed around technical tools, without considering the business needs or operational implications. Metrics were developed that told the CSO how many attacks were blocked and from what sources, while the real focus needed to be "Which attacks weren't blocked; which parts of the business were impacted; and what were the financial, legal, regulatory, and reputational costs?"

Instead, the cybersecurity governance model needs to be inverted to a top-down approach. This is the essential definition of organizational leadership:

- Understand and identify the challenges and opportunities.

- Establish priorities.

- Promote collaboration and innovation around solutions.

- Lead by example.

Leadership needs a full, transparent, and real-time understanding of the risks faced and the measures in place to protect the organization. If that information is not being clearly communicated to the C suite and the board, then leadership needs to find ways to ensure the right information is provided, typically by the CISO or CIO in today's corporate frameworks—or find someone else who will.

If implemented correctly, a top-down governance framework will eliminate most threats and provide a mature, defensible, and flexible structure for protecting sensitive data. It will also help to ensure compliance, establish good legal protections, and encourage good cybersecurity hygiene among employees, partners, and suppliers.

Adopting and "Living" the Right Security Framework

Security frameworks are important because they embrace the full set of issues necessary for good cybersecurity: business operations, legal, regulatory, risk management, and technical processes.

While there are numerous good frameworks available for leadership to evaluate—and keep in mind that all frameworks should be adapted to each organization's unique business conditions, operating procedures, and priorities—the most relevant and actionable one comes from the U.S. National Institute of Standards and Technology (NIST). This voluntary framework is the most broadly accepted and most widely implemented around the world, and has its foundation in five pillars:

- Identify the assets to be protected.

- Protect those assets with the proper safeguards.

- Detect incidents quickly, reliably, and comprehensively.

- Respond to incidents in a way that minimizes their impact.

- Recover from incidents and restore business operations as soon and as completely as possible.

There are plenty of actionable steps and best practices organizations can and should deploy in their cybersecurity governance model, such as assuring that appropriate security patches have been applied, end-of-life systems have been deactivated, and strong encryption and access control tools have been put in place and are being used. Still, those are technical solutions, most typically handled by the security and IT organizations.

The real power of the NIST model from a governance standpoint is that it creates an opportunity—or, depending on your sense of urgency—it provides a flexible framework for executives and board members to internally mandate and be used to hold business units accountable. The importance of the NIST Framework as a tool of self-assessment is that it places cybersecurity objectives in the context of the organization's overall business objec-

tives. The framework's inherent flexibility guides business leaders and the technical management responsible for cybersecurity to focus on actions that will best position their organizations to manage their unique cyber risk, and to direct resources to areas where they can be most impactful to the business.

Addressing the Organizational Structure

It has often been said that you can learn a lot about any organization's priorities by looking at their org chart. This is becoming more and more true every day in the realm of cybersecurity governance.

Increasingly, corporate leaders are driving change by rethinking and realigning who is responsible for cybersecurity and how the role is positioned within the enterprise. For instance, the idea that physical security, internal investigations, and cybersecurity should be merged into a single organization **reporting directly to the board** is gaining in popularity, and has many advantages. Independence is an important motivation for this approach, of course, but it also facilitates a more complete approach to security that takes into account people, business functions, priorities, and technical factors.

There is little question that announcements of changes in reporting structures make people sit up and take notice. Some of that is office politics, but much of it centers on the notion of what—and who—is gaining importance within the organization.

Elsewhere in this book, there are some excellent recommendations on how to identify and hire the best possible CSO in order to keep with a vigilant governance model for cybersecurity that ties business and technical requirements. In the chapter from executive search firm Heidrick &

Struggles, the authors offered some clear-headed advice:

"Boards need to exercise even more diligence than ever when determining who to hire, how to structure their roles and responsibilities, where to look to recruit them, and which tradeoffs are appropriate to make in order to land the best possible candidate."

And Adobe CSO Brad Arkin offered helpful advice to boards and C-suite executives: Listen closely to how your cybersecurity leader talks about problems and solutions. His pragmatic takeaway: If you're getting a lot of technical jargon instead of framing the discussion around business goals, you're talking to the wrong person.

Getting Smarter So Business Leaders Can Ask the Right Questions

As has been emphasized repeatedly throughout this book, security is a business issue, not a technical one. While we need the right technology tools to identify threats, protect against them, and remediate their impact, cybersecurity practices and policies must be planned, measured, and governed against business benchmarks.

Doing that requires strong, vocal, visible, and constant support from business leaders and the board. But it also necessitates that top management and board members put more energy and resources against expanding their own knowledge about cybersecurity's impact on their business.

Remember: You can't get the right answers if you ask the wrong questions. Or, in the context of this chapter, you can't govern if you don't know what you're supposed to be governing.

Now, no one is suggesting that the CFO or the head of marketing go back to school to get an advanced degree in cybersecurity, or that every board member have to pass a Security+ certification test. But the days of leaving cybersecurity responsibility to the technical people are long past. Regulations and legislation have changed the accountability quotient, and as we've seen too many times, an organization's very reputation—which has been carefully honed and crafted over decades with untold sums of money—can unravel after a cybersecurity glitch.

Some people have gone as far as to recommend that every board should have at least one member with extensive cybersecurity expertise in order to "keep the CSO honest." That concept may have some merit, but it still involves most board members and executive leaders turning to the "one wise man or woman in the room."

Business leaders and board members don't simply default to the CFO when a financial crisis hits, and they don't just assume the chief legal officer or outside counsel has everything covered when an embarrassing lawsuit pops up. In those and other scenarios, executives and board members jump in with both feet because, among other reasons, corporate governance demands that they do.

The same is now true with cybersecurity.

One of the important ways business leaders can get smarter and ask better questions is to have a commonly used prism of business issues through which cybersecurity issues can be analyzed, discussed, and acted on. For instance, discussions with the CSO on topics such as distributed denial-of-service attacks should be centered on how the business was impacted in areas such as downtime, lost productivity, revenue, and profit impact, and whether cybersecurity investment priorities should be re-examined.

Of course, this is a two-way street. Not only do board members and business leaders need to take steps to better educate them on cyber issues, but CSOs and other technical leaders need to re-imagine and re-engineer how and what they present to the business side. Things that have often been taken for granted, such as how a CSO's PowerPoint presentations look or why an organization is changing its policy for using public cloud services, must always be framed in a business perspective—ideally one that aligns with the organization's core values and business priorities.

What Boards Should Do Now

What should boards be doing in order to receive regular, appropriate security metrics around monitoring and detection?

First, the board needs to understand what cyber threats exist inside their organizations. A good starting point would be to obtain a report on current cyber threats impacting their industry and some recommended safeguards. Importantly, a search of any data on the Dark Web—passwords, personal data, confidential documents, or financial documents—that have already been exposed should be conducted by a reliable third party, and mitigation controls put in place.

Second, keep in mind that employees are almost always targeted for attacks. Board members need to receive regular updates on the level of staff security awareness through steps like controlled phishing exercises. The board also must ask if management is fully committed to this kind of organizational cyber hygiene in order to emphasize the importance of good security habits.

Third, internal and external resources should be deployed to regularly hunt for threats already on the networks but undetected, rather than simply relying on metrics around detected security events. Experience has shown us that attackers are often already inside networks for many months before real damage takes place. These hunts should be based on actionable intelligence and real-world knowledge of current threats.

Conclusion

Corporate governance has changed a lot in recent years, driven by such issues as increased regulatory oversight, more active and involved board members, and a need to apply healthy doses of both skepticism and support in an increasingly complex business environment.

And cybersecurity may be the single biggest thing to reshape corporate governance in decades.

Unfortunately, we still don't have enough clarity for actionable advice that corporate leaders can implement from the word go to help ensure the security of their organization and its data. But taking a more business-centric, inclusive, top-down approach to cybersecurity corporate governance will take us a long way toward achieving our respective organizations' goals. When cybersecurity is considered as a business issue, rather than isolated as a technical problem that has to be solved by technical people using technical tools, we will have a much greater chance for success.

---

[1] "A time for boards to act," McKinsey, March 2018

PART 3
Make Sure You're Covered Today

Part 3 — Introductions

22

Welcome to the Frontlines of Business and Cybersecurity

Pablo Emilio Tamez López — Chief Information Security Officer, Tecnológico de Monterrey

Digital transformation. The Internet of Things. Big data analytics. Cloud computing. Artificial intelligence. Machine learning. Somehow, we have come to think of these innovations as the future, the defining technologies of the next iteration of business, and the foundation for what the World Economic Forum aptly describes as the Fourth Industrial Revolution.

Guess what? The future is now.

Every one of those technologies is in practical use today. Type a search on Google, and you'll immediately see ads related to that search. It happens automatically—you might even say surreptitiously. All of the underlying technologies and business models that are transforming our world act like an invisible hand guiding almost everything we do in the Digital Age.

But take a second to look at it from the other side. From the perspective of our adversaries, those who would harm us for profit, geopolitical warfare, ego, or even just to create mischief. For them, digital transformation, the IoT, and big data analytics mean a greater attack surface. For them, cloud computing, AI, and machine learning are simply more weapons to use against us—and more sophisticated ones at that.

The situation has the potential to become more precarious in the near future, unless we act now, as leaders, to address it. Consumers and enterprises are spending more and more on IoT and mobile devices. The growth is exponential—with all of these connected devices generating information and, on the other hand, adding incremental attack surfaces. CISOs must understand this evolving risk environment, how to handle this data, and how to protect their assets. So, it is very important to implement adaptive and scalable technologies for this growing attack surface, either in the cloud or in the physical data center.

Now's the Time to Act

I share this viewpoint not to create fear or cause alarm, but to make sure we are all aware of today's reality and urgency. The audience for this book, *Navigating the Digital Age, Second Edition,* represents leaders in business, academia, and government who are not only directly affected by cybercrime, but are empowered to do something about it.

In Part 1 of this treatise, we focused on the future. In Part 2, we focused on lessons learned from the recent past and today's world. In Part 3, we focus on applying those lessons—what is happening now, how we can address today's rapidly evolving threat landscape, and, perhaps most importantly, how we can prepare for what is coming next.

Business leaders and board members are in a unique position, approving investments, guiding the vision for digital transformation, striving to build environments where innovation and opportunity can flourish. That also means being at the frontlines of cybersecurity.

You don't have to be a technology wizard to understand the vital role that cybersecurity plays in business today—or to provide leadership for your organization. In fact, as many of our authors express, you *must* provide leadership. If not you, then who?

For too long, it seems, our adversaries have been one step ahead of us. Now is the time to reverse that trend and put *them* on the defensive, make it more difficult, costly, and risky for *them* to attack *our* data, privacy, elections, infrastructure, business operations, or wherever else they may seek to expose vulnerabilities.

Making Sure We Are Covered Today—and Tomorrow

How do we do that? What can we do now to make sure we're covered today and also build the right foundations—in people, processes, and technologies—to give us the best chance of protecting our future and fulfilling the promise of the Fourth Industrial Revolution?

Many of the answers to these profound, provocative, and paramount questions are contained in the chapters ahead. In Part 3 of *Navigating the Digital Age, Second Edition,* we hear from leaders across the cybersecurity spectrum—business executives,

government officials, legal experts, technologists, chief information security officers, and others.

Each author shares his or her individual experiences to collectively create a compelling guide designed to spur action, communication, and innovation. The hope is that organizations of all sizes, locations, and industries can leverage the wisdom and practical advice contained in Part 3 to become better prepared to successfully navigate the challenges of the Digital Age. Some of the ideas that are sure to resonate include:

- **Trust:** How do we ensure that trust is no longer an issue for users?

- **Communications:** How do we get business and cybersecurity leaders on the same page, speaking the same language?

- **Regulations:** How do businesses work cohesively with regulators?

- **Technology:** How can the good guys leverage technology innovation to thwart the bad guys?

- **Preparation:** How can we prepare for attacks and limit the damage if a successful attack takes place?

- **Business enablement:** How can we transform cybersecurity from business risk to business advantage?

Conclusion

We've come a long way in a short period of time to reach the critical juncture in the Digital Age that is now before us. Many of the organizations that are using connected digital technologies to redefine industries weren't even in business as recently as 10 years ago. Now some have valuations in the billions of dollars.

At a time when our world is moving so quickly, when digital technology is transforming our lives and work, we must ensure that cybersecurity does not stop our progress. That's why today, this moment, is a critical time in our journey. If we are to move forward safely in the Digital Age, we must make sure we are covered today. When it comes to addressing the challenges of cybersecurity, *our* future is now.

23

In Today's World, Every Company Is a Cybersecurity Company

Mark Anderson — President, Palo Alto Networks

The theme of this third and final part of *Navigating the Digital Age, Second Edition,* is "Make Sure You're Covered Today." In the pages ahead, you will read about technologies, regulations, communications, processes, and people. You will hear from leaders who have been through breaches, helped draft regulations, developed innovative cybersecurity solutions, and remain at the forefront of driving progress in a vast number of ways.

As you forge ahead, both in reading the remaining chapters in this book and in addressing the cybersecurity challenges facing you as a leader in your organization, I would urge you to keep one thing in mind: If your organization is stuck in legacy constructs, if you are doing things the same way you did them five years ago, or even two years ago, it is time to reassess what you are doing. In order to make sure you are truly protected today, you must look forward to the future and not backward at the past.

Cybersecurity can't be an afterthought. It must be built into the priorities of the business at the ground floor. Cybersecurity can't be just about risk management. It must be about business enablement. And it can't be the sole province of technology pros. In today's world, everyone is responsible for cybersecurity. In particular, business leaders and board members must set an agenda and an example.

I could provide more examples, but there are many chapters preceding and succeeding this one that are quite eloquent in explaining and illuminating the cybersecurity challenges facing all of us today, whether we are in private industry, government, academia, technology, or cybersecurity. I would, however, like to share some thoughts on what business leaders can do now to move their organizations forward—making sure you are not only covered today, but are also prepared to deal with the cybersecurity challenges that loom on the near horizon.

Make Cybersecurity a Core Part of Your Business

There was a catchphrase that caught on several years ago to the effect of "Every company is a software company." It is time to think about cybersecurity in the same way. As Mark Rasch discusses in his upcoming chapter, every aspect of the business is tied to cybersecurity because every aspect of the business is touched by digital technologies.

Cybersecurity can't be an afterthought; it can't be an add-on; it can't be a silo.

Those are legacy constructs that will cripple you. Think in terms of the future state of your business. What are the outcomes that are most important? Where do you want to invest your dollars? What kind of corporate culture do you want to create?

When you set those priorities and build those future constructs—especially if you are evaluating or already well on your journey to the cloud—cybersecurity must be a part of every discussion and decision. You wouldn't think about planning your future business without considering sales, marketing, or customer service. Is cybersecurity any less important to your future and success?

Stop thinking of cybersecurity in terms of risk management or compliance, and start thinking of it as a core competency of your business—no matter what business you are in. In today's world, every company is a cybersecurity company.

Adapt Your Organizational Structure

In order to truly make cybersecurity a core competency for your business—as well as a potential competitive differentiator—you may have to shake things up in your organization. Again, it's a matter of getting rid of legacy constructs in which information technology and operational technology (OT) are typically separate silos (and "cooperation" can be made to feel like a four-letter word).

While it's true that cybersecurity is the responsibility of everyone in the organization, it is also true that OT and IT teams have more at stake than almost everyone. They are not just users of technology solutions; they are builders. If they fail to build in the proper cybersecurity protections, they bring risk to the entire organization.

With innovations such as the Internet of Things, machine learning, and artificial intelligence, OT and IT teams are more intertwined than ever—and cybersecurity must be one of the strong binds that ties them together. If your organization still thinks about OT and IT as separate silos, you are still mired in one of those legacy constructs we've been discussing.

Silos drive territorialism, and territorialism is a losing strategy for fighting today's cybercriminals. You need all the cooperation you can get, both internally and externally. If people inside your organization aren't collaborating, you won't be able to ensure that you're covered today and tomorrow. Fix it now.

Make Sure You Have the Right People—and Make Sure You Train *Everyone*

Look closely at the cybersecurity leaders you have in place. Are they forward-thinking? Do they like interacting with other teams and leaders across the organization? Do they emphasize training, awareness, and openness? Can they speak the language of business? Are they as comfortable in the boardroom as they are in front of a computer screen?

Today's cybersecurity challenges require a different kind of leadership than was appropriate in the past. Fear of change can be profound, yet we are in an environment when change is inevitable. Today's cybersecurity leaders should be excited by change, not overwhelmed by it. The skills that might have worked well for a CISO in the past may not be the skills that will help propel your company into the future.

It's not just about the people who are directly responsible for cybersecurity. It's about everyone, and it's about creating and maintaining a corporate culture in which cybersecurity is ingrained everywhere. If cybersecurity is to become a core competency for your organization, you have to treat it that way—starting at the top and extending all the way down, through every level and to every employee.

You must have a commitment to training, give your people the best tools, test them on a regular basis, measure the results, and keep track of your progress. If you're not improving every quarter, it should feel uncomfortable, and you should start questioning if your approach to training is adequate.

When It Comes to Technology, Look Ahead, Not Behind

One factor that can really hamper organizations is an insistence on holding on to older technology. If the attitude is, "We paid for it, we might as well use it," then you've got a real problem. Hanging on to legacy equipment that doesn't address today's threat environment is costly, inefficient, and likely to give you a false sense of protection. And it may be exposing you to even greater risk.

What does a "look-ahead" technology vision look like? Here are some key elements:

- **Automation:** It's been said time and again throughout the pages of this book: You can't fight machines with people. Our adversaries are becoming more automated; we must do the same.

- **AI and machine learning:** These are similar to automation. Our adversaries are using these technologies to their advantage, we must use them to defend ourselves.

- **A SaaS consumption model:** You can't buy new tools and put them one on top of the other. As Nir Zuk explains in his chapter, cybersecurity needs to be consumed quickly, easily, and cost-efficiently. Software-as-a-service is an enabling technology.

- **Cybersecurity-as-a-platform:** Openness is critical to driving cybersecurity innovation and enabling us to keep pace with our adversaries. A platform model supports an open environment and dramatically accelerates our ability to consume innovation.

Encourage a Culture of Openness

Embracing a cybersecurity-as-a-platform model is one aspect of leveraging openness, but it can also go further. Another one of the truisms that comes up time and again in this book is the idea that when it comes to cybersecurity, we are all in it together.

We have adversaries that have no qualms about sharing information, tools, and attack methods on the Dark Web. Shouldn't there be an equivalent Light Web, in which we work together to shed light on how we can all be successful, where we can talk about best practices openly across various industries and share real-time information about emerging threats?

There is a consortium made up of more than 15 different security vendors called the Cyber Threat Alliance. This body was built in the spirit of openness and sharing, with the belief that no one company can do it all. We must work together and share strategies and threat data to stay ahead of our adversaries. This organization produces playbooks, analyses, and reports for every member to consume and benefit from. If your security vendors are not sharing threat intelligence with the CTA, then it might be time to work with one that is more open and interested in contributing to our communities in this way.

Conclusion

The days of cybersecurity as an add-on are gone. There's too much at stake—and things are moving too quickly—for any organization to remain wedded to older models of cybersecurity. Whether it's people, technology, or processes, the only way to make sure you are covered today, is to look ahead and plan for tomorrow. Cybersecurity must be embedded in the DNA of your company to facilitate the business outcomes that will meet the expectations of your customers, employees, and shareholders in the years to come.

24

How You Should Expand Your Cybersecurity Talent Pool: A Lesson of Supply and Demand

Ed Stroz — Founder and Co-President, Stroz Friedberg, an Aon company

This is a story about supply and demand. It's a story about how to address critical resource imbalances in the face of mounting global pressures, complexities, and impacts. I'm not talking about the supply and demand of economic commodities, but rather the supply and demand of the next generation of cybersecurity talent.

Almost anyone reading this book knows something about the gigantic chasm between the needs of organizations' in-house teams compared to cybersecurity service providers, and the availability of smart, creative, talented men and women to fill the more than two-million-person global cybersecurity talent gap estimated over the next few years.[1]

Undoubtedly, your CISO has pled their case for a larger budget to identify, recruit, hire, and train cybersecurity staff. You've probably listened attentively to their arguments, and you've more than likely approved at least some of their requests. However, current attempts by the cybersecurity industry to fill this gap are simply not working, and the issue is not going to be remedied by ramping up what we've been doing to date.

There are two sides to the problem: To solve our growing cybersecurity challenges and to bolster personnel resources, we need increased talent on both the supply side and the demand side. In cybersecurity circles, the supply side is made up of the third-party cybersecurity firms that provide for-hire expertise in such roles as forensic analysis, digital investigations, third-party tools development, cyber risk assessment, and threat intelligence. Across the ledger is the demand side of cybersecurity, which is made up of the consumers of those capabilities and other security tools and services, including on-staff security experts who team with both internal business stakeholders and outside cybersecurity suppliers. Both sides need to evolve the ways they define, identify, and attract sought-after talent.

Supply-Side Cybersecurity

Now, in the interest of full disclosure, our firm is one of those supply-side cybersecurity service providers. We've been fortunate to have hired a lot of very smart, talented, and dedicated men and women who have helped save our clients from potential catastrophes; some of them have also gone on to important cybersecurity and business leadership roles on the demand side.

But I won't kid you. Despite our solid track record, it's getting harder for us to keep up with the demand for talent, and we like to think we've been pretty clever in where we look for new people and the process we go through to ready them for prime time. So we've had to update what we do, how we do it, and the kinds of people we target. You should, too.

A lot has changed for supply-side firms such as ours to make us rethink how we nurture and hire a new breed of cybersecurity professionals. Just 20 years ago, cybersecurity was a pretty immature field. A single cybersecurity practitioner could do quite a bit to help their clients because the state of the art wasn't that advanced. Maybe you had some digital forensics training, perhaps you gave expert testimony at a trial; for many supply-side firms, that was the pinnacle of their skill set, and it didn't require that big a net to find the right people.

Today, cybersecurity is a whole different ballgame. I don't have to tell you about the expanding threat vector, increased vulnerabilities, intensified risk management, and the need to turn cybersecurity from a cost center into a competitive differentiator for your entire enterprise. We've had to hire more specialists, in much the same way law firms and medical practices had to diversify across different areas of unique requirements. That has meant that organizations like ours have had to create and build methodically planned approaches to bringing new skills into the organization so we can deliver more value to our customers.

But that does not mean we're just looking for more college graduates with degrees in cybersecurity or the equivalent. That approach simply won't close the gap in an era of increased cyber risk. We need new and different types of people.

That's not to say we don't need people with deep technical skills; obviously, our clients rightly expect us to have the technology chops necessary to solve a wider array of problems faster than ever. That's particularly true when you consider the tightly integrated role of information technology across all organizational functions and in situations such as controlling critical infrastructure. But it's not enough.

We've supplemented and expanded our traditional mindset to recruit people who have studied in fields such as business, economics, or law. Even college students not studying technical disciplines have taken courses in technology, and let's face it: The millennial generation is far more technology-savvy and aware of cyber risks than those of us who graduated college in the last century. And this isn't limited to recent college graduates, either. We believe there is great benefit to taking people with the right "soft skills," like good judgement, inquisitiveness, and a bias for creative, alternative solutions, and having them work alongside colleagues with deeper technical training.

Of course, we have a detailed training plan that not only covers the technology issues, but also our clients' business challenges. I can't stress how important training is for firms like ours—and for those of you on the demand side, as well. After all, you don't take a recent Yale Law graduate, as talented and as well-educated as they may be, and have them argue a case before the U.S. Supreme Court.

Naturally, we want to hire people whose skills and expertise put them in the bullseye of our recruiting target. But there's a lot to be said for hiring people who may be found in the ring or two just outside dead-center.

Demand-Side Cybersecurity

On the demand side—from global corporations across different industries to smaller organizations with mounting cybersecurity risks—recruiting and training the next generation of talent is just as hard, for all the reasons I cited on the supply side. In many ways, a lot of internal security organizations have been set up like in-house security service providers, treating their business users as "customers." Things like internal charge-backs and restrictive security policies and procedures further promote the idea that the cybersecurity staff is somehow "different" from the business side of the organization.

That's a mindset that has to evolve. And one of the ways I think it has to be done is by expanding the profile of who is recruited, hired, trained, and nurtured on the demand side of cybersecurity.

We need to get away from traditional definitions of internal security operations teams as the techie people. Instead, we have to position these people as business peers and colleagues charged with achieving business goals. And we have to look for new types of people whose prioritized skills include business acumen, a problem-solving mindset, an ability to balance risk and opportunity, and just really sound judgement. That may be found in your latest cybersecurity graduate student ... but it might not.

Similar to what's happening on the supply side, the demand-side cybersecurity gap should be filled with more businesspeople. Having technical skills is, of course, great and necessary. But it shouldn't be a bar to limit the potential talent pool. On the demand side, you already probably have a wealth of technical talent, and you probably already hire some external security service providers for specialized expertise.

Demand-side organizations should place a higher emphasis on identifying and recruiting problem solvers with business expertise; you can always backstop them with people who can break down botnets or use automated monitoring tools to spot advanced persistent threats.

Not only is there more ability for demand-side organizations to look for a new breed of cybersecurity specialists from non-traditional backgrounds, I believe it is essential to do so. The harsh truth is that most businesspeople have worked in organizations that have been struck by a data breach, a distributed denial-of-service attack, or a ransomware demand. They understand far too well the impact of these and other threats on business outcomes, and they also know how some security policies lack the necessary operational context to reduce user friction and improve business agility because everyone is required to change their passwords monthly.

Remember what I said earlier about supply-side firms such as ours broadening our target audiences a ring or two away from the bulls-eye? The applicable rings can and should be expanded a bit further on the demand side. In fact, real-world experiences tell us that being too immersed on the technical side of a solution can prevent you from seeing the real enterprise-level issues. It's a bit like medicine; in recent years, doctors have received criticism for treating the symptoms, but not the patient. They feel they are curing cancer, but they need to also cure the person lying in the bed.

I also talked about the growing specialization in cybersecurity, just as the case has been in fields like medicine and law. And while that's true on the supply side, I think we need more generalists on the demand side. When I say generalists, I obviously don't mean people who are technical Luddites, but I do mean people who focus more on finding new ways to spot and solve problems, typically in close collaboration with business colleagues and technical specialists.

So How Do You Do It?

As business leaders, you can't just sit back and wait for your CISO to come in with yet another request for bigger college recruiting budgets or authorization to increase staff salaries to raid other organizations' experienced staff and to protect the ones you already have. Instead, there are a lot things you can and should do proactively to build your pipeline of cybersecurity talent.

Whether you're on the demand side or the supply side, it's time to rethink the kinds of people you seek to fill your yawning cybersecurity talent gap, or how to identify and retrain non-cyber-specialists to take on new roles.

Hire smart. Start by identifying smart people—even those without deep technical expertise. You can teach smart people enough technical detail so they can have good discussions with their more technically astute colleagues. But your best and brightest security engineer by themselves may not make much of a difference in your bottom line if they either don't have a grounding in business skills or don't have a good business mentor. Smart people will always find a way to figure it out.

Culture matters. Your organizational culture is vital in determining (A) if you can retain your good people, (B) if you can attract good people from the outside, and (C) if you can position your cybersecurity people as trusted peers who care about improving the organization's business performance, rather than in hunting bugs. Value these people, reward them, involve them in early-stage business planning, and treat them like they are vitally important. They are.

Create a diverse ecosystem of talent and skills. You need a web of relationships and abilities to solve the increasingly diverse and head-scratching challenges of cybersecurity. The new breed of cybersecurity talent is going to come more and more from disciplines like law, economics, statistics, accounting, operations, and finance—and you need them tightly integrated with smart, technical talent from both inside and outside the organization.

Value experience, not just expertise. Think about how many times you sat in a boardroom discussing a problem. Didn't you often gravitate toward the man or woman in the group who had lived through that problem before? This kind of experience is invaluable in cybersecurity; could your organization learn something from a business professional who worked at places like Sony, Target, or Equifax during their times of crisis?

Redraw your bull's-eye. Ask your heads of HR and cybersecurity to sit down and look at all the job descriptions of your open spots, and have them think how to redefine those roles in light of the rapidly changing cybersecurity landscape. Your "ideal" job candidate should probably look and act differently today and in the near future than they did even a few short years ago.

Don't worry (so much) about the cost. Hiring cybersecurity talent is expensive. So is fighting the aftereffects of a breach. In order to get a return on investment, you need to first invest. Not everyone is looking to face off salary offers against each other; some people just want to know they work in a place that values their input and their contribution, offers them the best chance to succeed at their job, and makes them proud to be part of the organization.

---

[1] "The Fast-Growing Job With a Huge Skills Gap: Cyber Security," Forbes, March 2017

Language

25

How to Articulate the Business Value of Cybersecurity

Mark Rasch — Cybersecurity and Privacy Attorney

Every aspect of business today has an IT security component. Every business relationship, product, hiring decision, and marketing program. Every customer interaction, communication, product design, and executive decision. Keep going: supply chain management, manufacturing, distribution, customer service. And more: finance, human resources, insurance, product safety, worker safety, and employee collaboration.

In fact, anyone reading this book would be hard-pressed to come up with a single business activity that is not, in some vital way, connected to a computer or computer network—and, therefore, to cybersecurity.

Yet, in far too many cases, we think of cybersecurity the same way a compliance officer sees cybersecurity—as a necessary evil. General counsel sees it as a cost associated with contractual or other compliance. Chief risk officers may take a risk-based approach to cybersecurity spending. Those involved in insurance or loss prevention may see cybersecurity and its related concepts of data protection and privacy protection as a potential loss to be managed.

All of these approaches lead to inadequate attention to resources and manage-

ment for cybersecurity. If the goal of cybersecurity is simply to prevent a reportable breach of personal data, then a company will only likely do the bare minimum to prevent or mitigate such a breach. If the goal is merely to comply with a legal or regulatory standard, then we will do no more than necessary to say that we have, in good faith, complied.

In the competition for scarce corporate or government resources—money, technology, people, and attention—we still fail to think of cybersecurity in terms of how we can use it to empower and differentiate the business. And we still tend to judge our chief information security officers (CISOs) and other security professionals based not on how well they've propelled the business forward, but on how many phishing attacks they've deflected.

Something's got to give. We have to shift our perspective and make sure we are talking and thinking about cybersecurity in a language that ties into the goals of the business: profitability, customer retention, corporate culture, brand reputation, and product innovation. And we have to create new ways of measuring the effectiveness of our cybersecurity teams. When you look at the concept of cybersecurity strictly through the lens of preventing harm, it will only get you so far. It's not that risk mitigation is a bad thing. But when it comes to cybersecurity, it can't be the only thing.

What can we do to change the language, adapt the cybersecurity culture, and shift our perspective? How can we modernize the way we look at cybersecurity to appropriately address today's rapidly changing world? I thought you would never ask.

Where We've Come From; Where We're Going

Compare the workplace of the 1960s with that of the 2010s. Think *Mad Men,* the U.S. television series that faithfully depicts the former era. Lots of low-wage, moderately trained workers moving mail, typing, filing, taking stenography. Pools of secretaries, rows of clerks, people in the mailroom. Fast forward to today. Those jobs are all gone.

You now have IT and security professionals who have, in effect, replaced those people. IT director, CISO, CIO; these are all jobs that didn't exist in the 1960s. Instead of 20 secretaries and 30 clerks making low wages, we now have a handful of people making higher wages. Only, we're far more heavily dependent on them—and the technologies they provide for us.

But this progress has resulted in what could be called "tyranny of the technologists," wherein technology becomes our greatest asset and our greatest potential liability. The goal of computer security is not to secure computers; securing computers is easy—unplug them and lock them up. The goal of security is information security as part of overall information management. And the goal of information management is business enablement.

If you manufacture widgets, you need IT for everything, from payroll and internal communications to business process flow, supply chain management, manufacturing automation, marketing, sales, HR, recruiting, and customer interface. Rather than asking how infosec can ensure compliance, CISOs need to ask how responsible security practices can enable new efficiencies, products, services, and customers.

The CISO needs to align metrics and goals with those of the core business. Thus, the CISO can show how an effective VPN solution empowers telecommuting, which reduces downtime and promotes efficiency and—guess what—sells more widgets. A secure virtualization platform enables the mobile workforce and customers to access their data, which promotes customer satisfaction and—wait for it—sells widgets. A secure payment system permits online ordering and—you guessed it—sells widgets. Security empowers sales, promotes efficiencies, and enables business processes that enhance products, cut costs, and, oh yeah, also ensures compliance and risk reduction. But mostly, it sells widgets.

With technology embedded in your business, you can adopt new business models. You can have a third of your workforce working from home and still maintain a critical mass of workers, social engagement, and collaboration. You can provide dedicated service to customers at any time from any location in the world. You can connect your supply chains in a constant loop of real-time information and advanced analytics. You can do virtually anything you can imagine, as we've seen with companies such as Uber and Airbnb, which have leveraged connected technologies to disrupt decades-old business models.

In reality, however, you can only do those things if the connections and flow of data are secure. That means cybersecurity becomes an enabler—of collaboration, efficiency, productivity, agility, cost reduction, product development, innovation. Security enables the organization to drive revenue and profits through the exploitation of data in new ways. Back in the *Mad Men* days, once you made the sale, the hard work was done. Now, the sale is just the start of the relationship. Data collection, storage, and analytics become critically important—as does security.

Aligning Cybersecurity With Business Objectives

If the end game is to align cybersecurity strategies and investments with business objectives, most companies are still discovering how to make the leap. Part of the challenge has to do with the metrics we use to measure CISO performance.

This becomes a problem when we build our budgets based on hardware as opposed to value; when we measure cybersecurity performance on criteria that has nothing to do with the actual risk mitigated or the overall value provided to the business. Have we done a good job if we prevent 98% of the attacks, but the 2% we miss are devastating? If we stop 90%, but the 10% have zero impact, have we done a bad job?

When it comes to budgeting and metrics for cybersecurity, we often fail to place the right value on the things we value most highly as a business. Part of the problem here is the "stovepiping" of data security: too many, or more accurately, too many different, chiefs. We have a chief privacy officer, chief information officer, chief information security officer, chief risk officer, chief executive officer, etc. Each "chief" has his or her own domain to protect—often with overlapping responsibilities. Each chief believes that her problems

or solutions are the most critical for the company.

The CEO—and ultimately the board of directors—has to balance these competing concerns. Recent SEC guidance in the U.S. has suggested that cybersecurity needs to be a primary concern of the board of directors of a company, and that those responsible for cybersecurity should report directly (or more directly) to the CEO and the board, who should be periodically briefed on the company's security status.

But before such briefings are going to be effective, the CISO and security personnel need to learn how to speak the language of the CEO and board—or educate them on speaking the language of the security personnel.

As a community, we still haven't figured out how to value certain essential aspects of our businesses, particularly when it comes to cybersecurity. I would suggest that most organizations are comfortable placing a value on tasks such as data collection, processing, and analytics, but struggle to place a value on something more esoteric, such as privacy.

We don't value privacy because we don't place a value on privacy. Sure, we can assess the cost of a data breach. We can say a breach will cost $15 per record, that we have 100,000 records, and that therefore a breach will cost $1.5 million. This helps, but it is imperfect.

We need to develop the right metrics for valuing privacy, because if we don't put a dollar value on it, it means we don't value protecting it. We measure privacy based on the cost of not protecting it, rather than the value of it intrinsically. Privacy protection—real and abiding privacy protection—promotes confidence. Confidence promotes trust. Trust promotes sales. And sales promotes the CISO.

Focusing on Business Enablement

Outside the cybersecurity realm, business enablement is typically a factor in just about every decision. Say the company is considering opening a plant in a country where it has never before done business. Management will address a series of questions: What are the risks? Is the government stable? Is there sufficient electricity and transportation? Is there a large enough pool of workers? How will this decision affect our profitability, revenue growth, customer relationships, and partner relationships?

Cybersecurity must be included in each of those discussions. Does the country have cybersecurity laws? Does it prosecute cybercriminals? What are the data retention requirements? Can we safely do business on the internet? Can we hire cybersecurity professionals in the region? Is there a legal structure that will protect the confidentiality of our data? Will law enforcement work with us if we are attacked? Can we get appropriate insurance? Are our partners reliable, and will they protect our data?

We should go a step further and attach a cybersecurity component to *everything* that gives the company value. When we develop a new product, we have to embed decisions about what data is collected, how that data flows through the service, how it is secured and monitored, how we will manage secure payments, and what the risks are associated with data loss.

The same is true with privacy. We treat security and privacy as separate concerns at our own peril. While you can be secure without protecting privacy, (you can securely violate privacy rights) you cannot protect privacy without security. This is the principle behind "privacy by design" requirements in government contracting and in data privacy laws.

It means looking at products, services, solutions, and new technologies and asking: What data is being collected? How is it being collected? What is the impact of collecting, storing, and processing this data? How is the data to be used? How long will this data live? From a security standpoint, does it mean asking who has access to the data? How do I audit access to the data? Is the data encrypted or secured, either in whole or in part? How do I protect data confidentiality, integrity, and availability?

If business enablement is the goal, then we have to use the language of business. Security reduces costs because it increases the efficiency of moving data and enabling collaboration. Security accelerates speed to market, which means we can make more profit. Security empowers us to do things routinely today that we couldn't have done a few years ago. Security enables us to hire the best people because we are not limited by geographic constraints. Security allows sales and marketing to leverage analytics and be more responsive to customer needs.

The Language of Business Enablement

We shouldn't *stop* talking about risk mitigation and regulatory compliance. These will always be critical to the success of our cybersecurity teams. But if CISOs *start* talking about reducing the overall risk to the company, they will be far more effective in speaking the language of business.

How do we change the conversation? Here are some suggestions for IT security professionals:

1. **Closely examine the overall objectives of the business.** Determine how the security function fits with what the business does and how it operates. Develop a framework for articulating the role cybersecurity plays in

key business functions—hiring, operations, sales, marketing, distribution, etc.

2. **Look ahead.** Where is the company going, and how can cybersecurity be a business enabler? Is the company looking to leverage robotics, the IoT, artificial intelligence, big data analytics? Is it looking to break into new global markets? Perhaps there is a new security technology that will enable the company to do something it couldn't before. *Let security drive the conversation.*

3. **Take a more expansive view of the regulatory environment.** Perhaps your organization is not operating in the European Union now, so there's a sense you don't have to worry about GDPR. But you may have business partners doing business in Europe; you might decide to open offices there; you may collect data there. Be aware, be comprehensive, be expansive. Don't look at privacy as a separate discussion, but embed it in your security posture.

4. **Talk business.** Focus on sales, profits, innovation, corporate culture. If the security team does a great job and there are no breaches, what will motivate corporate management to invest more in security? The selling point shouldn't be that nothing happened; it should be that security enabled and empowered the business to achieve these specific quantifiable and measurable results.

5. **Quantify the value of risk reduction.** At some point, the conversation will inevitably turn to risk. When a CISO can effectively quantify the value of risk mitigation, he or she can be more articulate and insightful in explaining overall return on investment. You truly change the conversation when you attach real numbers to risk mitigation and combine that with values associated with profits, sales, speed to market, hiring, product development, and improved operational efficiencies.

Conclusion

Business enablement through cybersecurity is not an option in the Digital Age. It is a fact of life in doing business. If you are involved with other companies, they will demand that you have a comprehensive cybersecurity program. Failure to have one means you won't be able to do business, period. However, if you merely place cybersecurity in the bucket of either "cost of doing business" or "risk mitigation," you may be missing the real opportunity at hand.

Cybersecurity can and should be about driving revenue, achieving greater profitability, attracting and retaining new customers, operating more efficiently, empowering innovation, hiring the best people, transforming the workplace. Only when we think of cybersecurity in those terms, can we truly leverage the power of the Digital Age.

If the only thing we're trying to do is not fail, that doesn't necessarily mean we're going to succeed. It's time to transform our language, mindset, and perspective. When it comes to cybersecurity, whether we are on the board, in the C-suite, or on the frontlines, we should all be speaking the language of business enablement.

26

Language, Please: How You Talk to Boards and Executives Can Make or Break Your Cybersecurity

James Shira

It's 4 a.m. on a quiet Sunday, and your Hong Kong office is suddenly offline. A fringe political group has hacked the local electrical grid, cutting off power to fans and cooling systems in the local data center. All production systems are down.

The result: Your global banking operations are not available. Dead. Not functioning. And the organization is bleeding money by the second.

As your organization's CISO, you get that panicky, middle-of-the-night call you often have nightmares about, and the cybersecurity playbook that was so neatly designed and prepared six months ago goes into effect. With good planning and tight execution, the disaster recovery and business continuity plans are enabled—hopefully automatically—and everyone jumps to attention to find the source of the problem, remediate it, and stanch the damage.

As you contact your boss to let them know what's happened and that a catastrophe has been averted, remember this: What you say next may be the most important step toward ensuring the organization is secure—as well as your career.

What you say to the business leaders of your organization—and how you deliver the message—must give them confidence that you:

- Know what happened.

- Know how it happened.

- Can determine and measure the impact on the business.

- Have a clear, defensible recommendation to ensure it doesn't happen again.

And you can't do that with a litany of technical terms, jargon, and "Don't worry, I've got this covered."

Cybersecurity Is Not a Technology. Don't Talk About It That Way.

Unfortunately, the scenario sketched out above is occurring far too frequently—and often with an unhappy ending. Too many organizations treat cybersecurity as a technical problem, one that is ideally addressed by technical people applying technical solutions to technical threats. And too many CISOs talk about cybersecurity with a technical voice, not with one of a respected business operator.

Cybersecurity isn't about firewalls, intrusion detection, authentication, malware prevention, or even threat intelligence. Oh, those are all important components of a good cybersecurity framework. But CISOs often fail—and their organizations suffer as a result—when they look at cybersecurity solely through a technology lens and talk about it that way to business leaders.

Instead, I strongly urge—no, I implore—you to rethink how you, as your organization's firewall against cyber risk, talk to C-suite business executives and boards about cybersecurity. Your language has to help bridge the gap between the technical underpinnings and the business implications. And the first thing you need to know is that it is not the responsibility of the CEO or the board to come to you and tell you what they want to know.

It's on you.

You must take the first step—and the second, third and however many it takes—to close that gap of knowledge for the non-technical executives. And you can't do that without arriving at a common language for communication.

For instance, let's go back to our nightmare scenario at the beginning of this chapter. When the CEO or a board member asks you, "What happened?" it's important not to talk about unanticipated data exfiltration, buffer overloads, or IRC-controlled botnets. Instead, your reply should focus on the business implications of operational missteps or technical failures, such as loss of online banking services for two hours, which resulted in spikes to our call centers and a 4% loss of revenue.

As a CISO, you must operationalize cybersecurity from a business perspective, rather than through a technical lens. You must describe the problems the organization is confronting in plain language that is rooted in business outcomes. You must be able to monitor, measure, and improve those outcomes, and it is up to you to turn cybersecurity into a strategic discussion, rather than a technical reaction to a problem none of them truly understand.

The words you choose, and how you communicate with the board and other business leaders, will be some of the most important steps you can take toward becoming viewed as a business operator in the same way the heads of functional areas, such as finance, operations, marketing, legal, and others, are regarded. If you don't use the right language, you will not be successful as a CISO.

Preparing Your Audience

In working with many CISOs in both the private and public sectors, I've learned that good communication, based on the most appropriate language, is aided significantly by following a familiar refrain: Know your audience.

As a CISO, you have to talk to a lot of different decision makers, colleagues, and influencers throughout the organization. So it helps to understand how best to get through to your audiences. One important way is to ask yourself if you are talking to someone who is a "reader" or a "listener."

A reader is someone who takes in information visually, reading position papers, case studies, situational analyses, and status updates before a board meeting or a gathering of executive staff. The reader comes prepared for the meeting by arming themselves with pertinent facts, opinions, options beforehand, and is armed to discuss options and consequences.

By comparison, a listener likes personalized discussions, often one-on-one, with the CISO so they can hear from you directly and ask questions as they are processing what you are telling them. With listeners, it's a good idea to have private pre-meetings, so they are prepared for the broader discussion with their peers.

You know the saying, "All politics is local?" Well, a good CISO should remember that "all communication is personal." So be prepared to tailor your language to the needs of the person who is processing what you're telling them.

The Power of Language

Interestingly, one place where cyber professionals and non-technical leaders have understood this requirement and have taken important steps to operationalize cybersecurity through language is the U.S. military. Security has been pulled into the normal chain of command so it's part of the core set of functions undertaken by the U.S. military branch. It's not an IT activity that resides on the edge of the operational framework; instead of talking about "information assurance," everyone speaks the language of "mission assurance."

How else can the CISO use the right language in the right context to be viewed as a true business operator, rather than as a technical guru?

First, don't give in to many business executives' stereotype of the CISO as a technical kingpin, perhaps a little eccentric, and probably biased toward technology solutions that fail to account for business realities. This means you should minimize acronyms, avoid hyperbole, steer clear of run-on sentences, and focus on how cyber risk affects business operations.

Second, understand your organization's business environment as well as the heads of any business function. Become knowledgeable and articulate in issues, such as competitive strengths and weaknesses, customer behavior, sales and profit trends, dis-

tribution channels, and branding considerations.

Third, build professional ties with colleagues based on personal empathy. Learn your colleagues' business challenges and frame your cybersecurity discussions and recommendations in their terms. Talk about how an investment you recommend will increase e-commerce application availability by 20%, ensuring that the organization won't bleed revenue like its competitor did last week when its ordering platform went down for two hours. Or talk about how a modernized data protection approach will make it easier and faster for the legal department to produce documents during the discovery phase of a lawsuit.

Finally, remember that you must back up your words and "own the fix." When you talk to your board about a recommendation for a cybersecurity investment or new policy, take ownership of implementation and accountability: "With your support, I am prepared to do the following." You can't be the person who opines on what to do but isn't prepared to own it.

Language Skills Will Be a Prime Requirement for the CISO of the Future

It's natural for us to play to our strengths as we conduct ourselves in business every day. After all, our strengths are what got us to this place. If a CISO sees himself or herself as the cybersecurity technical guru, they will talk that talk and walk that walk.

But I'm seeing important new trends in how CISOs are being put in place. For instance, I fully expect that more and more CISOs will come from top MBA programs, rather than from computer science programs. I also expect the CISO to be trained, mentored, and recruited internally, within organizations from non-technical disciplines such as finance, operations, and even sales and marketing.

That's because the CISO of the future is going to need to have stronger business skills and, especially, greater communications skills to build the coalitions and collaborations necessary to have the technical and non-technical disciplines work together. Without them, organizations will struggle to properly and proactively identify sources of risk, weigh the possible solutions, evaluate their impact on the business operations, and make difficult decisions on factors other than the best technical fix.

The communications skills are going to be particularly important as the CISO acts as a "translator" between the technical and business sides, as well as communicates up to the CEO and the board about balancing business opportunity with business risk. To make knowledge power, you have to make it understandable. In security, too often we've made it less understandable. The lack of technical knowledge of your audience such as the CEO and the board means they have to trust the person presenting the technical issues to them, which often means they miss the opportunity to ask the right questions that could avert a disaster down the road.

In the context of cybersecurity, great communication skills are required to promote better, faster, and more impactful decision making. The most specific things a CISO needs to communicate, clearly and compellingly, revolve around the need for appropriate investment, the requirement for shared ownership of cyber issues, and a bias for action in a time of crisis. Raising your game in communications is essential in order to move cybersecurity from a reactive mode to a proactive, strategic discipline.

Ultimately, the CISO needs to be the general manager of the full spectrum of security—not only information security, but physical security as well. Again, this is where having a CISO with strong business skills—communications, prioritization, political acumen, delegation, and collaboration—comes in handy. As CISO, you need to demonstrate managerial DNA, which highlights a comfort level with assuming operational responsibility for security.

And here's something else to keep in mind—something potentially controversial: Many current CISOs, as well as candidates for that job, don't want operational ownership.

Many CISOs still see their role as providing technical leadership in the areas related to information security. For them, it's about firewalls and advanced persistent threats and identity management. Too many "traditional" CISOs learned their craft at a different time, when security threats were often well known and their business impact limited.

No longer. And any CISO who dodges operational responsibility and the tight integration with all business functions within the organization does so at their own peril.

To be a successful CISO from this day on, you can't cringe before power. You must hold the organization accountable for a smarter, more effective balance between risk and innovation. And, you can't act like you're the only one in the room who understands the bits and bytes. You don't want to be seen as a CISO who is so comfortable lapsing into the next hype cycle.

Finally, remember that the most successful CISO is "prepared for why." Sitting in a boardroom, or having lunch with the CEO, you may be prepared to argue for new investments in tools, training, or staff. You may have compelling data to highlight a problem or anticipate the next threat. As important as those are, you will not succeed unless, and until, you are able to articulate the reasons *why* your recommendation makes sense. And the people who make those decisions are going to demand that you can defend your recommendations; they are not in the habit of giving you what you want because you dazzled them with your technical brilliance.

Elsewhere in this book, USAA Chief Security Officer Gary McAlum uses a particularly apt way of describing how to close the gap between what a CSO says and what the business executive or board member hears. He calls it "So what?" and he explains that everyone must be ready to explain the business significance of any problem, recommendation, or course of action to ensure rock-solid cybersecurity.

Your "why" must be concise, sober, and grounded in business benefits that are in lockstep with the organization's strategic goals. If not, freshen up that resumé.

Conclusion

In Part 1 of this book, SAP Chief Security Officer Justin Somaini told a very important story about how he set out to build strong relationships—and foster credibility—with business colleagues by asking to join SAP's sales organization.

Justin's rationale was brilliant: "Protecting the company from security breaches and ensuring compliance is actually not a very good description of my job, nor the job of my peers and colleagues around the globe … How could I enable sales if I didn't understand sales?"

As a CISO, it's important to step back and acknowledge that, at the end of the day, your job is to ensure that your organization achieves its most important goals. You may do that by reducing and managing cybersecurity risk, just as the head of sales may do that by creating new sales channels or the head of logistics streamlines global supply chains. It's a means to an end—not an end itself.

27

Using the Right Evidence to Make the Right Cybersecurity Decisions

Mischel Kwon — Founder and Chief Executive Officer, MKACyber

Security: It's been an evolution. At times, cybersecurity leaders have struggled to tell the story, because it's complicated. Moreover, we have to tell this story throughout the organization to executives who have vastly different levels of technical understanding and vastly different leadership priorities.

Too often in the past, security professionals have largely told the story of fear. We have also told the story of right and wrong, black and white. Don't get me wrong: The story is often scary. But this approach has backfired, because it isolated the security team's good, analytical thinking and kept smart people out of vital business conversations.

We know security professionals need to change the way they talk to business leaders, because we need to gain the trust of those leaders. We in security are contributors to digital business and facilitators of new sources of digital revenue. We need to participate in this conversation, and to do that, we have to take an evidence-based approach to those talks.

If we look at classic business decisions, they are made by analyzing facts—usually based on some statistical analysis, and measured by metrics. For years, security professionals have said that this is nearly impossible. So instead of providing meaningful measures and metrics, we have told stories of adversaries and attacks. Although this part of the story is inarguably important, it is not the part of the story that will help businesses understand how to make the right cybersecurity decisions.

Business leaders need security professionals to provide real, meaningful evidence—not descriptions of how bad the malware is, its country of origin, or what the user did to get infected. Statistics from IT and security must be viewed, analyzed, and presented in a way in which leaders can understand the risks. Subjectively made security decisions must give way to truly objective ideas, programs, and policies—based on quantifiable threats and risks—in a way that will seem familiar to business executives.

So why hasn't this been done before? Security executives focused on educating non-technical colleagues, but lacked the necessary data to generate meaningful metrics to measure cybersecurity. Times, however, have changed. Today, our IT systems, which often aren't even on our networks, but in the cloud, are more important to the business than ever. They are the backbone of digital revenue. Both the chief information officer's (CIO) and the chief information security officer's (CISO) responsibilities have changed from roles of delivery to roles that contribute to the top and bottom lines. As these roles have changed, so must the presentations of the work done or needed to be done by the security team.

Security executives must standardize their approaches to illustrate what is happening in cyber by embracing an organized reporting methodology. The need to tell stories and continually educate will ultimately diminish. It won't take long to set the expectation that cybersecurity reporting will be almost entirely focused on those systems, people, and data that are at high risk. Messages must be expressed as use cases, rather than the scarier term of "attack type." The CISO and their team should avoid discussing fear-inducing things that are irrelevant to the organization's business models and threat profiles.

Security and business executives, together, must embrace this use case organization, from high-level reporting all the way down to the data living in and transiting your network. It will change the security organization, because everything will have to be mapped to these use cases: the reporting, the security controls, the tooling, the analyst processes, and, yes, the data itself. This approach will spawn a rich array of statistics that, in turn, will allow organizations to measure cybersecurity and generate metrics that will ultimately provide the evidence for factual, business-like reporting.

Security leaders who follow this blueprint are simply taking a lesson from their business brethren, trying to understand what leadership actually wants to know,

and presenting them with the facts they need to hear so they can understand the business's risk. Let's just look for a moment at the chief financial officer (CFO) role. They use key performance indicators to report on liquidity, productivity, and profitability. How do we as security professionals present this picture for cybersecurity? **State of technology, security spend, and risk.** If you look at liquidity for a finance person, this is basically the state of cash. Cash is king in running a business. If you translate this to cybersecurity, then we're talking about the **state of technology** where data is king. **Security spend** can be articulated by use case, illustrating how spending on technology and people improves security capabilities or diminishes exposure to **risk,** which has been historically articulated based on compliance.

Aligning everything, including security controls, to use cases will enable data-based facts to enter into compliance and risk reporting. It is critical to understand what use cases are affecting which systems and, therefore, how certain parts of the business and revenue are impacted by cyberattacks. If your security leadership can articulate this, then reporting cybersecurity matters up to the executives and the board will become much easier and systematic. It will become much clearer that certain business areas are being impacted by security incidents, which systems are being targeted, which use cases are causing the most problems, where you are improving, and where there are gaps. Business executives should expect the CISO and cybersecurity teams to always provide recommendations for improvements in reporting, and to show the ways security is working collaboratively with IT, legal, and the other business segments to improve these measurable indicators of security progress.

There are, of course, challenges to this approach. It will be difficult to get access to the requisite data to establish this objective reporting methodology. It can also be difficult to map these various data to their corresponding use cases, but there is a tried-and-true method that we call the Maturity Model Matrix Assessment, which enables cybersecurity organizations to understand, and see if they have access to, the actual IT data in the correct format and in the correct place that is needed in order to detect each use case.

If you map the data you need to monitor each use case and to determine their effect on the organization, you will quickly determine you do not have access to some of the data you need and that your tooling doesn't always align with what you want to be doing from a security perspective. You have to see this as a good thing. Moving away from shiny-object syndrome, from spending frivolously on the latest and greatest tools, will be a wonderful side benefit of organizing and aligning IT and security data. As business leaders, you may have asked for this data before from your IT organization, but failed to receive it, because systems may not have been architected in a way to detect these use cases.

This assessment model is a near-perfect way to elevate these issues in a factual, unemotional, non-confrontational way. It's almost entirely certain that tooling, architecture, and process corrections will need to be made in the quest for use case–based detection. That's why I always recommend starting with a visibility project roadmap. You can then report on the execution of this roadmap and then slowly, as you become more mature, you can begin replacing road-map updates with real, use case–based security reporting.

Nirvana comes when your threat intelligence and the defensive content created for the security architecture and security information event manager (SIEM) is all tagged by use case, when you are able to map tactics, techniques, and procedures (TTPs) to indicators of compromise (IoCs) and, when needed, further map these to their relevant to common vulnerability enumeration (CVE) identifiers. With everything organized, you can really prioritize your vulnerability scanning, narrow down the threats you need to be looking for, and map the security controls to each of the problematic CVEs. Then you'll have a truly complete picture. Once all of this mapping is complete, you can measure the statistics and arrive at something new—operational compliance.

Use cases become your true key performance indicators—your evidence—and they aren't arrived at by conducting reviews, audits, or interviews but by analyzing data. Ideally, you will have a dashboard where you can see system hygiene, business risk, and use-case detection, essentially demonstrating where you are weak and how you can improve, charting your progress over time.

Maintaining access to the data you need can be a challenge in this new world of data center–driven networks that look very little like the in-house enterprise networks in traditional organizations. This kind of resource distribution is a challenge, and it means, more than ever, that security is a team sport, where cybersecurity experts partner with other business units to ensure proper network visibility. The assessment model, therefore, should be a regular (I recommend quarterly) event, where you can assess or reassess your access to the business' expanding array of technologies, whether they're on premise, in the cloud, or some enterprise app someone else built for you.

Let's use a hypothetical healthcare organization—a conglomerate of hospitals, researchers, physicians' operations, and educators—as an example. They would report on high-risk use cases such as ransomware, data exfiltration, distributed denial-of-service (DDoS) attack, phishing, and malware. They have one network where the four businesses live. Segmentation is non-existent, and they are detecting incidents based on intrusion detection system (IDS) alerts. They have a large number of Health Information Portability and Privacy Act (HIPPA) findings that have nothing to do with the actual incidents they are facing. This seems like an impossible situation, a fire fight where they will run out of water and, inevitably, the CISO will lose his or her job. We have heard or experienced this situation many times.

Their first action should have been to identify the use cases. Then they could review the vulnerability scans and map them to the IOCs that were mapped to the use cases that they were looking to detect. This would enable them to focus in on the highest priority use cases. They could then map the data in their SIEM to the use cases through the assessment model, which would show them where they are missing critical data. With the CIO's team, they could review all of their tooling, the state of their architecture, and put a roadmap together that would lead them to full use case monitoring. They would inevitably find massive savings in re-aligning their tooling to support use cases. The CIO and CISO could work on the architecture and tooling to improve visibility, detection, and their ability to measure these. Until they have clear use cases to report on, the duo would instead report on their architecture improvement.

Once the security team is able to detect by use case, they can then report not only what they are able to detect but also on where they are blind, demonstrating their overall capabilities and how they can be improved. When a lack of visibility hinders their detection capability, they could signify as much in their event ticketing and keep statistics on these blind spots. This, in turn, would be useful data in their detection capability reporting. Once they mapped their vulnerability scans with their IoCs, CVEs, and security controls, the focus of their audits changed too, focusing on that which is high-risk and requires more immediate fixing.

In the end, their reporting would have come from the actual function of the organization. The agreement of the use cases, the alignment of goals across the organization. This methodology would allow clear and meaningful reporting at all levels of the organization, based on facts, data, statistics, metrics, and improvement.

Over time, this hypothetical healthcare organization would reap many benefits. The improved architecture could eventually lead to a better-segmented network. They could migrate certain aspects of their business to the cloud. They would be able to work as a team, supporting the business as it corrected its spending on IT and security tooling. They would also be able to eventually report to the board together, offering a single, all-encompassing technology report.

This is truly a story of more than just reporting and evidence. This is a story of aligning the organization, organizing security, and ensuring that the requisite data is available for the security team to make fact-based, impactful remediation recommendations. The byproduct of this is that leadership can feel confident that they are making the right cybersecurity decisions—based on real, measurable data—for their digital business.

28

Building Empathy and Trust Among CISOs and Business Leaders

Brad Arkin — Vice President and Chief Security Officer, Adobe

The hallmarks of a great relationship are trust and confidence. That's true whether we're talking about business, geopolitical, or personal relationships—they all require a strong sense of trust and confidence in order to take root and thrive. And building trust and confidence in a relationship revolves heavily around the notion that all parties must develop a strong sense of empathy for how others feel and what they need. Could you imagine how negotiations between businesses would fare without a sense of empathy? Or between spouses?

The same is true in cybersecurity, where efforts often succeed or fail based on the state of the relationship between CISOs and their business colleagues, particularly in the C-suite and the boardroom. After all, technology comes and goes, threats evolve, and strategies are often redrawn in response to new vulnerabilities and changing business priorities.

But without open, honest, and two-way communication between the technical and business leaders, empathy will be impossible to achieve. And without a relationship built on empathy, progress toward optimal cybersecurity readiness will be fleeting, at best. How do we do it?

Bridging the Gap

Just think, if a major security incident occurs, who will be the one explaining it to the high-level business executives in the room? Questions could be as simple as, "Have you checked all the servers to ensure they are set up right?" This is where the security executive would need to patiently explain that there are hundreds of thousands of servers around the world, even a maxed-out Excel spreadsheet only opens up to ~64,000 cells. To help develop a sense of empathy, security executives will want to find a way to bridge the gap between what the business leaders know and what they need to know in order for us to make smart decisions together. And unless we find a way past certain knowledge and language barriers, we will be stuck in this no-man's land of mistrust and misunderstanding.

Technical details overwhelm and confuse non-technical executives, so it is often best to try to avoid having technical discussions. An alternative to technical discussions is the use of analogies, where one can take the unfamiliar and convert it into something non-technical that business leaders and board members are more familiar with. For example, in an attempt to stay away from the minutiae of security, one analogy that can be utilized is that of home renovations—something many people are very familiar with. The homeowner doesn't need to know what tool the contractor used, or what he did to meet the engineer's requirements to align with local zoning regulations. What the contractor needs to do is give the homeowner a sense that their work achieved the homeowner's goals—more open space, modernized design, bigger closets. It's all about giving them a feeling of confidence and trust that the contractor did the job properly—making it more likely they will do business again in the future.

Looking Out for Warning Signs

What happens when the C-suite and board don't trust the CISO to have security practices and policies that reflect business goals and realities? Aside from some potentially uncomfortable conversations, there's a lot of confusion on all sides about the status of the organization's cybersecurity readiness. This reality often inhibits decisions on security budgets, governance and oversight responsibilities, state of compliance issues, and legal exposure—topics business leaders do not want to spend their time, money, and energy on.

For business executives and board members, there are some common red flags to recognize. For instance, business executives may hear members of different functions pushing back on the CISO's policies, like the engineering team fighting the CISO's recommendations on substantial security features to be built into their latest widget. The non-technical leader may not have the ability to sort out which side is right, but that level of observable friction becomes a big problem in the executive's mind. If the security leader is asking for reasonable things—and if empathy has resulted in trust and confidence between the negotiating CISO and engineering leader —then you're far less likely to observe friction.

That doesn't mean the engineers won't grumble a bit, but they probably won't claim the CISO is an idiot.

Another tell-tale sign of a lack of trust between the technical and non-technical sides on security issues is when the security leader can't construct a clear narrative around how proposed investments align with desired business outcomes. If your CISO comes to you asking for a big check, and the first words out of their mouth is that they need it to reduce MTTR to sub-2 hours after botnet attack, no one is going to feel like the CISO "gets it." But if they frame their request in something understandable and relevant, like, "The most recent regulation guidelines require us to notify regulators and affected parties in the event of a breach of personal information, so we need to upgrade to these monitoring and reporting tools," the board is going to understand. And more important for the long term of the cybersecurity "relationship," it will lay the groundwork for an air of trust because everyone will have exhibited some empathy. The business side understands that the CISO needs this in order to keep the organization protected, compliant, and insulated against legal and brand damage, and the CISO feels the business leaders take him or her seriously and respect their recommendations.

Ultimately, the board and C-suite has to feel that the CISO is concerned with business results rather than trying to sneak in what they want by layering in a lot of technical jargon. If the senior leadership doesn't get that feeling, they're going to realize fast they are talking to the wrong person.

Building a Language of Empathy: It's Not Just What You Say, but Also What You Do

Everyone's heard the saying, "Actions speak louder than words." Well, what we say is obviously important as a way of helping someone build a sense of empathy, ultimately leading to trust and confidence. But non-verbal language counts for a lot—probably more than people realize.

An obvious example of non-verbal communication that can either elevate or undermine the CISO is the reporting structure. If the CISO reports to the CIO, you're saying, "Security is a technology issue, best left to the techies." But if the CISO reports to the COO or CEO, or if they have dotted-line access to the board, that makes a profound statement to everyone that cybersecurity is a business issue. And, by the way, it reinforces that notion back to the CISO, who now has more confidence that the board gets it, too.

There are other forms of non-verbal communication that build trust and confidence. Governance structures, budget approval, and financial oversight are just a few examples. And then there are others that are less tangible—but no less meaningful.

Here at Adobe, we use the term "executive presence" to describe someone who carries themselves with confidence and who projects an air of gravitas. I wish I had known how important that was when I was a 25-year-old technical nerd, without good communication skills and not particularly adept at translating what I wanted to say to the level and language of my audience. It was as if I was talking to myself—not a good thing for one's career, and not a good way to demonstrate empathy.

In their interactions with CISOs, business leaders want to see that they are prepared, that they are on top of any issues, that they have the confidence in themselves and their teams to be able to answer clearly, concisely, and in business language. And business leaders should be extremely wary of CISOs who try to bluff their way through an answer to a tough question. It's far better for the CISO to simply say, "I don't know. But I can get that information for you."

If your CISO is a bundle of nerves or is overly excitable after discovering a security event, that is not going to reassure business executives and board members that they've got it covered. As we all know, business leaders are like good poker players: They look for any "tell," any subtle sign of insecurity or confusion, that they're not getting the full story.

How Do You Recognize Success?

The signs of a successful relationship are often easy to spot: A long marriage with a lot of expressions of love and respect between people who like spending time together. An historic peace treaty between long-standing enemies. A political compromise that crosses party lines for the good of a nation.

There are similar measures for success in building a trustful relationship between the CISO and the business leadership—and some of these are as intangible as the very notion of empathy.

For instance, when your CISO has established and maintains the respect of business peers and organizational leaders, you'll be able to "feel" the confidence bestowed upon the CISO for the work they're doing.

That shows up in things like colleagues including the CISO in their business planning meetings (without being directed to do so by the CEO), or doing joint presentations to the board on the delivery of new business services. When the board members see Tom and Mary standing up in front of the room, easily playing off each other and finishing each other's sentences, they'll immediately feel more confident in their CISO and their relationship with the business side.

Of course, the CISO also has to deliver the goods. They have to make sure they are actually protecting the organization against undesired results, and when bad things do happen—as they inevitably will—your CISO must take the right steps to ensure things don't spiral out of control.

To facilitate those kind of results, we can identify a few important steps that have to happen along the way in order for that sense of trust and confidence to develop and grow.

- Does the CISO make the kind of rational arguments for security investments that allow the board to say yes, even to large requests?

- Is proper security being implemented across the organization, not just in the data center or the SOC?

- Can the CISO get the access they need to escalate matters? Are they "clicking" with their peers, as well as with executives and board members?

- Do executives feel a need to micromanage the CISO (and not just because they may be obsessive micromanagers)?

Finally, there are some hard metrics that we all recognize: How fast can your CISO

identify the existence of a threat, close up a vulnerability, and remediate the problem? How much money do they contribute to the bottom line by keeping systems and applications up and running, or by ensuring customer confidence in new services?

But even those have to be weighed against "soft" actions, such as how they conduct post-mortems after a breach, or whether they can convince development teams to design security into their new products before they are released.

Speaking the Language of Trust, Confidence, and Empathy

In all relationships, there often are crossroads where things can go the right way or the wrong way. Maybe a couple faces financial difficulty, forcing them to weigh some very tough choices about where to cut back. Or perhaps an inadvertent border flare-up sparks tensions between long-standing enemies who are just coming to grips with their new status as peaceful neighbors.

Cybersecurity is the same way. There will always be security incidents, breaches, high-profile ransomware attacks, and other potentially devastating events that will test the very nature of the relationship between business leaders and their CISOs.

What all parties do to build iron-clad trust and confidence will depend largely on their ability to establish a feeling of empathy: Yes, things may look bad now, but I trust you, and I know you trust me.

Strategy

29

To Get Ahead of Cybersecurity Threats, Focus on Preparedness and Sustainability

Heather King — Chief Operating Officer, Cyber Threat Alliance

Megan Stifel — Attorney; Founder, Silicon Harbor Consultants; Cybersecurity Policy Director, Public Knowledge

Everyone understands natural disasters are inevitable. Hurricanes, tornados, flash floods, wildfires, and other extreme weather conditions happen frequently and at different levels of severity, and the economic, human, and social impacts can be enormous, if not deadly. So it's imperative that representatives from all parts of the community share the responsibility to prepare for the onslaught of any threat or hazard.

Ultimately, greater individual and organizational preparedness contributes to a stronger, more resilient community. Doing that means everyone has to get out ahead of the problem, prepare for a wide range of potential challenges, and ensure that protective actions and defensive measures can be sustained in wave after wave of potential disasters.

Wave after wave of potential disasters: Sounds like the current state of cybersecurity, doesn't it?

We all have to rethink our strategies to ensure our organizations and our communities can achieve and maintain a stronger state of cybersecurity. And, those strate-gies must be built on resiliency, and subsequently, the twin pillars of preparedness and sustainability. Unless leaders move toward a mindset that emphasizes long-term planning and sustainable cyber-resilience, informed by the lessons learned from any given event, we will continue to fall further and further behind.

In no other institutional function would we accept such a downward trend without meaningful change. If company sales and profits were trending down, we'd find a way to plan and execute a sustainable path to financial health. If our house was repeatedly robbed, we'd either get an alarm system or we'd move. And if a country's economic and social position deteriorated, we'd look at things like job training, educational opportunities, import/export strategies, and an entire array of policies and programs.

But far too many organizations realize too late that they are behind the curve when it comes to cybersecurity, and yet they continue to cling to outdated, inefficient, reactionary, and ultimately unsuccessful approaches. Since all organizations experience incidents or intrusions, it's not surprising that many chief information security officers often feel overwhelmed by the sheer volume of actions necessary to better prepare.

It's time for a change.

Preparedness and Sustainability

Many organizations still view cybersecurity through a perimeter security lens, where the focus is on securing the network against intruders—an outdated castle-and-moat approach. Too many organizations have built cybersecurity defenses focused on addressing individual problems or reacting to specific threats. Unfortunately, that has created numerous cybersecurity silos and stovepipes—a solution for advanced persistent threats, another for mobile malware, another for phishing, and still others for threats in specific geographies or vertical industries. Intruders and malicious insiders exploit the seams and gaps this approach creates. Thus, it is inefficient, ineffective, and not sustainable.

Today, we must dramatically expand the focus of cybersecurity, so we can not only secure our networks but also secure our products and services used by other businesses, organizations, and individuals. And we're not just talking about the influx of tens of billions of connected things—it's nearly every aspect of how we work and interact using technology. Moreover, in order to change our strategies, it's a transformation/shift in how we think and approach doing business. For instance, instead of "first to market," think of it as "secure to market," putting a premium on providing the most secure products and services. At the heart of our recommendations on how to improve cyber resilience are the concepts of preparedness and sustainability.

By preparedness, we mean getting out in front not only of today's cyber risks, but also to anticipate what may be coming next. Together, these steps help organizations determine the potential business impact of cyber risks, and enable them to put in place heightened business continuity plans and incident response plans that are tested through training and exercises and updated regularly—not just after the latest incident.

The concept of sustainability is intricately tied to preparedness because it also recognizes the need to engage today in order to ensure the same or better opportunities tomorrow. Sustainability management expands the aperture of a company's product—whether hardware, software, or service—from the moment just before it goes to market to the point at which the company expends resources toward the product. Companies adopting sustainability management practices work across business lines to assess supply chains, interoperability and scale, consumer engagement, and regulatory compliance to ensure what goes to market today will withstand tomorrow's challenges and that the product's lifecycle is fully understood.

An organization's cybersecurity preparation must be sustained over time in the face of new threat vectors and rapidly changing business requirements. It's like shifting thinking of your business processes that support the enterprise from the view of IT acquisition, to extending supply chain risk management to your entire business operations—truly knowing who your vendors are, who they rely on, knowing your product's lifecycle, and how you will support it throughout, including managing vulnerabilities and patching to data collection, retention, and use.

The harsh reality is that our business leaders are far too optimistic about their organizations' current state of cybersecurity resilience. As a result, they often fail to see the upside of developing cybersecurity strategies in the same way they develop long-term product roadmaps or multiyear market development programs. Ultimately, organizations should be integrating cybersecurity into these and other business operations. Leaders still too often see cybersecurity as a cost of doing business rather than as a step toward improving customer experience, enhancing workforce productivity, maintaining trust with customers, or protecting the organization's brand.

To counter this mindset, business leaders and board members need to discard the all-too-prevalent, "what is this going to cost us?" reaction to cybersecurity measures to "how can cybersecurity investments improve our business competitiveness and deliver a better ROI."

To support such a shift, we need a more holistic approach to cybersecurity, which is informed by successful approaches from other disciplines, including preparedness and sustainability. When our organizations are prepared for as many eventualities as we can imagine, and when we take the long view about securing the organization and its digital assets, we begin to reassert control over the challenges confronting us.

Moreover, adopting sustainable business management practices has helped organizations achieve higher profits, in addition to improved environmental, social, and governance ratings. It stands to reason that organizations that adopt a broader vision toward sustainable cybersecurity practices can do things like anticipate and adapt to changing threat vectors more quickly and effectively, because their cybersecurity framework is built on holistic preparation, agility, and an ability to scale their programs as conditions change.

A sustainability-framed approach to cybersecurity enables these resilient characteristics because it is shaped not only by lifecycle, enterprise, and supply chain risk management, but also by user interaction and anticipated experience.

Rethinking and Re-architecting the Approach to Cybersecurity

Experience has taught us all that information sharing is fundamental to an organization's ability to build a new cybersecurity strategy upon the concepts of preparedness and sustainability. No sole organization can spot, react to, and remediate the impact of risks in real time on their own. Without a commitment by organizational leadership to collaborate with colleagues, partners, and even competitors to share relevant threat information, we will continue to fall behind malicious actors.

At the Cyber Threat Alliance, we recognize that information sharing supports an organization's preparedness efforts, and ultimately, its resilience. In fact, information sharing—whether human-to-human or near real-time automated machine-to-machine—demonstrates an organization's confidence in its own products and services. Moreover, it's no longer how much data an organization has access to, but it's what their products can do with the data. Furthermore, it communicates a realization that the threat is growing exponentially, and organizations can no longer tackle these threats individually, but that we have a shared responsibility to share information from our different perspectives and confront the challenges facing the digital ecosystem.

For instance, through its members, CTA enables near-real-time actionable cyber threat and incident information sharing among highly competitive cybersecurity providers. These competitors have voluntarily come together to improve the cybersecurity of the digital ecosystem in an effort to better prepare and protect customers, and ideally, achieve a more digital resilient world. They all believe this collaboration will improve their profitability, not weaken it. Further, CTA's information sharing facilitates analysis aimed at disrupting malicious actors, enabling more effective and collective defense actions, and forcing adversaries to invest time and money in new infrastructure and how they do business.

A good application of information sharing as a preparedness action is VPNFilter in May 2018. Cisco's Talos Group, one of CTA's founding members along with Palo Alto Networks, Fortinet, Check Point, McAfee, and Symantec, notified CTA of the VPNFilter threat that was targeting network equipment all over the world, and shared their analysis and malware samples with CTA members. As a result of the incident information sharing done through CTA, all of CTA's members were able to rapidly develop protections and mitigations for their customers and quickly counter the threat.

Moreover, as Megan wrote in "Securing the Modern Economy: Transforming Cybersecurity Through Sustainability," reliance on technology to do both mission-critical and everyday tasks in business, at home, and in our communities will only accelerate. Without a commitment to organizational preparedness and sustainability, organizations and individuals and the internet ecosystem will be put at greater risk as we are exposed to more and more public instances of information security problems: "Maintaining public trust in technology relies, in significant part, on all stakeholders maintaining cybersecurity."[1]

As organizations commit to a cybersecurity mindset based on preparedness and sustainability, executives and boards must challenge each other to rethink their most basic assumptions about technology usage and cybersecurity resilience. For instance, they must:

1. **Make cybersecurity a C-suite priority with their active participation.** A number of chapters have talked about why cybersecurity should be a C-suite priority. But their active participation is critical. This starts with conveying in management meetings, employee all-hands, and even your reports for publicly traded companies how serious you regard the cybersecurity threats facing your organization and ultimately, what you're doing to prepare and sustain your organization, both when an incident or breach occurs and when you take products—services or devices—to market. As we all know on any management topic, when executive leadership prioritizes and actively engages on an issue, it delivers a sense of urgency.

2. **Make cybersecurity intuitive in your day-to-day business operations.** Organizations should maximize opportunities for educating and raising awareness within the workplace, so that employees better protect the organization while "on the job" and understand how they can reduce their own digital risks "off the job." Software vendors should be required to demonstrate that they have secure development processes, supported by a software bill of materials. Next, organizations should communicate what is expected of employees by requiring best practices in the enterprise environment and following

product deployment, and encouraging their adoption at home. Organizations can develop "cyber civics" programs that emphasize using two-factor authentication and password managers, thinking before clicking on suspicious links, and being cautious about what they post online about themselves and their families' status and activities (e.g., limiting communications about travel).

3. **Recognize that cybersecurity underpins all business operations.** As Siân John of Microsoft points out in this book, security is a business problem, not an IT problem. Therefore, it's important to remember that a great risk management framework integrates technical solutions with business goals. Putting security first in all business operations enhances confidence in the processes that develop products and services, which results in better products and services that support the brand and ultimately leads to increased profits. Failing to incorporate security throughout the organization risks the confidentiality, integrity, accuracy, and authenticity not only of information within the enterprise, but also of the very products the organization depends upon to earn a profit.

4. **Inform your approach to cybersecurity planning with worst-case scenario consequences.** Consider not just the enterprise network, but also everything it depends upon (vendors, employees, power, physical structures) and attaches to it when assessing cybersecurity risk. In addition to adopting the Cybersecurity Framework promulgated by the National Institute for Standards and Tech-

nology to manage enterprise risk, get incident response and continuity plans in order, practice them regularly, and update plans, policies, and processes appropriately. Acquisition and plans must be collaboratively developed by all business functions within the organization, not just by the CISO. And don't forget to include product and service security upgradability and patching in these "dooms day" scenarios.

5. **Actively participate in an information-sharing organization ... or two.** Business leaders often struggle to get past their innate discomfort at sharing information with others. But as indicated earlier in this chapter, in the rapidly evolving cybersecurity landscape, this reluctance can no longer be tolerated. Invest now in learning some best practices about what, when, where, and how to share information, because going it alone is no longer an option. Sherri Ramsay says it clearly in her chapter of this book: The bad guys are collaborating; why aren't we doing the same?

As you undoubtedly imagine, this kind of holistic, integrated, comprehensive, and deliberate change in the way an organization thinks and approaches its business demands the support and active participation by every organization's executive team, from the corner office to the boardroom. We've not only tried to raise awareness about the need to confront threats in a more proactive, end-to-end manner, but we've also offered tangible ways organizations can challenge their own assumptions and create more cybersecurity resilient organizations based on the underlying pillars of preparedness and sustainability. And, it's essential for executives and board members to embrace this mindset; otherwise you risk leaving your organization to expend countless resources on a defensive posture that's always going to be playing catch up to the bad guys.

Conclusion

Too often, business leaders continue to take the castle-and-moat approach to enterprise cybersecurity. But modernizing that philosophy by adopting the preparedness and sustainability principles we've talked about in this chapter is essential because it enables executives to look around the corner and anticipate the impact of existing and emerging threats on business operations.

As we institutionalize this kind of mindset and reinforce it in our discussions and interactions with customers, investors, employees, vendors, and third parties, we take major steps toward a more resilient cybersecurity posture that is proactive, analytical, and self-reinforcing. It's like preparing for extreme weather conditions. The more you plan, and the more you put measures in place—not just for a point-in-time event but for the long term—the more routine this will all become and the more successful your organizations will ultimately be in managing cyber risk and, as a result, achieving their mission.

---

[1] "Securing the Modern Economy," Public Knowledge, April 2018

30

Learning and Leveraging the Wisdom of "So What?"

Gary McAlum — Chief Security Officer and Senior Vice President for Enterprise Security, United States Automobile Association

As cyber threats become more frequent, more sophisticated, and more impactful on business operations, organizations need to adopt a practical approach if they are to make sense out of what promises to be an uncertain and confusing future.

Yes, many business executives and board members will convene meetings with their chief information security officers and other senior IT executives to consider financial investments and changes to business processes. And many of those discussions will be riddled with technical buzzwords and talk of things like intrusion detection systems, UEBA, multi-factor authentication, next-generation firewalls, network segmentation, and machine learning, just to name a few. Your top IT and security experts will undoubtedly impress you with their depth of technical knowledge and give you an array of solutions to "defend the perimeter" and establish "multi-layer security frameworks." And every vendor has "the last piece of the puzzle that you need" in your security technology stack to solve all your problems.

And when those buzzwords start flying and the acronyms dominate discussions, your reaction and response should be simple: "So what?"

I don't mean you should ignore or belittle the technical expertise of your CISO or CIO, or disregard their requests for smart and even potentially large increases in security budgets. "So what?" is just the lead-in for a series of questions that need to be properly addressed. As important as technology solutions are in establishing stronger cybersecurity, it's essential that business leaders and board members focus on the operational implications of cybersecurity challenges and keep the technical issues rooted in a business context.

- How is this threat impacting or how could it impact our business?

- How are our customers and partners going to be affected?

- What are the financial, operational, regulatory, legal, and brand implications of the threats?

- What is our risk exposure? What is our residual risk?

- How will we know if we are succeeding in defending our most valuable assets?

- How can we look around the corner at what's next?

- And the hardest question of all: How are we measuring success? In other words: So what?

How USAA Learned the Lesson of "So What?"

Several years ago, the financial services industry was attacked—not by masked thieves breaking into our vaults under the cover of darkness or by smash-and-grab robberies of our branch offices. It was a cyberattack—a distributed denial-of-service (DDoS) attack, to be precise, targeting the U.S. financial services sector. And it was a real mess.

Seemingly, no financial services organization was immune—and that includes where I worked at that time. In fact, we were hit twice. Believe me, the fact that we had plenty of company did not make it any easier for us.

As the first wave of attacks hit organizations throughout our industry, we could see the writing on the wall. The media started picking up on the attacks, so there was a daily dose of reporting and an increasing tone of fear, uncertainty, and doubt (FUD). We knew it was going to be a board-level issue, that they'd want clear answers, and they'd want them fast. So we began to prepare our presentation.

I sat down with my SecOps team, and posed an open-ended directive to them: "Give me a short presentation for the board, no more than three slides." I knew this was a challenging request, and I felt it was a good teaching moment for my team to gather information they felt was relevant for senior leaders and to give them an opportunity to develop strategic communication skills.

I wasn't surprised when the team came back with a technical presentation on botnets, how they occur, what they do, and all the technical considerations. There was a great deal of detail on the types of DDoS attacks that were occurring: UDP Flood, Ping of Death, NTP Amplification, HTTP Flood, etc. What the brief didn't include was an answer to the fundamental question: So what? In essence, we were telling the board how the watch worked, but not what time it was.

It would have been easier for me to give them more explicit instructions—especially considering the sense of urgency of the moment—but I felt it was crucial for our team to see and "feel" the impact of not providing the right information in the right context. I challenged some of the leaders within my group to go out and talk to business teams, to understand the financial, operational, and reputational impact of being offline, let's say, for eight hours. In fact, I suggested that the Business Continuation team would be a great place to start, since their annual Business Impact Analysis would be an authoritative source of valuable data.

They learned their lessons well. They came back with a tight, business-oriented presentation that was short on technical minutiae and long on business impact.

By the way, it was a single slide. They boiled down the "so what" to its essence, and that's what we presented to the board. Essentially, they answered the question, "So what if our customers can't get to their online accounts for eight hours?" There were very definite answers pertaining to lost business, inability to service customers, impact to money movement transactions, etc. Any downtime due to the DDOS, regardless of type, was going to be a big deal. They got it.

We know they got it because we were able to easily demonstrate the business impact of not taking action in dollars and cents, and what it would mean in terms of pain for our customers if we didn't take stronger steps. More importantly, it allowed the conversation to change to "Are we ready to deal with this? And if not, what resources are needed?"

Creating a Culture of Cybersecurity Using a "So What" Approach

In another chapter of this book, Patric Versteeg writes compellingly about the importance of setting a strong "culture of cybersecurity" throughout an organization. I think he has hit on an important requirement, and our "so what" discussion can be applied in the area of cybersecurity culture, as well.

Using our "so what" yardstick, how can business leaders and CISOs build and nurture a culture of cybersecurity? I have a few suggestions that may work for your organization.

- **Demonstrate that it is a top-down strategic initiative.** Sending out memos and approving policies on good cyber hygiene are fine, but they lack "so what" impact. Your organization needs to see its leaders "walking the walk" by doing things like engaging security team members on new-product development teams from the start, rather than simply having them eyeball your new IoT initiative as it's about to be released to the market.

- **Real leadership goes beyond writing checks.** Again, having business leaders and board members approve important cybersecurity investments is essential. But it fails to deliver the "so what" impact of steps like having your CISO report to a senior executive outside the typical CIO chain or having regular interactions with the board.

- **Making the right personnel decisions means everything.** It may sound counter-intuitive, but I believe we are all often better served by having fewer, rather than more, FTEs devoted to cybersecurity—as long as they are the cream of the crop. Maybe this is a vestige of my days in the military, but I always want an elite team rather than a large number of average performers simply to have enough eyeballs to monitor and manage security events. Business leaders have every right to ask "So what?" of the CISO who puts in a request to expand his or her team. So, what will this expansion do to decrease risk, improve business operations, or enhance products and services?

- **The executive team and board members need to commit to continuous security education.** Regularly scheduled presentations to the board and continuous conversations with business executives are good, but self-initiative on the part of the board and C-suite executives is better. Don't just sit back and ask your CISO for a briefing; take the lead and get educated on your own. Visit with the security team on-site and ask questions. Spend some time reviewing threat intelligence reports with your CISO. Attend conferences and listen to podcasts. Professional organizations like the National Association of Corporate Directors offer an increasing number of training and awareness events around cybersecurity. Your board and executives won't know how to evaluate the answers to "so what" questions if they are not committed to going beyond becoming cyber-aware and actually becoming cyber-centric. It's that important.

- **Adopt a "secure-by-design" approach.** This should be applied to everything from new-product development to how you use technology for everyday operations. Policies like changing passwords quarterly are annoying to your employees, in large part because they don't hear their "so what" pleas answered. The same is true with your system engineers and application developers. They will push back on your well-intentioned edicts, for example, to strengthen authentication for that new online loan approval application, unless you make them understand the implications when security defenses are breached or customer accounts are compromised.

Framing "So What" Questions for the Best Results

As is true in nearly every type of relationship, your ability to get everyone on the "so what" bandwagon is influenced heavily by how you send your messages. Different people on the receiving end of a "so what" missive can interpret that in different ways, and the results can range from instant learning and embracing the spirit of "so what" to hostility, confusion, and fear.

What you say matters. But how you say it may matter more.

- Is your "so what" message motivational, challenging, instructive, and benefits-oriented, or is it threatening?

- Is it framed in business implications, such as financial impact, operational efficiency, company risk, or brand reputation?

- Do we need to shore up our defenses by increasing financial and manpower investments, or maybe re-prioritize the use of existing resources?

At the end of the day, "so what" is really a metaphor for an operational methodology that frames three key points:

- What is the business impact of this security situation?

- What are the risk implications?

- What are we doing about it?

For C-suite executives and board members, what you don't want or need is a growing cascade of reports, dashboards, and metrics. CISOs already have a vast amount of information that they are sending to business stakeholders about vulnerabilities and risk; just dumping more data on the desks of decision makers isn't going to work. Board members and executives have to walk that fine line between getting "so what" answers and wallowing in tactical details. And, time is always a limited commodity.

One way to help is for business executives and boards to train the technical presenter—the CISO, CIO, or anyone providing security information to the business side—not to pull the crowd into tactical, technical discussions. Board members, in particular, have a limited amount of time, and they need to have confidence and trust in the people accountable for ensuring the organization and its assets are secure. Coach your CISO and their team on how to deliver strategic answers to the "so what" question.

Moving Ahead With Your "So What" Methodology

Taking a "so what" approach to cybersecurity isn't about downplaying risk or minimizing the importance of smart technology investments. Instead, it's a pragmatic way to prioritize how, where, and when to utilize key resources (money, time, people, technology) to spot and prevent problems before they impact business operations.

When I was first exposed to "so what" in my Air Force career, I'll admit it was a little uncomfortable and occasionally disconcerting when my superiors challenged me in this way. If you're technically focused, you tend to think and respond in what you know best—technical terms. But CISOs and their teams have to force themselves to think and present information differently, even if it's not easy for them. I know it wasn't always easy for me. When you are sitting in front of a 4-star general and having to explain why it's really important that computers supporting a major weapon system have to get patched (which means risk), you very quickly learn to cut through the technical details and answer the "so what" questions.

Ultimately, business leaders and board members should use the "so what" methodology—wisely, strategically, and non-judgmentally—to help CISOs and other security professionals sift through all the technical details and present only the information needed to make smart, fast decisions. For business leaders asking "So what?" may not be an easy process. Your technical leaders have a tendency to want to give you the whole story, to tell you everything. You have to help them pare that down.

After all, a DDoS attack may be right around the corner, and no one wants to hear about the history of botnets and how an ICMP flood attack works.

31

Junk the Jargon: In Today's World, Money Talks

Diane E. McCracken — Banking Industry Executive Vice President and Chief Security Officer

When it comes to cybersecurity in today's world, money talks.

Most cybersecurity professionals, like myself, come from a technology background. We are comfortable talking about hardware, software, networking, applications, databases, next-generation firewalls, cloud computing, artificial intelligence, machine learning, and the like. In many ways, it's our native language.

But when it comes to communicating with business leaders, particularly board members, tech talk does us no good. In fact, the more we speak the language of technology in the boardroom, the less successful we will be in advising these leaders about the risks around cyber. These are business leaders who, while consumers of technology, have no practical knowledge about the subject.

In today's environment, cybersecurity professionals need to learn a new language. The language of money. That's when board members and executive management pay attention. They are interested in the bottom line and need to know what the investment is really buying and whether it will protect the organization.

To Walk the Walk, You Have to Talk the Talk

For CISOs and other cybersecurity professionals, the only way to learn to interact with the board is to interact with the board—often, and with great purpose. In my organization, I speak with the board on a monthly basis.

Just like any relationship, trust must be built and a common understanding of roles, accountabilities, and, most importantly, expectations will be negotiated over time. Only through consistent interaction will you and board members start to speak the same language. This evolution is unique to each organization and CISOs must drive it.

Advice for CISOs

Get smart quickly about how to talk the language of business. Nothing makes board members and executive management sit up straight in a board meeting like the subject of how risk can impact the bottom line for their business. Have numbers ready and be prepared to answer their questions. Just like a good attorney, anticipate what they will ask, be ready with an answer, and watch out for questions from left field.

Advice for Executive Management and Board Members

Establish a regular cadence that includes the topic of security in your meetings. Insist that the security teams present information in language and formats that are clear, simple to understand, relatable, and focused specifically on the value to the business.

Support your cybersecurity leaders. They are fighting a nameless, faceless adversary on your behalf. They have to be right thousands of times a day; the bad guys have to be right just once. In order to be successful in the cyber world, both parties must be in sync, and only through these conversations will that be possible.

If It Helps, Use Taylor Swift

In addition to speaking the language of business you should use whatever references you can to engage meaningfully with your leaders. I'll give you an example: Taylor Swift is a huge icon and the queen of social media. When I was making a presentation to the board about the risks of moving certain operations to the cloud, I was able to invoke her name to make my case.

Can you imagine, I told the board, if a photograph of our logo was on an umbrella that Taylor Swift carried out of a restaurant. She has 240 million followers on social media. Her fans would look up our brand, maybe even choose one of our products. With our existing infrastructure, we wouldn't be able to ingest that much business at once. It would shut down our systems.

However, moving to the cloud would give us the flexibility to meet that demand without requiring us to make huge investments in hardware and personnel. I was talking about elastic scalability, but putting it in terms that the board could relate to.

The second part of that conversation was about risk, because risk, along with cost, is what needs to be managed. With the cloud, the point we made is that, just because we were physically moving our environment to a third-party, it didn't mean we were also moving our risk. The reality is that we *always* have risk, whether physical infrastructure is on site or in the cloud. It's a matter of managing risk properly and ensuring that we always have control of our data and visibility into the environment, regardless of where it lives.

Use the News

As a CISO, there are many ways to get the attention of board members, but you must take the time to understand what makes them tick, what inspires them, what scares them, and what will make them sit up and take notice.

One of the things I've found among board members with whom I regularly interact: They follow the news, whether it's *The New York Times, Wall Street Journal, Bloomberg* or *60 Minutes,* CNN, or CNBC. If there is something about cybersecurity above the fold, on the scroll at the bottom of the screen, or highlighted on a news-magazine program, I know it is something my board members will have questions about—in particular if what was reported affects our business.

In our discussions, I make sure to address the news and tie it back to what we're doing at our organization. They want to know: "Is it possible that something similar could occur here?" The answer is typically "Yes." I explain up front what we have in place to deter it and how we are prepared to react to a similar event if it impacts us directly. I always make it personal and in the language of business—

money, risk, reputation, customer relationships, employee morale, productivity, and compliance.

Cybersecurity Education 101: Risk Mitigation

In the language of business, there are two areas that are always bound to resonate. One is risk and its consequences. The other is business enablement.

With risk, I often compare cybersecurity to an insurance policy. When you buy car insurance, for example, you are mitigating the consequences of risk in case something bad happens. But you are not doing anything to specifically reduce the risk or the likelihood that something bad will actually happen.

Cybersecurity investment is a different type of insurance policy. By investing in cybersecurity, you are actually taking steps to prevent something from happening and protecting the business, not merely mitigating the consequences. This differs from an insurance policy in that you are reducing risk, not transferring it.

What does that mean, in language that relates to the board? I tell board members that we spend a lot of money on state-of-the-art technology, yet without the right investment, we could be vulnerable to an attack if a single person in our organization clicks a link in the wrong email.

How can that be prevented? You need multiple layers of cybersecurity protections, focusing on people, technology, and processes. If someone clicks on a malware link, you have to have the pieces in place to ensure this does not have an adverse effect on the business. You need a cycle of incident response with technology to detect anomalous behavior, the processes to respond to it, and the people trained to investigate and take the necessary steps to contain it.

This is what the board is paying for. I would also recommend walking your board through a cyber incident response exercise. This will especially help them understand the consequences of a real-world event and the pieces you've put in place—with their funding—to defend and respond.

Cybersecurity Education 102: Business Enablement

Business enablement is the other area that will always get the board's attention—if the CISO presents it properly. In our organization, we brought software development in-house and identified the need for secure lifecycle management and assurance. This was a complex undertaking and required investments in technology, people, and processes to build this program from scratch.

After presenting the need, we focused on the money. We showed the board that the cost of addressing a potential security problem at the beginning of the development cycle costs much less than addressing just prior to launch. If the application security team doesn't look at the project until the end, it could be a showstopper. It could delay a launch while the problem gets fixed or, worse, put the business in the position of possibly launching a product with a vulnerability.

We worked hard to convince the board that it makes more business sense to find out if there's a problem at the beginning, fix it, and get the product to market. We showed the cost of remediation early, midway, and at the end of the development lifecycle, and the board fully funded our program.

In a case such as this, it is clear that the role of the CISO is as a business enabler. It's not our job to say "No." Our job is to advise on the risk and put the controls in place to appropriately limit that risk.

When the business needs the board's sign-off, I must be able to address the risk in language the board members understand.

Conclusion

In our organization, we include the board members, at their request, in communications we send to our employees about how to protect the organization and themselves from cybersecurity risk. They not only want to understand what we share with our fellow team members; they want to improve their cybersecurity chops as well.

Because we've taken the time to educate our board on cybersecurity and speak their language, they understand that everybody has skin in this game. That's really the only way to get folks to buy in—to ensure that they understand that this directly affects them and that they have an obligation as users of the internet to secure their piece of it.

Our security team works hard to engage with everyone in our organization around cybersecurity. We always make sure that our language is not too technical or filled with jargon. With the business leaders and the board, money is the universal language. However, it is our obligation as security professionals to clearly articulate cyber risk, regardless of the audience.

32

Zero Trust: The Strategic Approach to Stop Data Breaches

John Kindervag — Field Chief Technology Officer, Palo Alto Networks

Addressing today's cybersecurity challenges requires a new approach, one that is focused more on strategy and less on tactics. At a high level, strategic thinkers agree that there are four basic levels of engagement:

1. **Grand strategy:** This is the ultimate goal of any entity. The grand strategic direction of an entity—whether it is a corporation or a nation-state—is determined at the highest levels. For nations, it's done by presidents and prime ministers; in corporations, it is done by CEOs and members of the board of directors. A grand strategy provides the vision and direction of the entity.

2. **Strategy:** This is the big idea that is used to achieve the ultimate goal, as defined in the grand strategic objective. It is done at the next level down in the entity. For nation-states, it's done by agency heads, legislatures, or generals. In companies, vice presidents and line of business leaders provide strategic vision. Strategy provides the ideas that give tangible momentum to the grand strategic vision. More importantly, to be strategic, the idea must resonate with the highest

levels of the organization while being fully implementable at the levels below.

3. **Tactics:** These are the things we use to execute on the big idea, so that we are able to achieve the ultimate goal. Most people confuse strategy and tactics: They think they are strategic when, in fact, they are tactical. Tactics are implemented in the organization at the next lower levels in the organization.

4. **Operations:** This is the way in which we use the things we have. The operational aspects are often overlooked because we are focused on stuff, or tactics, without understanding the importance of operational integration. Tactics and operations align at this level to execute the strategic big idea so that the grand strategic goals can be achieved.

So, what can those of us in the cybersecurity community do to align with the grand strategic initiatives of the entities we are duty-bound to protect?

First, we must articulate a grand strategic objective for cybersecurity in the Digital Age; and it must be this: **to stop data breaches.**

213

To stop breaches, we must update what we think a breach is. Often, we cling to the old-school castle/moat analogy: "Someone breached the castle walls and they are inside!" This is actually an intrusion, not a breach.

The term "breach" is now a term of art in the legal and regulatory professions. Think GDPR. The breach happens when data is exfiltrated from an organization's network or systems and placed into the hands of unauthorized entities, especially malicious actors. Therefore, to be successful in cybersecurity, we must prevent sensitive or regulated data from falling into the wrong hands. To do this we need a strategy.

That strategy is Zero Trust.

The Broken Trust Model

There exists in our industry a broken trust model for security, built on the axiom, "Trust but verify." This model of anthropomorphizing the network and giving it attributes of trust is the fundamental problem we have in cybersecurity today. Trust is a vulnerability. It serves no purpose for your organization. Trust is not necessary to move packets across a network.

The only users who benefit from trust in our systems are the malicious actors who exploit it for nefarious purposes. We must eliminate the idea of trust from our digital systems if we have any hope of protecting sensitive data and assets from exploitation and breaches by malicious actors. To do this, we must adopt the Zero Trust model.

I will describe the concepts behind Zero Trust in further detail. First let me discuss why it is essential connective tissue for the chapters on transforming cybersecurity from a cost center into a business enabler. To achieve this transformation, business and technology leaders need to rethink their approach to security in several important ways, including:

1. Security must align with the business function.

2. Security must be embedded in the design of networks and applications.

3. Security must be agile and dynamic, with the flexibility to design for change.

We can achieve each of these goals, and others, with the Zero Trust model. With Zero Trust, organizations can position themselves for a future in which they are not in constant reactive mode to threats, but instead have cybersecurity built into their technologies, cultures, and operations.

Why Zero Trust, Why Now?

Today, business-level decision-makers must be on top of the challenges facing their IT and security teams, particularly this important paradigm shift: When it comes to cybersecurity, the biggest issue facing practitioners is the breakdown of their traditional trust model, which is based on the "trust-but-verify" approach to cybersecurity.

In this model, the network was broken into two sides, an external side—the "untrusted" network that connected the organization to the public internet—and the "trusted" side, where all internal users had access to sensitive resources. This is best illustrated by the labeling of the interfaces of early firewalls. They generally had two interfaces: One interface was labeled "trusted," and the other was labeled "untrusted."

This pervasive model means that almost all negative security events—including data breaches—are an exploitation of that trust model. External attackers know that if they can get their packets of code past the "trust" boundary, they will be given privileges—trust—based upon the location of the packets as they traverse the network.

Additionally, threats from malicious insiders are a really big deal, but cybersecurity professionals are conditioned to think of the internal network as "safe" and the internet as "evil." Users of internal network resources are even called "trusted" users. But some of the most highly visible incidents of our time—including the Chelsea Manning[1] and Edward Snowden[2] data breaches—happened by so-called "trusted" users on a so-called "trusted" internal network.

Zero Trust is built upon the idea that security must become ubiquitous throughout the infrastructure. The model is designed to be strategically resonant at the highest levels of any organization, and yet be tactically implementable by practitioners using commercial off-the-shelf technology. The concepts of Zero Trust are simple:

- All resources are accessed in a secure manner, regardless of location.

- Access control is on a "need-to-know" basis and is strictly enforced.

- All traffic is inspected and logged.

- The network is designed from the inside out.

- The network is designed to verify everything and never trust anything.

Zero Trust is designed to stop data breaches. Stopping data breaches must be the grand strategic objective of cybersecurity because a data breach is the only IT event that can get a CEO or company president fired. Therefore, Zero Trust is the only cybersecurity strategy. Everything else is just tactics.

Transforming the Security Model

Rebuilding security from the inside out means that the Zero Trust model replaces traditional perimeter defense with ubiquitous treatment of security throughout the organization. When assessing how to best redesign the network, companies often choose the Zero Trust framework because:

- **Security needs to align with the business function.** The working environment needs security to align with the business function. Most organizations are split into different departments and not all teams require the same amount of privileges. Enforcing strict access privileges where necessary and doing so efficiently is a priority for those adopting Zero Trust.

- **Modern organizations require elasticity and the ability to design for change.** Different SLAs, admins, audit requirements, regulations, and certifications necessitate flexibility and transparency for auditors and management. Infrastructure and security teams need an architecture that allows for quick changes and optimizations unhindered by controls and complexity.

- **Zero Trust is not rigid.** Another important aspect of Zero Trust is that it doesn't have one single approach. It is not cookie cutter and can be designed specifically around the data, applications, assets, or services that an organization needs to have protected.

Business Drivers

Today, companies are looking to leverage technology to position their internal technology management toward better security and manageability. Many organizations are trying to reimagine security outside of traditional parameters and redefine their security practices to meet both current threats and dynamically changing business needs.

But to get from here to there, organizations must rethink legacy network security to make it simpler and more efficient. When businesses attempt these types of transformational projects, they typically face onerous challenges. Zero Trust initiatives help address these challenges in the following ways:

- **Cost management:** Security teams often face significant restraints on financial, budgetary, and organizational resources. Zero Trust initiatives help maximize resources. Many companies adopt a startup mode when beginning the Zero Trust journey. Therefore, they handle their money very carefully, making sure spending is in line with the team's core competencies, in terms of manageability, maintainability, and scalability.

- **Personnel resources:** Working teams are already lean. Companies face staffing issues and most of the staff is already strained by daily operational needs. Zero Trust teams must start small and leverage the existing architecture and technology to address the environment in a new way.

- **Legacy architectures:** Traditional IT is inefficient. Most existing networks have grown organically and are not designed to be agile and efficient enough to meet business needs. New innova-

tions, such as cloud computing and user mobility, mean that organizations can no longer stay within the bounds of old IT's capabilities. Zero Trust uses technology and architecture to its advantage to make IT a business enabler instead of a business inhibitor.

- **Cloud enablement:** Server virtualization and cloud services change the rules of the game. Most organizations want to collapse the network infrastructure to reduce the number of servers by leveraging virtualization and public cloud infrastructure. The security aspects of these technological shifts remain challenging. How do you put security controls in a virtual environment? How is traffic going to be managed? What happens when applications and data are in multiple clouds? How do you maintain visibility and control? Zero Trust network architecture is virtualized and cloud-friendly.

Conclusion

One of the keystones of protecting our digital way of life is preventing the breach of sensitive data. It is a core of every business strategy that relies upon connected digital technologies. To do this, incorporate a Zero Trust model to ensure that all resources are accessed in a secure manner and all traffic is logged and inspected. With Zero Trust, we can take the next step forward in trusting that cybersecurity can be a true enabler of business success and differentiation.

---

[1] "Everything you need to know about Chelsea Manning," ABC News, May 16, 2017

[2] "This is everything Edward Snowden revealed in one year of unprecedented top-secret leaks," Business Insider UK, September 16, 2016

THE CASE FOR THE ZERO TRUST MODEL

- A broken trust model is the most urgent issue facing cybersecurity today.
- All users are effectively "untrusted."
- Security must be embedded throughout the network, not just on the perimeter.
- Networks must be designed from the inside-out, based upon the elements in the network that need to be protected.
- Networks must be designed with compliance in mind.
- All resources must be accessed securely.
- All traffic traversing the network must be inspected and logged.
- Zero Trust is the future of cybersecurity.

THE BUSINESS VALUE OF THE ZERO TRUST MODEL

- **Visibility and security:** The new infrastructure allows network administrators tremendous visibility into users and systems. With enhanced visibility, the environment is more lenient in terms of monitoring and allocating resources. Along with better visibility, Zero Trust forces the application, systems, and security teams to work together more effectively. Zero Trust encourages interdepartmental communication and breaks down silos that inhibit innovation.

- **Cost-effectiveness:** Companies that deploy Zero Trust typically see tangible capital and operational cost benefits. Zero Trust networks require fewer people to manage large, complex, and more secure deployments. Companies experience reductions in people and equipment costs, as well as improvements in uptime and failure rates.

- **Assessment and compliance:** Implementing Zero Trust makes auditing much more straightforward, simple, and quick. Zero Trust networks often have fewer audit findings because auditors can understand and conceptualize them more easily. Many compliance items are built into a Zero Trust network by default, and many current audit requirements were designed to uplift legacy networks and are not applicable in Zero Trust environments.

People

33

Making Boardroom Changes Today to Ensure a Cyber-Secure Tomorrow

Kal Bittianda — Head of North America Technology Practice, Egon Zehnder

Selena Loh LaCroix — Global Lead, Technology and Communications Practice, Egon Zehnder

William Houston — Advisor, Technology and Communications & Industrial Practices, Egon Zehnder

Go to our firm's website and click the "What We Do" link. The first three words you'll read describe the key drivers that frame our scope of work as management consultants and executive search experts:

Globalization. Convergence. Disruption.

We could just as easily apply those words to the tumultuous state of cybersecurity—and, in particular, the unique demands now faced by and debated in every boardroom. In fact, it would not be an overstatement to say that cybersecurity is reshaping how boards assess risk, practice governance, advise management, and ensure the very long-term viability and prosperity of their organizations. In cybersecurity, global risks are being accelerated by technology convergence at a rate never before seen, causing untold disruption in our work, our lives, and our communities.

And, as is typically true of all forms of dramatic change, board members face critical questions that will determine if the board—and the overall organization—is going to thrive in an era of intensified cybersecurity risk, or be steamrolled by it.

As boards typically do, sorting out the issues, debating the options, and arriving at the most appropriate recommendations involves asking and getting answers to high-impact questions. But instead of simply posing those questions to management, now boards have to look inward and ask those questions of themselves.

And one thing we have learned during our collective years of experience at advising the C-suite and board members is this: Not every board member is going to embrace this kind of change easily. And in some cases, not at all. Get ready.

Why Changes Are Necessary at the Board Level

Aligning your board with the dramatic changes going on in cybersecurity risk is a strategic issue, one requiring a lot of thought, deliberation, debate, cajoling, and even a little good luck. Making the right moves in how the board operates is a *facilitator in risk management.* The technology shaping cybersecurity issues is undergoing dramatic change—AI, machine learning, blockchain, Internet of Things, and more. The technology risks are getting more complex and dynamic, but at the same time, they reflect important new business opportunities that cannot be shunted aside simply because of new/greater risk.

The right board composition, coupled with setting the right mandate for leadership and action, is the best way for board members to make the greatest impact. It's about making the *right* choice, not the *safe* choice.

After all, nothing comes with zero risk. Boards have always had to deal with geopolitical, financial, regulatory, and product risks, and cybersecurity is the latest addition to the mix. The experience, expertise, mindset, and attitude of your board is critical to juggling the classic risk/reward equation.

There's another important factor—one that is a bit "delicate," to say the least. Although the pace of technology change in the past 20 to 30 years has been dramatic, this is nothing compared to what we will experience over the next few years. That's extraordinarily difficult for anyone to manage, even experienced people. The reality is that the mean age of board members is creeping up in many organizations and industries, and it is becoming harder and harder for some to stay on top of the changes. Yet as the threats grow in number and sophistication, with new types of bad actors and threat vectors, people with current operating experience, fresh ideas, and greater comfort with technology will be needed to help guide policy and priorities.

Although many boards understand the need to come armed with fresh perspectives, not enough board members actually know what to do. This is likely to become more and more urgent as cyberattacks have material impact on an organization's financial performance, regulatory standing, legal exposure, and customer confidence. The next shoe to drop may be successful lawsuits aimed directly at board members for failing to meet their fiduciary responsibilities in a cyber breach situation. If you're a board member, that will undoubtedly make you sit up and take notice.

This is where board dynamics become very important. If you have a board whose members are honest, open, and willing to listen to "different" ideas, it's far easier to deal with the uncertainty and magnitude of cyber risk. Board members need to be fearless in proposing ideas that may seem unconventional, or even radical. That can be a very powerful force for debate and change, even when your board is properly composed.

How You Know You Are Succeeding

Truth be told, a very small minority of companies proactively come to us and ask for help in defining their board composition with an eye toward the future. An initial step we believe bodes well for a board readying itself for the impact of cybersecurity risk is recognizing the need for an orderly board succession plan and then laying out a methodical execution plan over a two-to-five-year period. Savvy board chairs will meet their evolving needs, such as in cybersecurity risk evaluation and governance, by thoughtfully planning around upcoming retirements and departures.

A successful board transition begins with a documented strategic plan that defines the board member archetypes who will be recruited to the board over the period, and sometimes even identifies specific/aspirational people to approach. Unfortunately, too few organizations actually think this through and invest the time and energy to map it. Often boards realize, "Oops, this person is retiring next year, we need to find an audit committee chair." Or they may have been dinged with a poor diversity score from ISS or Glass Lewis that triggers a search for a female board member.

Experience has also shown us that successful transition plans involve creating and maintaining synergies and strong working relationships in the boardroom. While it doesn't mean everyone has to spend quality time together outside the boardroom, it does mean avoiding adversarial, confrontational meetings where personalities and perceived slights get in the way of doing productive work. Give a lot of thought to the intellectual, personal, and political dynamics of your board.

After all, the days when board members spent 20 years in their seats and then retired gracefully are quickly passing us by. These are ground-shaking times, requiring a more proactive board willing to explore new ideas and new ways to achieve success.

Remember: We're not recommending overhauling your board by orchestrating a palace coup in the boardroom. We've all seen examples of how messy those can get and the kind of unproductive, even hostile, environments they can create. The evolution of the board needs to be designed with its future desired state in mind, in conjunction with managing affected board members in a thoughtful, respectful, and personal manner.

Make no mistake: It has to be done. The very future of your organization and its success depends upon it.

ESSENTIAL QUESTIONS FOR THE BOARD ... ABOUT THE BOARD

We've often seen that boards that are most successful at anticipating and coping with sea changes of the magnitude in cybersecurity risk are willing to look inward and ask very tough, often uncomfortable, questions. Four come to mind:

Are the right people on our board? A successful board starts with having the right people around the boardroom table. However, the answers to the question, "Do you have the right people—and if not, who should they be?" will vary widely depending on the type of organization you have and the current mix of experience on your board.

- If you decide to bring a cyber expert onto the board, unless you are actually expanding the board, that's a board seat you're giving up to a specialist. If having that kind of expertise is a strategic differentiator in your industry (e.g., technology, financial services), or if you want to dramatically shift the cyber posture of your company, that may be a smart decision.

- But if your organization believes it has less cyber risk, you may not want to devote that seat to a cyber expert. Instead, you may decide to focus on ensuring the company has a world-class organization with strong cybersecurity credentials (and the business acumen to match), including strong leaders who will regularly meet with and brief the board.

Do you have the right committee structure for evaluating and governing cybersecurity risk? Committees and sub-committees are important to give weight and light to such functions as audit, HR, regulatory, strategic planning, risk, and cybersecurity.

- If you're in an industry where the risk of a cyber breach could have a devastating impact on the company, you'll probably need a technology committee.

- It may be harder for boards in industries that have traditionally not relied as heavily on technology, such as retail and trucking, to justify a dedicated technology committee. Ironically, they could be the ones that need it most, as they probably don't possess sufficient technical talent in their organizations.

- Cybersecurity could also be incorporated into an existing committee, such as the risk or audit committees.

What should board members talk about? Board discussions around cybersecurity must be proactive and center on such issues as:

a. **Organization structure:** Have the CEO and CISO properly structured the organization to address information security? Do we have the optimal reporting structure and the right people in the right roles?

b. **Investment:** Are we allocating the right budgetary resources for our current and future risk profile? Are we making the right budget allocation, and do we know what we get from/for this investment? (Hint: Setting security spending levels is not a mathematical exercise.)

c. **Accountability:** Do we have the right person in the CISO role? Do they have the right goals, and are they properly incented for the desired outcomes?

d. **Improvement:** How do we know that our "non-mitigated" risk footprint is shrinking? What metrics are we using to determine this, and are they still appropriate? (For example: What portion of issues are resolved once and for all? Are the resolution times decreasing over time?)

Of course, the board also needs answers to forward-looking questions: Which threats are imminent that we have yet to address? What would happen to our bottom line if we lost our ability to take orders online for an hour? A day? A week?

What are the responsibilities for the rest of the board? Even if you're not the board's resident cyber expert or you don't sit on a relevant committee responsible for cybersecurity oversight and governance, you have a critical role to play.

- Every board member needs to be involved in the discussions and deliberations around cybersecurity.

- You may decide to let your colleagues take the lead on the issues, but you still can and must ask good questions.

- And don't assume that because a fellow board member experienced zero-day attacks at their own company, they are the only one qualified to ask questions about the organization's threat detection, prevention, and remediation practices.

- One smart practice we've seen some boards take is to have the less-technical board members spend a day, at least once a year, with the cyber team to watch what they do, ask questions, and get a practical education from people on the frontlines.

34

Creating a Culture of Cybersecurity

Patric J.M. Versteeg, MSc.

Creating a culture of cybersecurity across an organization is not only doable—it is essential!

When it comes to cybersecurity, culture is a huge deal, and it is a very real component for creating a more secure organization. All people across an organization, regardless of their roles, are responsible for being vigilant and taking the right steps to securely use technologies and processes.

Defining and "living" a cybersecurity culture requires viewing the issue from two different, yet interdependent, perspectives—as **senders and receivers.**

Senders in organizational hierarchies are the leaders—the business C-level executives, CISOs, and board members. They are the ones who set policies, enforce processes, ensure governance, and set the general direction for the rest of the organization. Moreover, for senders, there are two significant things to remember about the culture of cybersecurity.

- **First, when it comes to cybersecurity, culture is neither a democracy nor a dictatorship.** Senders establish baselines for requirements that act as the foundation for the organization's cybersecurity, in alignment not only with business goals, but also with cultural values and behavior. After the baselines

have been implemented, the senders should be open for a dialog with the receivers about the next level of cybersecurity to be achieved throughout the organization.

- **Second, leaders must learn to listen—or, as an homage to organizational guru Simon Sinek, learn to speak last.** All too often, business leaders—and many CISOs, also—come into organizations with their ideas fully formed: "We're going to do this with access and identity management; this with authentication; and change all processes according to X, Y, and Z." It's essential for senders to prove to the rest of the organization that their perspectives matter. Great ideas and effective policies must be the product of multiple points of input, each coming from a unique perspective. Listen first, speak last.

Receivers are those who take in, process, and "live" the directives and priorities established by the senders. And it is important that they see themselves as actively participating in the development and promotion of a cybersecurity culture, not just passively accepting the rules and regulations.

In a culture of cybersecurity, receivers have skin in the game. Their day-to-day responsibilities are profoundly shaped by the policies, processes, and procedures set forth to govern good cyber hygiene—and not only as a benefit to the organization. Those steps also must protect their digital safety, so they do not become reliant on cybersecurity technology and processes to keep them and their organization safe. If the senders do their job right, receivers are not the weakest link but the strongest, in the cybersecurity chain.

Learning how receivers shape, and ultimately fit into, a culture of cybersecurity isn't easy, given the seemingly infinite differences between how any two people interpret processes and are motivated to contribute to the building and caring of a cybersecurity culture. Fortunately, there are several effective models that help us understand how culture is defined inside an organization. One is the Competing Value Framework by Quinn & Rohrbaugh. There is an important synergy between this framework and the challenge organizations face in creating a culture around cybersecurity.

For instance, the Quinn & Rohrbaugh model in Figure 1 shows us how an organization's culture can be defined. Depending on the organization's culture—specifically, about how that culture affects people's ability to embrace change—the culture of cybersecurity is shaped accordingly. This model centers on four distinct, yet interwoven, organizational culture models:

1. Open Systems Model: This model is based on an organic system, emphasis on adaptability, readiness, growth, resource acquisition and external support. These processes bring innovation and creativity. People are not controlled but inspired.[2]

2. Rational Goal Model: This model is based on profit, emphasis on rational action. It assumes that planning and goal setting results into productivity and efficiency. Tasks are clarified, objectives are set, and action is taken.[2]

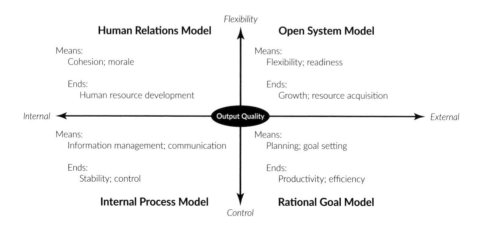

Figure 1: An overview of the Competing Values Framework by Quinn & Rohrbaugh[1]

3. Internal Process Model: This model is based on hierarchy, emphasis on measurement, documentation, and information management. These processes bring stability and control. Hierarchies seem to function best when the task to be done is well understood and when time is not an important factor.[2]

4. Human Relations Model: This model is based on cohesion and morale, with emphasis on human resource and training. People are seen not as isolated individuals, but as cooperating members of a common social system with a common stake in what happens.[2]

Using the Quinn & Rohrbaugh framework, it is possible to define leadership roles (Figure 2) that have the most positive outcome when it comes to supporting a company's culture and therefore shaping the most effective culture of cybersecurity.

The exact definition of the mentioned leadership roles (Innovator, Broker, Producer, Director, Coordinator, Monitor, Facilitator, Mentor,) is beyond the scope of this chapter. But to give some more insight, you can probably imagine that if the tone at the top (senders) is driven from the Director Role (lower right, in Figure 2), it will not be adopted well or easily for receivers in a company that has a Human Relations Model (upper left, Figure 1).

The models illustrate that defining and understanding the organizational culture is an essential step toward getting a better grasp on how to steer the organization toward a more cyber-secure-centric culture.

The Power and Necessity of Change Management

Despite most everyone's best intentions, many cybersecurity programs languish or outright fail to keep the organization and its digital assets secure because people on

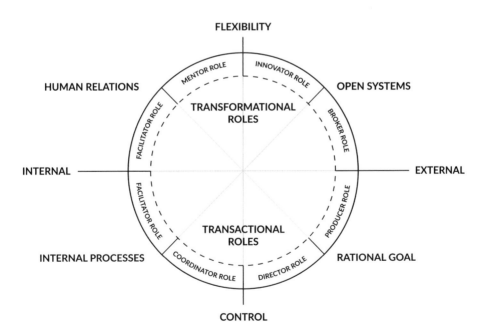

Figure 2: Leadership roles mapped in the Quinn & Rohrbaugh model[3]

both the business side and the technical side are reluctant to change. It is this intransigence that puts up the biggest roadblock in getting people to agree on the delicate balance between prudent cybersecurity and business opportunity.

After all, people are creatures of habit. We all love to do things in a certain way, and senior management is often the most likely to dig in their heels against change. "I've been running this business my way, it's working well, and we haven't had any issues," I hear over and over. Unfortunately, very often this attitude gets translated into statements like, "We can't do that," or "No, that's not allowed," when it comes to cybersecurity.

And let's be clear: We need changes in how organizations plan, implement, and measure effective cybersecurity because the threat vectors are always expanding and the cyber attackers are bolder, more resourceful, and even more collaborative than ever. Our rate of change must exceed theirs if we want to keep our businesses sustainable.

Cybersecurity culture is all about change management, from the executive leadership on down. Whether we want to admit it or not, many of us crave change or we risk stagnation, boredom, and losing our competitive edge. I know I need this: Every few years, I move into a new company to enable myself to learn new things and apply my skills in different environments and different cultures. If I'm not willing to change as a business leader, I'm going to fail terribly.

And in today's high-pitched cybersecurity environment, failing is unacceptable!

Getting to Yes

Ultimately, one of the best ways to think of a culture of cybersecurity is to talk about what I call getting to "yes." This may sound counter-intuitive in cybersecurity, where the emphasis has always been on what not to do, and why that can't be allowed.

But leaders have to fight against this tendency when creating a cybersecurity culture: We have to find ways to let people think they **can** do something, that they are allowed and even encouraged to do something, to take action, and to minimize a reliance on technology and processes.

In setting a culture of cybersecurity, leaders (senders) develop criteria—remember, by listening to their teams (receivers), rather than speaking at them—for what can be done, how it can be done, and under which circumstances. Leaders should focus more on goals than tactics, on facilitating rather than creating roadblocks, on outcomes rather than minutiae.

When leaders build and promote a culture that encourages teams to make smart decisions that assess and consider risks and rewards, it becomes easier to put reasonable limits around what can and can't be done in cybersecurity. We can more easily evolve to "Yes, in the following circumstances with the following xyz controls" or "Yes, but in this manner," when we have established that your culture requires you to start with "Yes."

Of course, there are some things that your culture of cybersecurity cannot and should not allow. You can't sell private patient information to data brokers; you can't break the law; and you can't put the organization into legal jeopardy. But even then, there are choices that can be made.

Let me give you a hypothetical example. Suppose your CISO, or their boss, reads about a data breach at an organization that was prompted by a security flaw with a public cloud file-sharing service. If you have a strong get to "yes" culture that promotes initiative and prudent risk-taking, your senior executives may have set data storage policies to establish a clear balance between risk on one side, and agility and empowerment on the other.

But if you don't have such a culture of cybersecurity, not yet driven by "yes," what your executives say may be a knee-jerk response to news of the latest public cloud security breach: "No one can use file sharing services."

It's OK and even necessary to raise questions about security, but when leaders (senders) issue directives without considering implications or alternatives, it undermines the culture of cybersecurity. Most likely it will create a (personal/receivers) shadow IT project that, in the end, might bring in even more risks.

To help the team get to "yes" leaders should think of the goal, which in this case is to have a secure, efficient way to transfer files between businesses or with customers. However, you have to trust your people to come up with appropriate solutions that balance risk with business opportunity. It's not about stopping the use of file sharing; it's about managing the risk.

Getting Started Toward a Culture of Cybersecurity

To empower change and drive a culture of cybersecurity, executives and board members need to consider some essential issues. For instance, business leaders should determine what type of culture for receivers is predominant within the organization; this will go a long way toward shaping how messages, directives, and policies should be presented and communicated throughout the organization.

At the same time, it's important to assess the tone set by the top (the senders) in talking about cybersecurity, and to ensure the leadership style is in sync with how the organization receives the message and gives life to the desired cybersecurity culture.

Board members and executives should use a mix of statistical analytics tools and old-fashioned "management by walking around" to get both a quantitative and qualitative assessment of how senders and receivers are aligned—or if they are aligned at all.

This alignment is critical to building a thriving culture of cybersecurity. After all, if senders set a tone that is directive, authoritarian, and overly top-down, this could foster a passive response by the receivers if they are used to a Human Relations Model organization culture.

Use engaging and interactive sessions to help senders experience situations and understand receivers' reactions, so senders can better understand the implications of their actions.

I am convinced that a culture of cybersecurity can be achieved where the human element is the strongest link in the cybersecurity chain, but only if your "yes" message is presented as a fit to organizational culture. If not, your "yes" message might be misinterpreted as a resounding "no." And nobody likes to hear—or receive— "no."

Conclusion

Any good venture capitalist will tell you that the most important thing they consider when evaluating all the investment proposals they receive is the quality of the leadership team. After all, products come and go, and markets continuously evolve. But a great team will anticipate and adapt to change to ensure the organization stays on track toward achieving its goals.

The same is true for creating a culture of cybersecurity. Business executives and boards, in concert with their cybersecurity and IT leaders, need to understand and shape their organization's culture in order to create the right cybersecurity mindset— even before setting policies, procedures, and priorities around cybersecurity.

Our apocryphal file sharing story is a good example of how culture can either inhibit or promote smart, successful cybersecurity. Organizations that build and nourish the right culture around cybersecurity find ways to get to the goal faster. They are also more cost-efficient, with less rancor and politics, than organizations that fail to understand the critical role culture—set both by senders and receivers—plays in their efforts.

Let's all find a way to get to "Yes."

[1] Quinn, Robert E., and John Rohrbaugh. "A Spatial Model of Effectiveness Criteria: Towards a Competing Values Approach to Organizational Analysis," Management Science 29, no. 3 (1983): 363-77. http://www.jstor.org/stable/2631061

[2] "Competing Values Framework," University of Twente https://www.utwente.nl/en/bms/communication-theories/sorted-by-cluster/Organizational%20Communication/Competing_Values_Framework/

[3] "Competing values leadership: quadrant roles and personality traits," Alan Belasen and Nancy Frank (2007) https://www.researchgate.net/publication/242337141_Competing_values_leadership_Quadrant_roles_and_personality_traits

35

Recognizing, Developing, and Deploying Good Cybersecurity Habits

George Finney — Chief Security Officer, Southern Methodist University

I'm a Chief Security Officer for a major United States university. I love my job, even with its frenetic, unpredictable twists and turns. I thank my lucky stars every day that I don't have a boring job where I know what to expect when I show up at the office or log in to my email.

And that's not all I do. I'm a writer—seriously. I've written books, short stories, crime novels, and screenplays. But since they tell me that writers should write about the things they know best, my last four books have been about cybersecurity. In my most recent book, *No More Magic Wands: Transformative Cybersecurity Change for Everyone,* I introduced the topic with something I knew would become more and more important as we continued to battle with cyber adversaries:

"If security is everyone's job, everyone needs to have the right tools to actually do the job. Not *some* of the tools. Not a *little* bit of the tools. All of it."

And one of the most important tools anyone can have—whether you're a CSO, a CEO, a board member, or anyone who uses technology to do nearly anything—is good habits. Yes, next-generation firewalls, automated monitoring, and threat intelligent services all are must-haves in any

organization's cybersecurity arsenal. But it's not enough. You also need everyone in the organization—and everyone the organization deals with outside the firewalls—to have well-honed and expertly deployed cybersecurity habits.

That's because cybersecurity is not a skill to be learned, nor is it a competency. How do I know this? Simple: Because we've always assumed that making employees undergo training sessions for good cyber hygiene will yield improved results. And that isn't happening, not in any way, shape, or form.

Cybersecurity is a habit, like getting up in the morning to exercise, showing affection to your children, and adjusting your car's mirrors before you back out of the driveway. And when you look at cybersecurity through that lens, it's not surprising at all that making your employees watch a short video on security doesn't change their behavior. It's like reading a manual about using a treadmill. It's not going to make you any healthier.

Getting Started: Identifying Good Habits

I didn't come up with this epiphany early in my cybersecurity career. Like pretty much everything else, I had to learn it through trial and error. Years ago, we were doing what everyone else did, delivering online cybersecurity training videos, brownbag sessions, and simulated phishing messages. But we continued to encounter cybersecurity events—just like everyone else, of course—so we knew we were missing something.

Two things stood out in my mind. First, I remembered my childhood experience of learning *tae kwon do,* especially the realization that simply learning the moves didn't really translate into success. I eventually figured out that the drills are what made the difference, and that I had to put in the time and diligence to see real progress.

Second, my HR colleagues and I decided to model our cybersecurity training around something that we knew had succeeded: wellness programs. These days, most HR departments have established health and wellness programs as employee benefits—partly because many employees like the idea of trying to take charge of their health, but more because they actually work. Wellness training succeeds in large part because we can educate and influence people about the benefits of eating healthier or working out, but also how to actually make it habitual. And they use incentives like free vacation days to give employees even more motivation to build new routines. These programs succeed because they force people to confront, acknowledge, and act upon the notion that wellness is a habit, not a skill.

To make wellness work in cybersecurity, we had to focus on identifying good cybersecurity habits and then doing drills with people. These habits need to be institutionalized, starting with top management and board members, not just the CSO having a monthly lunch-and-learn

session. If senior executives don't buy into this and send strong signals that cybersecurity is a potential threat not only to organizations but also to employees, we will have to confront a major challenge.

What are some good cybersecurity habits?

Don't react. Don't just look at something and start acting. Try to "see" what is happening by taking your time and noticing the details. If this sounds like "can't see the forest for the trees," you're right. Chances are you are not just seeing an isolated incident or two, but rather data points in a pattern that can be viewed in ultra-high-definition, if you take the time to see the big picture. Automated network monitoring has done great things to help identify abnormal data movement patterns in and out of your systems, but we still need to rely on smart, discerning, curious people to review the information before we allow that very large file transfer to the Ukraine to go through.

Trust your gut. Instincts are powerful defense mechanisms—if we pay attention to them. I'm not suggesting that you overthink everything, and fall into the "paralysis by analysis" mode. But if that email from the CFO seems slightly different from past communications, don't just assume it's legitimate. Reply with a question, or, better yet, pick up the phone or walk down the hall.

Rely on community. One of the big mistakes we often make, both in business and at home, is that we are afraid to ask for help—or even just validation. We don't want people to see us as less than confident in our knowledge, or we may feel that by bringing others into our thought process we are giving away some kind of "competitive advantage" as we seek to advance in our careers. We're not alone, and when it comes to cybersecurity, it's far better to get another point of view. For instance, organizations should consider joining a cyber-intelligence-sharing consortium. Don't worry, you won't be giving up the company secrets, but you may be learning something you didn't know.

Slow down. Because so many factors—including the pace of technology change—are accelerating the decision-making process, we too often feel the need to "ready, fire, aim." We often make decisions based on the "bias for action" philosophy espoused by business leaders. A bias for action is great, except when it results in bad decisions that were based on incomplete information and made just to be the first to market. Think about that when your product development team wants to roll out the industry's first IoT-enabled widget and they haven't baked in the security protocols.

Nothing is random; make planning a habit. When bad things happen—property crimes, shootings, motor vehicle accidents, and more—we ask ourselves, "What could we have done differently?" That kind of introspection is good, but only if it results in making scenario planning a systematic, thoughtful process. For instance, our employees and third parties accessing our proprietary data have to log on to Wi-Fi networks securely and with the right permissions. Everyone also must change their passwords in a thoughtful and sincere manner and avoid leaving those passwords on Post-It Notes on our screens. Good planning—and repeating good habits—is essential.

Let me give you a real-world example of what I'm talking about. I recently met a business journalist who had written about cybersecurity. We got to talking about the subject and my focus on good habits, and she excitedly told me a story about what had happened the night before.

Her husband received a text from PayPal, alerting him that a $1,000 transaction had been made in his account. He was initially confused and then immediately irate, convinced that someone at PayPal had made an error. He told his wife, sitting across the dinner table, what had happened, and said, "I'm going to see what they're talking about." Just before he could click the PayPal link in the text, the wife screamed, "Wait!" and grabbed the phone from his hand. As you can now imagine, her good cybersecurity habits warned her that something was amiss, and that her husband was a nanosecond away from enabling a phishing attempt.

This kind of thing undoubtedly happens all the time in our organizations, from the largest governments and multi-national corporations to small retail stores using technology to manage their finances, track inventory, and pay employees. We have become so dependent upon technology for everything in our business and personal lives that we sometimes let down our guard—often with catastrophic results.

What Can and Should Business Leaders Do?

While good cybersecurity habits are developed and honed by individuals, the C-suite and the board play outsized roles in promoting this kind of good behavior.

First, keep in mind something Patric Versteeg says in his chapter about creating a culture of cybersecurity. Patric notes that culture is shaped by management and then is embodied in the organization's people and processes. It's very trendy to talk about a bottom-up approach to problem-solving, and it often makes a lot of sense. But don't kid yourselves; we still are very prone to hierarchical organizations, and executives remain the most powerful and influential force in the enterprise. Executives need to exhibit "intentionality," based on the things they do, what they say, how they ask questions, and so on.

Second, it's unfortunate to say that too many executives display an air of entitlement when it comes to cybersecurity habits. It is often personified by that frightening word: Exceptions. Picture the stereotypical CEO. He or she may urgently need something done, so they demand action. Of course, they may feel they don't need to go through the proper cybersecurity protocols to request that large payment to a strategic vendor that is trying to deliver a critical part. When that email comes through to the treasurer or CFO, everyone jumps to attention, only to find out that the request is really from a hacker mimicking the CEO's email account.

Third, executives need to support the CSO and the HR director in institutionalizing training programs for good cybersecurity habit development—and they need to participate in them, as well. If executives are going to be taken seriously in promoting the importance of good cybersecurity habits, it must become a leadership mandate. In my book, *No More Magic Wands,* the main character of the book isn't the CSO, it's the business executive who champions and pushes for change. It is incredibly important for business leaders to be seen as the agents of transformation for good cybersecurity habits, not seen as just sitting back and directing the CSO to lead the way. Nobody wants the CEO to be a micromanager on cybersecurity, but a CEO who abdicates their leadership role in this area is a big, red warning light for board members.

Conclusion

Aristotle once said, "We are what we repeatedly do. Excellence, therefore, is not an act, but a habit." Today, he'd either be a $1,000-an-hour management consultant or a CSO.

Leaders must take big steps toward institutionalizing good cybersecurity habits throughout their organizations; without it becoming part of the corporate culture, it will never be actualized by employees at the office, on the road, or at home.

So, keep investing in cutting-edge technologies, sophisticated analytics, and innovative cybersecurity tools. Make sure your SOC is properly staffed, your business units have embedded security professionals, and your CSO is as well-versed on inventory turns and competitive differentiation as they are on botnets and spear phishing.

But also remember to put in place the steps covered earlier in this chapter:

Don't react.
Trust your gut.
Rely on community.
Slow down.
Make planning a habit.

Then, please give me a call to share your experiences. We can write a book about it.

36

Social Engineering Attacks: We're All Targets

Yorck O.A. Reuber — Head of Infrastructure Services & CTO, North Europe, AXA IT

In today's environment, professional attackers know how to avoid your security technology by using social engineering and picking out human victims within your company. In fact, human targets have moved ahead of machines as the top target for cyber criminals. As noted by IDG's publication, CSO, "Hackers smell blood now, not silicon."[1]

Your employees can be difficult to protect. Adversaries will use people's emotions and their readiness to be helpful to obtain information that helps launch a highly targeted and often believable attack. Process and technology alone will not address this. Raising awareness and increasing vigilance will help you protect your employees and your organization. More importantly, it will help you build a culture of cybersecurity.

Cyberattack Calling and Other Modes of Attack

Targets of a social engineering attack need not be executive staff or members of the research department working on a secret project. More often, criminals target a random employee they spied in advance to ensure the attack is formulated in a max-

imally convincing way. They use social media to discover details about projects, names, dependencies between departments and individuals, and friendships between colleagues. Once they have the baseline information, it's simple to approach an employee, appear legitimate, and obtain corporate information or access to corporate networks. Here are some examples of approaches used:

Cyberattack calling: A call via the switchboard results in what appears to be an internal call. In this call, an urgently required support activity will be referenced: "Our colleague, Mrs. X, has not given me the data I urgently need to finish the report for board member Y. She is now on holiday; I am sure I will be fired if I do not send it immediately. Please help me … I can't afford to lose my job." Far too often, financial, corporate, or personal information is then disclosed in an attempt to help the caller do their job.

Corporate network access: An employee receives an email from someone who appears to be working in the same company. The mail signature is correct, and the content fits with the daily routine of the recipient. The inhibition threshold to open the malware-infected attachment or to click the malicious link is very low. In 95% of all cases, this click will then result in a successful malware infection. This is the entry point for a far more sophisticated campaign, which gives the attacker backdoor access to the corporate network that may only transpire several months later.

CEO fraud: The cybercriminal pretends to be a general manager, CEO, CFO, or other high-ranking employee. The email might read as follows: "A secret company takeover is coming and only *you* have the trust of senior management. Further information will be transmitted to you from (pretend) Bank Clerk X from (corrupt) Bank Y." The follow-up email will contain bank account details of an account controlled by the fraud organization and an amount to be paid.

The consistent theme, regardless of approach, is that the cybercriminals will have used social engineering to make their approach appear as legitimate as possible. Unless employee's awareness is raised to be vigilant at all times, these attacks can be treated as a normal communication from a colleague or manager.

Defeating Social Engineering Through Training

Cyberattacks via social engineering are nothing more than old-school acquisition of information through hands-on research. Many attackers and social engineers try to take advantage of people's emotions and readiness to help others. And their successes come from the ways in which their attacks appear absolutely believable. Little hints can help the attacker move forward, such as:

- Colleague X is on vacation

- This is done by Department A

- Yes, our CFO is usually very impatient

- No, we use antivirus from vendor Z

Every name mentioned, every connection from day-to-day business, will help the attackers prepare the next call so it's even more efficient or targets a more fitting contact person.

Train your employees and yourself to always stay critical and never divulge anything to unknown parties on the phone. Managers, especially, tend to underestimate this type of attack as they consider themselves unlikely to ever reveal anything. This can be a very dangerous mistake.

Raising employee awareness to suspicious phone and email communications is key. Some of the triggers employees should be trained to look for include:

- Subtle errors or differences in URLs or email addresses that on first look seem normal. Sometimes the sender's name is correct, but when you look at the address, it's subtly different.

- Most attacks will be focused on getting you to click something within an email. If you are being asked to provide personal or corporate information via a link, or if the actual address you're directed to go to doesn't look legitimate, call to check its legitimacy first.

- While many emails and phone calls are well-created, look for language mistakes, as adversaries may not be using their first language.

- Use of corporate graphics or images to make their emails seem genuine.

- Use of language in the email that is designed to make you take action.

If there's any doubt, it's best to call and verify if it is real or not, even if it seems the email has come from within the company. IT security teams should continuously train and inform employees and colleagues. This can happen via employee meetings or via automated penetration tests that check password quality.

Especially effective are self-designed phishing emails. These are created by your cybersecurity team and used to increase employee awareness of potential phishing emails. You can use a variety of incentives to mislead the recipient to click a contaminated link—different people will respond to different stimuli. You might try to tap into an emotional response or offer a tablet or smartphone as a prize. A phone call after a click explaining how to avoid the mistake in the future will not only reduce risk that the employee will make the same mistake again, it will also encourage people to come forward and report a similar situation in the future. This type of targeted education is far more efficient than generic training and preaching the same doctrine to all employees in a sterile environment.

Every email the IT department can identify directly after—or even before—the first click lowers the chance of a successful phishing attack. As soon as the attack path is known, the IT team can block access to malicious web addresses, prevent the execution of the malware, and reset potentially phished passwords.

For these tests and training to be effective, it is critical that there be a no-blame culture. Employees must understand how to report a situation in the future. And you need a way of monitoring people who do not report when they have clicked a contaminated link so you can work with them to ensure they do report it in the future.

The combination of deploying different activities and repeating them regularly is key to success. However, don't go overboard or you will achieve the opposite effect. A tool that checks the quality of passwords, is too old, or is poorly con-figured is not only expensive, it can also frustrate employees to the point where they start writing down their keys again. In this case, the company would have to spend a lot of money while decreasing the level of security. With a much less expensive employee event, the company might have achieved far more. Events that thrill the employees with concrete examples help generate awareness of cybersecurity challenges.

It also helps to recognize behavioral changes of employees and colleagues as early as possible. Anomalies can be logins from unknown places or data accessed from previously inactive seats. Modern protective tools and processes can help by recognizing anomalies and automatically alert IT and security personnel to proactively shut security gaps and contain and limit the damage of a successful attack.

It makes more sense to watch the critical data with this type of process than to establish stronger barriers around the data center. These days, intrusions into the company network are hard to prevent; it is crucial to notice manipulations and data loss immediately in order to limit them.

Posing Critical Questions

To get a feel for the organization's vulnerability to social engineering, and the type of training that would be most effective, the IT team can pose specific questions to managers and employees, including senior-level executives and board members. Questions to ask include:

- What percentage of individuals have a general security awareness?

- What is the common understanding of cybersecurity across the people in your department? How does that change across the company?

- How well are the organization's security experts understood, or do the IT and security teams speak a different language than the business people?

- What obstacles have data security concerns created at work?

- Has the security situation produced concerns, and what overreactions has it created?

- Who are the in-house, social engineering or forensics experts, and how do they keep themselves updated?

The answers to these questions will be different, depending on the business unit. Executives at a regulated company handling health data might exhibit greater awareness than those at an unregulated company. The reality, however, is that every company is vulnerable, and every organization has data that needs to be protected.

The potential for harm is endless. The organization must be aware of the risk. To reduce this risk, it is important to prevent an overreaction, which complicates interactions with customers and reduces your employees' ability to work.

In addition to posing questions to employees, organizations can benefit when senior-level executives pose specific questions to their cybersecurity leaders. These questions can help determine what intentions and goals they are trying to achieve with their cybersecurity investments:

- What is your intent with this investment? In other words, what are you protecting?

- What is the business impact of doing so?

- What is the business impact of not doing it?

- What is the risk of delaying the investment—can we delay it six months, or can we speed it up?

- Do we have anything similar already in place? Why is this not already sufficient?

Raising Awareness for Every Single Employee

Top executive management needs to be willing to bear the consequences of cyber-attacks and ensure appropriate and balanced communications to all employees. There are some basic points I would urge all executives to look at within their departments and across their organizations.

Employees must be aware that information, such as, "Who is working where and with whom?" is extremely interesting for industrial spies and the people supplying them with background information. This is the same as it is in private life, where burglars are notified by Facebook when a house is empty due to a long-distance trip and where the house is located. This example can easily be transferred to work life. Pictures from the last company party deliver information regarding which employee knows which colleague and what their names are. This might already be enough information to tune a spear-phishing email with personalized information and provoke the fatal click.

Obviously, you can't prevent employees from using social media, but you can ask them not to post work-related information, i.e., people's roles, names of projects, etc. These days, every comment on the web can manipulate public opinion regarding the employer or provide important information that adversaries can use to start an attack against IT or other departments.

Conclusion: We Are All United

Every employee on every level of the organization must be actively aware that he or she is personally responsible for data security and the image of the company. Only with continuous and engaging communication can security awareness be established and a culture of cybersecurity be developed. Only by making employees aware of the risks and consequences can carelessness be prevented and sensibility raised. Only through constant vigilance can organizations ensure that security risks are identified and, even more importantly, reported.

It is also important that in-house security experts—and other leaders—network effectively and empower the right culture. By sharing information with colleagues from other companies, your IT and security teams will know what questions to ask internally. Leaders can learn from the failures of others, and also from their successes. In the war against cybercriminals, all companies must be united.

---

[1] "Top 5 cybersecurity facts, figures and statistics for 2018," CSO from IDG, Jan. 23, 2018

37

Hunting for the Cyber Leader With the Best Board-Level Credentials

Matt Aiello — Partner, Heidrick & Struggles, United States of America

Gavin Colman — Partner, Heidrick & Struggles, United Kingdom

Max Randria — Principal, Heidrick & Struggles, Australia

The billionaire founder of a New York-based online games business with a global franchise was deeply concerned. His company had developed market-leading and inspiring games that attracted millions of tech-savvy customers. But many of those avid customers were *too* tech-savvy: They had uncovered and exploited multiple ways of circumventing the paywall, and were playing for free.

The company's board knew they were facing a pivotal moment—one that demanded the combination of technical skills and business acumen of a world-class chief information security officer. Recognizing the critical business issues at play, the board initially targeted a specific, big-ticket CISO, only to discover during the recruitment and interview process that the candidate didn't have the skill set required to address cybersecurity at the highest possible strategic level.

Instead, the board held out for a different kind of CISO, one who was able to tackle the strategic issue of ensuring application security. He was recruited, not because he had the best all-around skills

portfolio but because he had the ability to deal with the highest levels of risk. Under his leadership, the business' revenue leakage was stanched. Crisis averted.

This real-world scenario illustrates why searching for and landing the right CISO is more important than ever. It also sheds light on why the process is challenging for even experienced board members and their organizations' C-suite executives. That's because there is no universal playbook for identifying the perfect CISO candidate.

In fact, there is no such thing as the perfect CISO candidate. What boards should look for—and what they should demand in executive searches for their next CISO—is a candidate who is perfect for their organization. After all, no two organizations are the same; each has different economic, operational, and reputational risks, and cybersecurity strategies must account for those unique circumstances. That means that the qualities, experiences, skills, and attitudes that make one candidate ideal for Organization A may make them a complete misfit for Organization B.

243

And there's another important consideration for boards to keep in mind. No matter who you tap as your next CISO, or what reporting structure you adopt for your new cyber chief, the CISO exists to serve the needs of the very top echelon of the organization.

As important as the CISO is, the ultimate decision-makers on cybersecurity remain the board and the CEO. If the CISO fails to execute their job well enough to protect the organization, its data, and its competitive position, the blame ultimately falls at the feet of the board.

That means boards need to exercise even more diligence than ever when determining who to hire, how to structure their roles and responsibilities, where to look to recruit them, and which tradeoffs are appropriate to make in order to land the best possible candidate.

In Defense of Reputation and Brands

As cyberattacks have become more audacious and damaging to organizational reputations, board members have had to embrace new responsibility for ensuring the protection of the business. Well-known brands have been targeted and attacked, raising the stakes for everyone throughout the organization—and often reshaping the way CISOs are viewed by their boards. CISOs, long accustomed to fighting for air time to talk about threats, now are being cast in the center stage at board and committee meetings.

This is an important development for business-savvy CISOs, who now are being seen as trusted advisors responsible for protecting the "corporate shield," rather than as doomsday fearmongers warning about technical weaknesses threatening to expose the organization's crown jewels to cyber thieves.

Instead of convincing fellow executives to take him or her seriously, the CISO now has a built-in, even eager, audience that wants to hear about cyber risk and, importantly, what is being done about it. This means that board members need to demand the hiring of a CISO with executive personality, not just one who spouts a technical vocabulary that does little but confuse people. While the CISO must have requisite technical skills, those can be identified and even "bought" far more easily than someone with significant boardroom presence.

And board members should be aware of the risks in elevating those who can "talk the talk," but who are out of their depth should a crisis erupt. The board must be confident that the CISO they appoint is both operationally sound and has board-approved procedures in place to respond to a major attack. This CISO must also be able to work in parallel with the CEO and other C-suite executives to ensure they are fully briefed on all eventualities. Most of all, the CISO needs to have the full confidence of their peers and the board that they have the full sphere of technical, financial, regulatory, and operational bases covered—and will be calm, reassuring, and confident when a crisis hits.

After all, your organization's brand reputation can rise or fall based on how good a job your CISO does in preparing the organization to respond appropriately and quickly when a data breach takes down your customer-facing systems for an hour.

When Demand Exceeds Supply of Elite CISOs

Most cyber leaders are trying to build robust teams of security professionals to handle multiple threats; but building those teams requires a willingness to search far and wide for the best and the brightest—starting with the CISO. There is a relatively small, finite number of prized professionals to fill the CISO role, and they are regularly on the move across national and even international borders. Our firm recently assembled a shortlist of top candidates to fill an open CISO slot, only to see our list whittled down every day as candidates were snapped up by rival offers.

As the cyber leader's role is maturing, the process of identifying and recruiting the next CISO is becoming more complex. But there may be lessons learned by looking at potential candidates through both industry and geographic filters. In Silicon Valley and other technology hubs, digital-native organizations employ security professionals who are charged with protecting their organizations against some of the most relentless and sophisticated attacks. And in financial services firms in New York and other financial centers, security professionals have had to up their game in order to withstand a broadening set of attack vectors.

In Washington, DC, government agencies are at the leading edge in the battle for top cyber talent, where a lot of this industry expertise has been forged under fire. These agencies are excellent places to find top cyber talent, though generally below the C-level.

Major European enterprises have experienced sophisticated and prolonged cyber-attacks from malicious actors, including rogue states, who are deploying massive resources to attack legitimate targets to extort money and data. Increasingly, private-sector companies depend on a collaborative cyber community, including European government agencies, such as NATO, NCSC-NL, and GCHQ, that shares cyber alerts and stays updated with businesses that are willing to step in to help those under attack. This kind of extra-curricular networking activity should be discussed and sanctioned by the board.

Cyber talent also is increasing in number and depth in other geographies—although it is still not able to meet the rising demand. For instance, Australia is known as an exporter of talent in the security industry. In the last two years in Australia, there has been an enormous increase in CISO positions in all industries and at all levels. Israel is another excellent source for security talent. Israel plays a dominant role in cyber-security, with high-growth start-ups and major product developments outsourced by the major Silicon Valley tech companies.

In order to attract the ideal CISO, boards increasingly are giving consideration to what type of reporting structure they should have with the CISO in order to ensure that cybersecurity receives its proper prioritization and attention, and that the CISO receives the right mix of resources, responsibility, and accountability.

We are seeing several iterations of this reporting structure, depending on the size and scope of the organization. Tech firms, financial services institutions, and consumer-facing companies dependent on tech transactions, such as retail, hospitality, airlines, and healthcare, are increasingly seeing the need for a board-level cyber leader. Rapidly catching up are large infrastructure providers such as energy, oil and gas, and large-scale manufacturing.

Reporting structures may not always be a perfect representation of the priority an organization places on cybersecurity. But there is a lot to be said for the message it sends to your ideal CISO candidate when they are told that they will have direct access and accountability to the board.

Don't Wait for Perfection

The French philosopher Voltaire is often credited with saying some variation of, "Perfect is the enemy of good." He must have been anticipating boards' current dilemma in their searches for the so-called "perfect CISO."

As stated above, there is no perfect CISO candidate, so boards and executives should not wait for perfection. However, they must not hire sub-optimally either, as the costs will vastly outweigh the benefits of a compromised hire. With such rapid change in cybersecurity threats, vulnerabilities, and risks, it is difficult for a "pretty good" candidate to have the luxury of time to grow into the CISO role. If a compromise must be made, focus on hiring for the skill set associated with the highest risk. Evaluate your operations and technology environment, and hire a CISO who fits that environment. Be open to restructuring the role around the person, as well.

Today's leading CISOs possess a blend of leadership traits, including an air of credibility, board-level presentation skills, and strong business acumen, and tomorrow's CISOs will need to lead more by influence than authority. Boards must look for agile, risk-focused people who are quick learners and are comfortable positioning security as a strategic advantage and marketplace differentiator.

The board also is looking for superior levels of personal integrity and ethical trust. It is vital to understand that CISOs are not always motivated by the size of their pay check, but by the mission and the higher purpose of the organization. Often, the cyber leader has a quasi-spiritual determination to defend the enterprise, the data, the customers, and the entire organizational ecosystem from malicious intent.

This results in the building of a strong fellowship of collaboration among those who embark on this mission.

Another important consideration is for boards to think down the road during their CISO-hunting expedition. As the rate of cyber-change accelerates and as threats rapidly transform, it's essential for boards to hire a CISO not just for today's needs, but particularly for where you want your business to be in three years' time. For instance, it might be better to "overhire" and pay more than feels comfortable to attract a candidate best suited for tomorrow's needs. Remember: Your cyber-security requirements will undoubtedly change over time.

Conclusion

Ask 10 board members which corporate role, after the CEO, is most critical to an organization's success, and you'll likely get 10 different answers. Sales, finance, operations, engineering, IT, marketing—they all are essential to the organization's long-term health and success, and the C-level executives overseeing those and other functions need to be top performers.

Now, cybersecurity must be considered at the same apex of the corporate organization. A board's decision on its next CISO can make the difference between market leadership and a badly damaged brand, profits and losses, customer confidence, or mistrust. It's a decision-making process that must be taken seriously at the board level.

Your organization's long-term health and viability depend upon it.

Process

38

How to Manage a Data Breach

Lisa J. Sotto — Partner, Hunton Andrews Kurth LLP

Every organization is vulnerable to cyberattack. But being aware that an entity is vulnerable is not the same as being prepared to manage such an event. The number of data breaches annually continues to skyrocket. According to the most recent data breach report by Verizon, there were 2,216 data breaches in 2017, across 65 countries. More than three quarters of those breaches were financially motivated.[1]

Managing a data breach is a major undertaking that can quickly overwhelm an organization in the throes of an attack. Depending on the size and scope of the incident, it could monopolize virtually all of management's time and energy for months. Worse, it could expose the organization to enormous risk—financial, legal, and reputational—if the appropriate steps are not taken from the beginning to help ensure a proper investigation, reporting, notification, and communication.

Among the most effective ways to prepare for a data breach is to have a clear understanding of the process involved in responding to an intrusion. There are many lessons to be learned from best practices that have evolved over the years and enabled organizations to successfully navigate global data breaches.

Event and Mobilization

To understand the arc of a data breach, it is important to consider each step in the timeline on the next page. Regardless of industry sector, every organization experiencing a cyber event generally will experience the stages set out in this timeline.

The response effort commences immediately following identification of an attack. The organization must quickly mobilize the proper resources for a coordinated response.

Businesses may learn about a cybersecurity event through a variety of channels. For example, the information security function of an organization may find an anomaly in the company's systems, signaling a breach of the system. Or the entity might be contacted by law enforcement officials who identified data linked to the company on the Dark Web. Alternatively, a company's customer service center might receive a sudden barrage of customer calls suggesting that fraud has occurred. The media also is active in identifying cyber events and notifying companies before they find the issue in their own systems. Although there are many different avenues by which an organization might identify an issue, the key is to respond immediately and start putting the right plan in place.

Data Breach Response Timeline

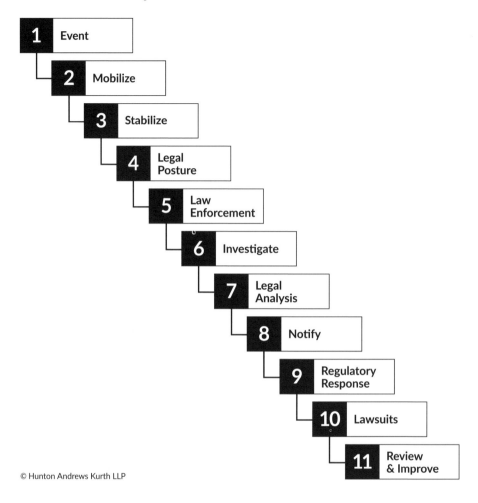

1	Event
2	Mobilize
3	Stabilize
4	Legal Posture
5	Law Enforcement
6	Investigate
7	Legal Analysis
8	Notify
9	Regulatory Response
10	Lawsuits
11	Review & Improve

© Hunton Andrews Kurth LLP

Once aware of an issue, the organization's chief information security officer and her team generally will take the lead, along with the company's general counsel. Outside counsel frequently is brought into the fray in an effort to preserve the company's legal posture, including protecting privilege—to the extent possible—around the investigation. If the breach appears significant, counsel likely will advise the organization to implement a legal hold, requiring that relevant records be preserved. Counsel also may raise the possibility that the breach constitutes a material event requiring disclosure under the securities laws. Finally, counsel may suggest notifying the relevant insurer.

Counsel will work with the organization to determine whether to retain an outside forensic investigator. For a major breach, several different investigative teams might be brought in, each with different areas of expertise. For example, some external experts have deep technical knowledge in finding and following the footprints of an attacker. Others may be adept at gathering intel and determining the attribution of a threat actor. Still others, such as certified PCI forensic investigators, may focus exclusively on the payment card aspects of a breach.

In addition to hiring forensics experts, it also may be appropriate to contact law enforcement authorities during the early stages of awareness and investigation. Depending on the circumstances, the company might choose to contact either a federal or a local law enforcement agency.

It is important that the group handling the incident be limited to need-to-know personnel. Keeping the circle of breach responders small can help to prevent leaks and speculation.

Notification

As the forensic investigation is proceeding, the relevant legal analysis is occurring simultaneously. Among the questions at this stage are the following: What type of data is involved? Is the affected information considered personal data? If so, what data elements are affected? What are the jurisdictions of the individuals whose data may have been impacted? How many people's data is at risk? Over what time period did the attack occur? Is the intruder still in the system? Myriad questions will need to be answered at this stage.

With respect to breach notification, in the U.S. alone, it may be necessary to analyze the laws of each of the 50 states (and a number of other jurisdictions with breach notification requirements, such as Guam, Puerto Rico, the U.S. Virgin Islands, and Washington, D.C.). In the EU, with the enactment of the General Data Protection Regulation (GDPR), companies are required to notify government authorities of a personal data breach within 72 hours of becoming aware of such an incident.

Given the aggressive timing requirements of certain breach notification laws, organizations often are in the unenviable position of having to issue notification while the forensic investigation is taking place. The difficulty of this position is that the findings from a forensic investigation frequently change as the investigation proceeds; entities would be wise to avoid relying on their first instincts when trying to scope the issue. The forensic investigation will need to unfold before the nature and scope of the breach can be properly understood and assessed.

In these early stages, counsel typically begins working to craft the appropriate documents, which could take the form of notifications to regulatory authorities; letters or emails to affected individuals; and notices to a variety of other stakeholders, such as business partners, enterprise customers, service providers, media, employees, and relevant government entities (in addition to regulators).

There may be many parties to consider and numerous stakeholders to manage. Crafting a communication strategy can be challenging, and external PR experts may provide sorely needed assistance. Adding to the pressure, this strategy often must be crafted within a tight time frame when the facts are not clear. As mentioned above, in the EU, there is a 72-hour-notice requirement for notification to the appropriate government regulator. In certain industries, such as the energy sector, notification to the regulator could be required in as little as one hour.

It is also important to understand that the evolving narrative may not be in the company's control. Social media plays a significant role in today's information environment. News of a data breach will go viral quickly, even before an affected organization has had an opportunity to coordinate a communication strategy. A third-party public relations firm may be able to provide assistance in helping to manage the message and craft the right PR framework.

The notification generally should be sent directly to the affected individuals. Alternatively, if the impacted organization does not have contact information for the relevant individuals, or the cost of mailing a notice to the affected population would result in expenses exceeding an amount specified by law, "substitute" notification is available. This enables the affected organization to provide the public with information regarding the data breach. The substitute notification rules require the affected entity to post information about the breach on its website, provide notification to statewide media (which is most commonly accomplished via a press release), and send an email to the relevant individuals if email addresses are known.

Sending the notification in a timely manner is essential. To assist with the mailing, companies often retain external mail houses. In addition, the services of third-party call centers are frequently invoked to assist with the inevitable barrage of calls following notification of a data breach. It is helpful to use skilled customer service agents, particularly those in specialty call centers that routinely handle data breaches.

Going Live

Once the event has been announced publicly, the affected company can expect an immediate barrage of inquiries—from federal regulators to state attorneys general to foreign data protection authorities. The company will be faced with myriad questions about the data breach, as well as the organization's overall security posture. Business leaders should anticipate a multi-month, or even a multi-year, exchange of information and dialogue with regulators.

With respect to regulator activity following a data breach, most government inquiries result only in an investigation, not enforcement. Should an investigation culminate in an enforcement action, fines may be imposed by some regulators (such as state attorneys general and some overseas data protection authorities). Other regulators, such as the U.S. Federal Trade Commission (FTC), have limited authority to impose monetary penalties and instead often seek equitable relief. In actions involving the FTC, enforcement associated with data breaches typically results in a settlement in the form of a consent order. The FTC could impose significant financial penalties for violation of a consent order.

In addition to regulatory activity, lawsuits are likely to follow most significant data breaches. These actions may be brought by affected individuals, issuing banks, shareholders, and other parties directly or indirectly impacted by the breach. Lawsuits resulting from data breaches can take years to resolve. Between litigation and regulatory action, organizations will be dealing with the ramifications of a breach long after the actual event.

Being Prepared

In addition to understanding the processes involved in managing a data breach, there are steps organizations can take to be better prepared before they suffer a breach and are thrust into response mode. Although some cyberattacks are inevitable and cannot readily be prevented, being prepared to identify intruders quickly and manage the fallout is critical in today's pernicious cyber environment.

One key readiness step is to build relationships in advance with cybersecurity experts. The better-prepared companies know which forensic firm, counsel, PR firm, call center, credit monitoring service, and mail house they will retain in the event of a breach. These breach response providers may be listed, for example, in the company's incident response plan.

Purchasing cybersecurity insurance also is a key cyber preparedness step. The organization's cyber insurer can play a significant role in helping to assemble a breach response team. Cyber insurers often have significant experience managing breaches; compromised companies can leverage that experience to help accelerate and coordinate the response.

Other key cyber preparedness steps include maintaining a state-of-the-art incident response plan. This plan typically is a dynamic document that should be revisited frequently to reflect the rapidly evolving threat landscape. It is also important to establish a relationship with relevant law enforcement authorities before experiencing an attack. Get to know local cyber law enforcement teams in advance, and begin building a collaborative relationship before an incident occurs.

Many organizations conduct tabletop exercises to practice their incident response plans and help ensure that the members of their incident response team understand their respective roles and responsibilities in the event of a cyberattack. Tabletop exercises help build institutional muscle memory and will serve to streamline an entity's breach response, mitigating harm associated with an actual event. Although cyber incidents are inevitable, practicing managing such an event through a tabletop exercise can serve to reduce inefficiencies and organizational stress associated with real events.

Conclusion

The threat of cyberattacks continues to grow. Whether criminal hackers, nation-states, or hacktivists, cyber intruders are often technically savvy, well-funded, and highly organized. Because of the potential havoc cyber attackers can bring, it is incumbent upon all companies, regardless of industry sector, to take appropriate steps to prevent successful attacks.

In today's precarious cyber environment, organizations need to be aware that the increased scrutiny that could result from a data breach could have a profound impact on a business's operations, financial position, and reputation. How an organization responds to a data breach is often a bigger test than the breach itself. By knowing what it takes to respond, business leaders can be better prepared to provide the leadership and guidance necessary to successfully steer their organization through a cyberattack.

---

[1] "2018 Data Breach Investigations Report," Verizon, March 2018

39

Incident Response: How to Deal With a Cyberattack

Dr. Andreas Rohr — Chief Technology Officer,
Deutsche Cyber-Sicherheitsorganisation GmbH (DCSO)

Compromised networks are the new normal. It does not matter which sector a company operates in or how large or small it is: Professional attackers find data in every organization that can later be turned into economic advantage or cash on the black markets. For some time, the question—from the criminals' perspective—has not been *whether* an organization can be successfully attacked; it has been only a matter of *when.*

While it may be uncomfortable to acknowledge this new reality, it is necessary. By recognizing that total protection is not economically feasible, leaders in business, IT, and security can focus on the real task at hand—minimizing the chance and impact of a data leak and getting back to the work agenda.

Of course, even in a world where successful attacks are a part of daily business, your organization cannot get by without security mechanisms such as firewalls, virus scanners, ID and access management, etc. These components generally ward off attackers that are not operating in a targeted fashion; adopting the watering-can principle (one of the sprays of water is bound to hit the target), these attackers search across wide areas for vulnerable infrastructures.

By contrast, professionals with a targeted approach can generally overcome these hygiene security mechanisms. In most cases, they do this by selecting one or more employees in the target organization and turning them into unknowing accomplices for the leap over the firewall, via social engineering. Another common mechanism is to use less-secure entry points at a subsidiary or supplier location that are connected to the corporate network.

Allow the Attacker to Have Their Moment

In such cases, attackers initially have one objective: remaining undiscovered for as long as possible in order to tap into company secrets. If data thieves have compromised your network, managers should take time to reflect on the situation. They should not act on their instinctive response to take the affected systems offline and delete or even dispose of them in order to keep the loss as small as possible.

Modern, smart attackers set up several back doors, allowing them to regain access to the network. In today's complex IT infrastructures, often distributed across countries, it is easy to set up various hidden access routes. So, if the company deletes parts of the criminal's toolkit or footprint, it does not take out the data thief's full arsenal of weaponry.

This takes the company into a more dangerous phase because people think they can relax. But that relaxation is, at best, deceptive. Think about it this way: If you discover an intruder in a bedroom in your home because his flashlight has given him away, your instinctive response is to drive him off. But in doing so, you may have overlooked an accomplice lurking in the darkened kitchen.

Waiting has the additional advantage of allowing your team to learn about possible additional back doors by observing the behavior and tools used. Moreover, by gathering information, it is possible for your team to gain insights into what is motivating the intruders, possibly even discovering their identity.

Plan Countermeasures in Secret

Naturally, you cannot allow the intrusion to progress to the point where data thieves are clearing out the company silverware under the gaze of company management. If criminals are starting to work on databases, design drawings, confidential contracts, or the entire customer base, you must disable the ability of the attacker to act, and cut connection immediately.

But shutting systems or connections down is not enough. In order to avoid data being copied again once the connection is switched back on, the data needs to be completely removed from the compromised network and a transitional structure created.

Nearly all attackers have the patience to wait until a company shuts down parts of its network, so a shutdown without rebuilding is insufficient. As long as the intruders are only creeping through the network by lateral movements, cybersecurity specialists can track their movements, making it quicker to identify the entry points and tools used.

In an extended organization, this process of illumination and tracking can take anywhere from eight weeks to six months. Admittedly, a waiting period such as this can be hard to tolerate. For that reason, if an incident does occur, company management needs to be united in its response, in advance of the attack. If the discussion starts when you learn about the intrusion, valuable time is being lost—especially since the outcome of the discussion could well be of questionable quality, due to the massive pressure from the crisis situation.

Who Turns the Tap Off, and When?

It needs to be clear who in the company is allowed to do what in the event of an attack being detected. Which committee or which employee is empowered to decide that the connection gets cut? Who releases what information to outside parties, lawyers, supervisory authorities, the stock exchange supervisory authority, customers, and the press?

It does no good getting together for the first time to thrash this all out as the intrusion is actually happening. Being prepared also means developing as detailed a scenario as possible for "pulling the plug," i.e., determining which data is not permitted to be transferred outside the company by thieves under any circumstances, and how the shutdown of the affected systems is to be carried out.

In most cases, you will bring on an external incident-response service provider to handle illuminating the network and the hoped-for detection of the attackers. This service provider should be tied in to the company under contract at an earlier stage, and should not be brought on board in a frantic rush as the damage is being done.

At the same time, it is the service provider's duty to protect the customer from misuse by overly curious employees. Confidentiality clauses are therefore essential.

In order to enable the inspection of systems, networks, and services operated by external service providers, these rights need to be firmly anchored contractually in advance under outsourcing arrangements.

Set Out Responsibilities and Get All Stakeholders on Board

It is necessary to decide who will be making decisions in the event of a crisis, because no matter how good the preparation, unique situations will always arise. In bigger companies, it is probably the CIO, unless the CISO reports directly to the executive board. In that case, preference goes to the CISO, since the CISO's area of expertise relates directly to the technical issues involved. If neither post exists, then probably the only option is the CEO or managing director, due to the significance of the decisions.

In all instances, it is important that the security specialists and experts running the IT systems act as a unit. Trust-based collaboration during times of peace is vital. Without it, when the crisis hits it triggers superfluous, time-consuming discussions and turf wars that detract from the actual objective.

You also need to determine how the crisis manager or the service provider entrusted with monitoring the environment can gain access to areas of the orga-nization for which separate administrator rights are required: network infrastructure, applications such as SAP, databases, etc. It is possible that specific areas are being operated by external partners. Advance clarification is needed with all these parties as to which rights are to be granted in the crisis situation.

Empowering a Crisis Team

Prior to a crisis, the organization should have an ad-hoc committee in place that has a clearly defined path for decision-making and can meet as soon as a crisis occurs. The chair of the committee—probably the CIO or CISO—must be empowered to make decisions even against the votes of committee members.

The crisis committee should comprise representatives of individual corporate functions, i.e. legal, IT, IT security/group security, finance, HR, communications, etc. The committee should meet regularly for sessions lasting a maximum of 15 minutes, delegating the matters discussed to the relevant departments for implementation. The decisions should not be discussed with the company's top management, but only within the committee.

Conversely, the organization should not spend too much time preparing for a crisis situation by devising various crisis scenarios. No matter how many employees take part in these planning games, they will still be surprised by the creativity shown and routines adopted by attackers. Accordingly, it should be sufficient to list the five or 10 most plausible attack scenarios (threat modeling) and play these through. Employees can rehearse some of these scenarios in a war game. It is more important to plan for response capabilities such as gaining visibility, given certain trigger information.

Steps for Dealing With the Crisis Situation

Preparing for the crisis situation includes defining the necessary steps and recording them so that no valuable time is lost if you are faced with the threat of data loss. It is true that every crisis involves something different, and every organization brings a different set of conditions to the table. Nevertheless, you can map out a viable plan in advance. Here are some key considerations that may not be apparent if you've never been through a cybersecurity crisis:

1. Never switch off the computers affected; instead, monitor the attackers by creating (real-time) visibility.

2. Do not waste time trying to elaborate on the root cause or assigning blame. This slows down your ability to deal with the crisis, because the people potentially affected will not be open about the situation, and they won't collaborate. Likewise, it is pointless to assign blame. Ultimately, it is the job of the audit team to answer this question during its follow-up.

3. Top management should sit down with the ad-hoc crisis committee at the start and then allow the team to get on with its work. That includes making all required resources available to the committee. It is as simple as it sounds: Give them two suitable rooms, a budget for catering, and release them from filling out irritating forms; tasks involving too much organizational detail should be handled by others.

4. The chair of the committee and his/her respective authorizations must be identified to the whole organization in advance.

5. It is not only IT security experts who need to work in shifts in a crisis situation; IT personnel running applications also need to ensure they can be contacted around the clock. Attackers often favor moving through networks at times outside their victims' normal office hours. If a monitoring sensor is triggered, an applications specialist may need to be brought on board to minimize the consequences.

6. Even if it is difficult for top management, the reporting that would normally happen needs to become a lower priority during the first two weeks after becoming aware that the network has been compromised. Perhaps a committee member can be available once a day for 10 minutes to bring management up to speed on the latest developments. One typical nail in the coffin in responding to an attack is when management wants individual reporting, which can require a great deal of time and effort. While it is an understandable stress reaction, it is a disastrous diversion from the work that is really essential.

7. Once you are past the first two weeks, a central control body should coordinate all further measures and, above all, obtain the necessary resources because, in most cases, there are no budgets for such situations. The employee entrusted with this role should have sufficient experience in having budget discussions with top management and in issuing instructions to the specialist departments involved. This normally rules out external consultants.

8. Another critical question is: Who pays for needed software or external experts? It is clear that the tendering process that would ordinarily be used has to be set aside, otherwise the organization will not be able to act in a timely manner in the event of a crisis. It is possible for a written power of attorney to be deposited in advance or, in the best-case scenario, even for a budget to be allocated. Alternatively, corresponding framework agreements can be put in place for possible support, which can then be called on as the process dictates.

9. A secure communications platform should be made available for communicating with everyone involved—the ad-hoc committee, employees in specialist departments, top management, external consultants, and auditors. The systems otherwise used for email or instant messaging should generally be considered as compromised, and therefore should be ruled out as a channel for exchanging confidential information. Suitable arrangements include internet data rooms and email SaaS platforms with two-factor authentication that are independent of the company infrastructure.

Conclusion

The time has come to acknowledge that complete protection against cyberattacks has become uneconomical and unrealistic. Instead of spending the entire cybersecurity budget on prevention, a good portion of the money should be invested in mechanisms for identifying successful attacks (detection) and after-care measures (response capabilities).

It is also important to remember that technology is only one part of the solution. People will determine your success in minimizing the damage of a cyberattack, so make sure you make budgets available for raising their awareness. Without the knowledge of what a social engineering campaign conducted by criminals looks like, employees can quickly fall victim to an attack.

In the face of an attack, standard processes within the company and otherwise customary methods of risk management come up against their limits. It may sound crazy and counterintuitive to allow cybercriminals to continue their work once they have been discovered, but that is often an important way to minimize damage.

If we are indeed at a time when complete protection is unrealistic, we must take the time and make the proper investments to ensure that we can respond quickly and appropriately if an attack takes place. In this case, it is an ounce of preparation that is worth a pound of cure.

40

Don't Wait for a Breach to Build Your Communications Strategy

Robert Boyce — Managing Director, Accenture Security, Accenture

Justin Harvey — Managing Director, Accenture Security, Accenture

When it comes to cybersecurity breaches, there are two types of organizations: those who've been breached and those who don't know they've been breached.

So, let's assume the inevitable: Your organization has been breached. An unknown quantity of data has been stolen, records have been compromised, potentially damaging information may now be on a Wikipedia page, and your customers' personally identifiable information is floating around the internet. It's time to plot your communications strategy. Oh, wait. Too late.

Unfortunately, no matter how many smart steps you've taken to shore up your cyber defenses—girding your networks, and protecting your data with sophisticated tools and services—it's important to plan for a breach, especially considering that data breaches are occurring more frequently and with increasingly insidious intent and impact.

Equally important, data breaches aren't one-time-only events. Successful compromises beget more hacking attempts and, thus, it's in every organization's best inter-

est to assume it will be hit—likely again and again—and have a detailed, actionable, and well-rehearsed communications plan already in place when a breach happens.

The Fundamentals of Breach Communications

Breach communications is more than sending letters to customers, talking to the media, or engaging lawyers. It is a comprehensive system of gathering, vetting, and sharing information with all relevant internal and external audiences. It also is designed to help ensure an organization's ability to recover and restore operations after a data breach, regardless of data loss or financial and brand damage.

In our many client engagements, we've seen a fair share of data breaches. We've seen smart, disciplined, well-planned, and meticulously executed communications strategies. But unfortunately, we've also seen some regrettable, unstructured, and poorly executed efforts. In assessing both the successes and failures, we can offer actionable advice in two main areas: components of a breach communications plan and potential landmines to avoid.

Please forgive the cliché, but we know that "hope is not a strategy." So, as you build out your breach communications plan or modernize an existing one, we encourage you to begin with a few fundamentals:

1. **Stay calm.** The first few hours following the discovery of a potentially damaging breach are critical, and you can undermine your organization's well-intentioned efforts to minimize the internal and external damage if you allow yourself to be overcome by adrenaline, fear, or a misplaced need to seem bold and aggressive. The ability to remain calm and proceed in an orderly fashion will instill confidence in your employees, customers, trading partners, suppliers, opinion shapers, and regulators. It also can help minimize the potential for shooting from the hip with incomplete or inaccurate information, which could cause even greater damage.

2. **Be prepared.** It is an egregious failure of an executive's or a board member's fiduciary responsibility to not take the time and energy to prepare an action plan that includes steps to take before, during, and after a breach. Earlier in this book, Exabeam Chief Security Strategist Stephen Moore laid out some sound advice about cybersecurity preparation, including a smart idea to write your breach notification letter *before* you suffer a breach.

3. **Engage** *all* **key players well in advance.** When a breach occurs, everyone must know his or her role—which requires that the right people are recruited for input on the plan's development, for involvement in

game planning the response, and for assigning the proper roles and responsibilities. Every functional group in the organization must be engaged, and the right external resources—lawyers, forensic analysts, crisis management communications firms—must be identified and recruited. Waiting until a breach happens to start communications planning is much too late, and if you're missing even one key contributor to the breach communications team, you risk leaving out critical elements from your plan.

Key Components of a Breach Communications Plan

At the heart of every breach communications plan is what you do before, during, and after a breach hits. Being prepared is a critical component of your breach communications strategy, but what are the actual steps you should put in place?

Assign roles and responsibilities. Once you've engaged all key players from all key functional groups, you need to decide who is doing what. At this point, don't worry about "committee creep" by including too many people. Some people and functions may participate in the overall communications planning, others may focus on customer outreach. Some may concentrate on governance, risk, and compliance-related matters, and a few may be involved in every element of the plan's development and deployment. The key is crystallizing everyone's role so that when a breach happens and time is of the essence, there's no ambiguity around who does what when.

Take a broad view of your communications targets. It's natural for organizations—especially large, well-known brands with global recognition—to put media outlets at the top of the list for post-breach communications. Obviously, consumer, business, and trade media are important, but they are far from the only people and groups with whom you need to communicate. Regulators will also be keenly interested in the status of your efforts, the extent of the breach, and your plan to stanch the damage. If you're a publicly traded company, stock analysts will be asking you questions while also answering others from the media about any potential impact to your stock price or competitive position. And don't forget law enforcement organizations, who may see your data breach as part of an organized digital crime ring or another data point in an ongoing pattern of cybercrime they are investigating.

Identify and engage experienced third parties. Crisis communications firms, outside legal counsel, investor relations firms, and cybersecurity consultants all provide valuable perspectives from different areas of expertise. Undoubtedly, they've all been involved in similar incidents with other firms in the recent past, so they will be able to share advice based on real-world perspectives.

Pressure-test your plan. Okay, you've done everything listed above. You've got a comprehensive plan and everyone knows their role. Now what? Do you just sit around and wait? Well, does the military wait for their country to be attacked? Do police forces wait for a crime wave to hit? Of course not. They all practice, practice, practice. They stage rehearsals under as close to real-world settings as they can manage—and so, too, should you. Pressure-testing your plan is one of the most important things your organization can do before a breach hits. It could involve something as simple as tabletop exercises, where a pseudo-breach is assumed and everyone talks about what they are going to do. Or,

it could be something more realistic, such as a full-on simulation where participants are not told it's a drill and might do everything short of notifying law enforcement.

Determine how you will communicate. Depending upon the type and severity of the breach, your normal communications media—email, internet, even phones—may not be available to you, either because they have been damaged or their security has been compromised. Have a plan to utilize out-of-band communications and, even, engage in face-to-face discussions. And be careful what you put in writing. While we certainly don't advocate doing anything illegal or improper, it's crucial to understand that written communications may become essential in legal discovery well after a breach has been resolved.

Keep the board informed. You're not necessarily asking for their permission on any aspect of your plan, but there's a good chance that some, if not most, of your board members have dealt with similar situations in their own organizations. Listen to their experiences and heed their advice about steps to take in developing a more effective breach communications plan.

Engage law enforcement. Depending on the nature of your breach and the expertise of the law enforcement jurisdiction, this step can be tricky. Not surprisingly, the increasing incidence of cybercrime has driven law enforcement agencies to treat digital crimes on the same level as crimes of the physical world—robbery, assault, and others. A local sheriff's department, for example, is not going to have the same capabilities—or maybe even the same interest—around data breaches as the U.S. Federal Bureau of Investigation or Interpol. While schools of thought are divided on how proactive organizations need to be in involving local law enforcement when a breach occurs, it's a smart practice to build relationships with law enforcement as part of your pre-breach planning. This way, you have a familiar voice on the other end of the line when you suspect your data breach may be part of something bigger.

Potential Landmines to Avoid

While it's unlikely that your planning will anticipate every potential twist and turn leading up to and following a data breach, there are some clear problem areas you should anticipate and plan to avoid when developing and implementing your breach communications program.

Fight the urge to overcommunicate. This recommendation may run counter to what executives are used to doing in their day-to-day business roles, but we've seen numerous instances of organizations saying too much, too soon after a breach. Let's say Company A has a breach and loses data on 100,000 accounts; they release a statement talking about those numbers only to discover two days later that 500,000 accounts were compromised. While companies may need to keep regulators well informed on a regular and timely basis, it's good to not have escalating data breach numbers played out in headlines, day after day.

Don't overlook the need to test your communications plan. We've covered this in greater depth above, but one of the biggest mistakes you can make is to develop a comprehensive plan and let it collect dust on a shelf until the inevitable breach occurs. It's important to update your plan on a regular basis; after all, people come and go, business processes change, regulatory requirements evolve. Don't assume the plan you developed last year will still work next year.

Manage and control your employees' use of social media. It's astonishing to think that your employees would go on Facebook, LinkedIn, or Twitter to post updates on their efforts to "help" in mitigating the impact of a data breach. Sadly, we've seen this happen more than once. Most often, employees are simply trying to be good ambassadors of the organization to customers and visitors. To avoid any potential issues, make sure employees know that all social media communications related to a breach must be authorized by a designated functional group.

In her chapter on managing a data breach, Hunter & Williams partner Lisa Sotto provides important advice on the right way to use social media as an integral part of a coordinated breach communications strategy. Her key point rings loudly: "News of a data breach will go viral quickly, even before an affected organization has had an opportunity to coordinate a communications strategy."

Take executive responsibility. Remember the actions of Johnson & Johnson in the immediate aftermath of the 1982 Tylenol tampering scandal? The company's CEO was front and center, embracing responsibility and even advising the public not to take Tylenol; his leadership gained the organization much-needed credibility and leeway in re-establishing consumer trust.[1] Contrast that with the ill-advised comments of a BP executive after the tragic Gulf of Mexico oil spill and fire, where he complained, "I want my life back."[2]

Don't Become a Cautionary Tale

We cannot stress enough how vital it is to have an honest, open, and brutally candid discussion among your executive colleagues about your breach communications plan. As so many authors in this book have emphasized, cybersecurity is a leadership test—not a technology glitch. It demands the full attention and resolute commitment of both business executives and the board, and extends to their involvement in the development of a comprehensive and actionable breach communications plan, which is too important and complex to be left to a single individual to architect.

Cybersecurity isn't a static state; your technology solutions are always evolving to meet the changing nature of threats and vulnerabilities. Your breach communications plan must be every bit as flexible, dynamic, and modernized as your technology infrastructure. If it's not, fix it—and fast. It's not an overstatement to say that your organization's very viability depends on it. Thoughtful planning, regular testing, and meticulous execution of a breach communications plan will separate the industry leaders from those that become cautionary tales in the wake of a breach.

---

1   "How Poisoned Tylenol Became a Crisis-Management Teaching Model," Time, September 2014
2   "BP CEO Apologizes For 'Thoughtless' Oil Spill Comment," Reuters, June 2010

41

Making Cyber Insurance a Strategic Tool in Reducing Risk and Improving Resilience

Robert Parisi — Managing Director and U.S. Cyber Product Leader, Marsh

If you magically found a spare $2 million to spend on cybersecurity, what would you do?

If your CISO was asked, their reaction would be immediate and decisive. "We'll expand our headquarters' security operations center (SOC) and those in our core international facilities. Then we'll install next-gen endpoint protection, institute biometric access controls to our data centers, harden our critical infrastructure, and expand our threat intelligence subscription services."

Those and similar technology investments *are* a smart way to go. But it approaches security as a problem to be solved rather than as a risk that needs to be managed. Managing any operational risk needs to be more nuanced. So let's look at it from a different perspective.

Now, what if your CFO and Chief Risk Officer were told that $2 million spent on a bespoke cyber insurance policy could take $100 million of risk off their books and, at the same time, improve the organization's operational resilience? In other words, you would not only be financially protected in case of a costly data breach but also ensure that the organization can withstand the financial impact of a disrup-

tion to business operations for a material period of time.

That's not a hypothetical scenario. More and more organizations are facing the harsh reality that their technology will fail, a vendor will not be there when needed, or they will be attacked—if it hasn't happened already—in the future, with potentially grave financial, operational, legal, regulatory, and reputational consequences. Certainly, having the right technology tools, services and protocols in place is essential to fortifying cybersecurity in the face of expanding threats. But the cold, hard truth is that bigger technology spending, in and of itself, isn't going to stop the problem. It may slow it overall, and it may even relegate certain specific threats to irrelevance. But that's not enough to keep your business humming after a supply chain meltdown, data breach, malware campaign, ransomware demand, or distributed denial-of-service (DDoS) attack. Cyber risks are not simply problems that can be spent away. These are operational risks that need to be managed with the same level of attention and diligence as any traditional risk that could potentially put you out of business.

Cyber risk has now overtaken other, more traditional risks and become the number-one nightmare for business leaders and board members. And that risk has now evolved beyond privacy breaches and lost credit cards. The modern commercial entity is now so heavily dependent upon technology—their own and others'—that the board's biggest concern is whether or not their organization is truly cyber resilient and up to the challenge from the myriad threats out there.

It wasn't that long ago that the C-suite's primary worries about ensuring continuous operations dealt with things like natural disasters and political risk, particularly for multinational conglomerates. And those things are certainly still material considerations, but they are no longer likely to be either the most probable or the most severe disruption a company faces. The Business Continuity Institute, which assesses factors that shape business continuity and their impact on organizations, recently concluded that unplanned technology and telecommunications outages now outpace natural disasters and political risks in disrupting local, national, and even global supply chains. And as severe as the impact may be when an organization is in a geography hit by a flood, hurricane, or tornado, the potential impact of something like a ransomware attack—as the 2017 NotPetya malware attack demonstrated—is likely to be even greater.[1] Not only that, but a ransomware attack is far more difficult to predict and defend against because its source is rarely known until after it hits. Imagine if the hurricane could pick and choose where it made landfall based upon where it could cause the most damage. Now you have an idea of why cyber risk is scarier than weather. But companies manage their risk across a spectrum, with technology, protocol, and procedures being the primary risk mitiga-

tion tools. At some point along that spectrum, those risk tools no longer prove effective. It is at that point—for the residual risk—that insurance comes into play. You need a cyber insurance policy that aligns with your risk profile and that is integrated into your overall risk management framework. Cyber insurance is no more an alternative to sound risk management principles than technology is a silver bullet against every threat or exploit.

Cyber Insurance As a Resilience Play

We all know the traditional insurance model. An event occurs that has financial impact on a person, a community, or an organization. The insurance coverage pays the affected party a sum of money in accordance with the terms of its policies, coverage limits, and so on.

But traditional property and casualty insurance has left a vacuum by not evolving its breadth of coverage along with the changing risk profile of its customers. This is where cyber insurance plays a critical role. Cyber insurance anticipates and accounts for the need for operational and financial resilience. There are massive hard- and soft-dollar costs associated with running your business in the Digital Age. Even very small companies depend heavily—and will depend even more heavily in the coming years—on the integrity and availability of the technology underpinning their day-to-day operations.

It is a lack of resilience, even more than security, compliance, and the threat of lawsuits, that makes organizations increasingly vulnerable to cyber risk. And that's why cyber insurance must be considered part of an integrated risk management strategy.

Recognizing, Acknowledging, and Acting on the Threat

The good news is that cyber insurance is increasingly being viewed that way—as part of a holistic approach to risk management on par with traditional governance, risk management, and compliance functions. Interestingly, research conducted by Marsh, with Microsoft, indicates that cyber insurance "take up" rates—the percentage of organizations in a particular sector that purchased stand-alone cyber insurance—have been trending strongly upward in recent years.[2]

In virtually every major industry, take-up rates have moved higher in each of the past three years, with manufacturing, education, and hospitality/gaming demonstrating the highest rates of increase. Healthcare, meanwhile, remains the industry with the highest take-up rates. There's a qualifier to this good news, however. The fact is, most organizations have yet to move to dedicated cyber insurance policies. In fact, only about one in three organizations have done so.

What Should You Do First?

Of course, acknowledging the risk and the need to close the risk gaps that even great technology, and incredibly dedicated and innovative CISOs, can't fully plug is the first step. This is truly a case in which denial is not an effective strategy.

Making smart and strategic decisions on how, where, and when to use cyber insurance to mitigate risk starts with some key learnings and actions:

Cyber risk has to be part of the board's normal operational risk discussions. It is business risk, plain and simple. Too often, executives and boards fall victim to a kind of cyber mysticism when confronted with cyber risk, throwing up their hands because they don't feel confident they understand the technology. But at the end of the day, it's about looking at the potential impact of a cyber event, and working backwards from that to plot out

how all the defenses and responses, including cyber insurance, mitigate that. It's not only about "How do we stop that DDoS attack that's going around our industry?" but it also has to cover "What is the financial and operational impact to our business if our global supply chain is cut off?"

Get help in assessing organizational risk. Cyber insurance is still a fairly young line of business, and as such, it lacks the rich actuarial data associated with fixed-asset valuation like cars and plants. But there are a lot of helpful assessment tools to evaluate risk, from both inside and outside the firewall. Cyber-risk modeling companies run non-invasive scans and scrapes, and knock on your virtual doors to see if ports are left open. They can give you susceptibility metric to estimate attack vulnerability, without being disruptive to day-to-day business operations. Think of it as CCTV cameras on your virtual world that can see where information is flowing in and out, and that help you determine what that means. For instance, if you learn that you've got a lot of data flowing from a particular port to Kazakhstan—and you don't do business with anyone in that country—it's a pretty good clue something's amiss.

Take the time to understand relevant cyber insurance trends on coverages, premiums, and services, and compare your organization with others. Examining your peer group, however you define it, is a good way to put your assumptions into context, and to frame decisions about how to work with your broker to create a customized solution. But that analysis should not be limited to just what cyber insurance your peers are buying. Some of the assessment tools mentioned above can benchmark your threat vulnerability against a peer group.

Do a thorough, ongoing evaluation of the organization's at-risk asset values. And be sure to stretch your imagination when identifying those assets. Do you have a lot of personally identifiable information of employees, customers, prospects, and trading partners? Do you have trading algorithms? What is your inventory of intellectual property? And be sure to reassess those assets' value regularly, especially when corporate "events" like mergers or the introduction of new products and services take place. In addition, NotPetya made it clear that physical assets are also at risk from cyber perils, with millions of dollars of smart phones, tablets, PCs, and servers "bricked" by the malware. Being able to understand the value of at risk assets and the potential financial impact of a cyber event are critical first steps in determining the right level of insurance.

Be honest about your pain threshold when it comes to cyber risk. Executives and boards need to be on the same page when it comes to evaluating how much cyber risk they are willing to accept and how much they want insurance to cover. One organization may decide to hold the first $25 million in losses as their pain threshold and expect insurance to step in above that, while others may feel uncomfortable waiting for a digital catastrophe before receiving relief through insurance. Regardless, waiting until the disaster hits is not a good way to make that determination; have that discussion now, and revisit it regularly.

Make sure all the key players are at the table to discuss cyber insurance issues and to make the critical decisions. Of course, insurance decisions traditionally have rested in the CFO's domain, but smart CFOs, CROs, and compliance officers are bringing CISOs to the table to get a better handle on identifying current and future sources of cyber risk, and to collectively assess the impact of that risk on their operations. And CEOs should do more than just stick their heads into the room when these discussions are taking place; they need to have skin in the game, too. And the same thing goes for board members. In another chapter in this book, Paul Jackson of Kroll talks powerfully about heightened levels of board-level corporate governance brought on by cyber risk. Ask a director at any organization that has suffered a debilitating and embarrassing cyberattack if they wished they had asked more probing questions about what their insurance policies did and didn't cover when it came to cyber risk.

Conclusion

Does anyone reading this book honestly believe that their organization's use of technology will do anything except skyrocket in the coming years? Of course not. So it's reasonable to assume that since the bad actors aren't sitting still, your cyber risk profile is going to expand and deepen.

Cyber risk is not a problem you can solve with quick technology fixes. You need to have a smart, sober, responsible plan for mitigating cyber risk that integrates technology, process, and cyber insurance. Evaluating cyber risk on an ROI basis is, of course, smart and necessary. But be sure you consider the full impact of a cyber event on business resilience when deciding what role cyber insurance plays in your enterprise-wide risk mitigation and management strategy.

---

1   "NotPetya tops list of worst ransomware attacks," ComputerWeekly.com, October 31, 2017

2   Marsh Microsoft Global Cyber Risk Perception Survey, 2018

Cyber insurance is the yin to traditional insurance's yang. The latter enables a company to transfer the risk associated with physical perils, while cyber insurance responds to risk from non-physical perils arising from the ever-evolving nature of technology. Born during the dot.com bubble, cyber insurance now extends to cover a wide spectrum of liability and direct loss and has at its core the premise that all of a company's technology risk should be insurable.

Liability

The heart of liability insurance is coverage for harm that a company causes third parties. In the case of cyber insurance, the harm is caused by either a failure of the insured's computer security or a data or privacy breach, including things like wrongful collection or unauthorized access to confidential data, be it personal or commercial. If such allegations are made against an insured, the insurance will provide a defense of the claim as well as indemnifying the insured for any damages it may be legally liable for.

Regulatory

With the abundance of privacy and data breach regulations, including the recent coming online of GDPR, the insured will likely face a regulator or the obligations imposed by statute before they face a civil plaintiff. Cyber insurance provides legal counsel to assist in responding to a regulator's inquiry and in determining the extent of any obligation under the statute. Insurance can also cover fines and penalties assessed against the insured. The underlying thought here is to avoid a misstep that could come back to bite you later in any civil legal action.

Direct Loss

Cyber insurance indemnifies an insured for loss or damage to its digital assets, as well as loss of revenue and extra expenses incurred because of a computer security failure, or any technology failure not caused by a physical event. Loss of revenue can also be insured if the cause is a security or technology failure at a business that the insured depends upon in its operations, such as technology infrastructure vendors and an insured's supply chain. This aspect of coverage has been evolving the fastest lately, with some insurers now offering coverage for loss of revenue due to either a voluntary shutdown or the failing reputation in the wake of a cyber event impacting the insured. In addition, insurers have added coverage that touches upon the "physical" with indemnification for bricking losses.

Event Response Expenses

Cyber insurance is unique in that it assists the insured almost from the moment an event is discovered or suspected. An organization will incur significant out-of-pocket expenses investigating the cause and nature of a breach or failure, responding to the various regulatory obligations such as breach notification statutes, and addressing the associated reputational noise. The cyber insurance market has developed two approaches in this area. The first and more traditional being to provide indemnification for incurred expenses, with the insurers also providing an insured access to a panel of expert service providers. The second approach, more popular with smaller companies, is to essentially have the carrier's panel step in to manage the event for the insured, with the insurer dictating which providers are to be used.

Miscellany

In addition, cyber insurance indemnifies the insured if it is the victim of an extortion threat to cause an otherwise covered loss or liability. Cyber insurance also is adept at filling the vacuum created as traditional insurance lags behind or fails to keep pace with the evolving risk profile of the economy. Two recent examples are the extension of coverage for liability arising from a company's use of IoT technology and the risk associated with blockchain technology. Finally, cyber insurance also has expressly adapted to align with traditional insurance as losses become more nuanced, where a physical injury has some cyber aspect lurking in its chain of causation, to ensure that an insured can achieve the maximum recovery for the loss.

Technology

42

How You Should Use Cybersecurity Technology to Improve Business Outcomes

Naveen Zutshi — Senior Vice President and Chief Information Officer, Palo Alto Networks

Throughout this book, you've read great advice from smart people about cybersecurity, with a recurring theme: Cybersecurity is a business issue, not a technical one.

That's correct, of course. But it doesn't tell the entire story.

There's no longer any debate that cybersecurity must be addressed strategically and in a business context by executives and board members, in close concert with their CISO, CIO, and security operations (SecOps) teams. But when it comes to cybersecurity, technology does matter—a lot.

The right cybersecurity technology can prevent a vast majority of attacks, detect vulnerabilities quickly, mitigate cybersecurity risks, and enable security of strategic business initiatives like digital transformation. If done right, these business outcomes can be achieved without impeding the speed of delivery. Of course, that's not to say that wasting investment dollars on yet another point product, or hiring mediocre security operations personnel to manually monitor networks for aberrant data movement, is the way to go. Security threats are dynamic, fast moving, and can be highly unpredictable for legacy and manual approaches to keep up with. With an increasingly machine-based adversary, cybersecurity approaches that are manual, highly fragmented, and point-product-based are doomed to fail.

Instead, we need to take a different approach—one that embraces a comprehensive view of security architecture, with new technology assumptions to make our organizations more secure, even as we use technology to surface new business opportunities. While I won't subject you to a chapter riddled with terms like containerization, micro segmentation, serverless compute, or service provisioning, I do feel it is important for business leaders to understand that there are some critical technology shifts underway that can help us create a more agile, scalable, and modernized cybersecurity layer.

And if we don't make some important technology shifts, we will:

- Waste money.

- Divert badly needed manpower to perform manual tasks.

- Fail to keep up with the breakneck pace of new security risks.

Without a commitment to a new cyber-security technology paradigm, we will put our organizations in peril, causing irreparable damage to our brands and destroying our customers' confidence in our ability to protect them.

Let me explain why and how.

Delivering Speed and Agility— Securely

In the digital world, success requires organizational speed and agility—more than ever before, in fact. Every organization wants, and needs, to move faster and become nimbler in spotting and taking advantage of new business opportunities. Technology plays a key role in making that goal attainable, as many of us learned over the past few decades.

But for a long time, technology needed a large footprint in order to deliver business benefits. Big iron. Big applications. Big data centers. Big staff to monitor and manage networks. These big capital expenditure (Capex) investments and large IT/security workforces were often considered competitive differentiators for companies. Unfortunately, this legacy of "big technology and large workforce" has become a boat anchor, weighing down our organizations and restricting our ability to achieve speed and agility.

Fortunately, new solutions, such as cloud computing, Software as a Service, and anywhere/anytime connectivity, are changing the technology paradigm by delivering breakthrough capabilities faster, less expensively, and with a smaller technology footprint. Additionally, software-based automation has laid to waste the traditional approaches of problem solving and are significantly reducing the need for massive security operations centers (SOCs).

But with the adoption of any new technology comes risk—specifically, cybersecurity risk. Take cloud, for instance. It has changed the way we work, and we've only begun to scratch the surface. Earlier in this book, Ann Johnson of Microsoft called attention to the fact that cloud computing has quickly evolved from a useful tool to an essential one, and is now entering a transformative phase of its development that will accelerate the pace of change and increase our business opportunities.

And, as she said, it will also increase our cybersecurity risks. With public cloud, there is risk in assuming that, because you are using someone else's infrastructure, you don't have to secure it. This is a false, and potentially dangerous, notion. Public cloud requires a shared security model. This typically means that customers are responsible for security above the operating system, including all customer data and IP, and the public cloud provider provides security of the underlying hardware and infrastructure.

Additionally, in using public cloud, access control API keys can be easily discovered and used to compromise vast amounts of compute resources in minutes, since hackers have automated tools looking for those vulnerabilities within systems. They can then exploit them in ways ranging from bitcoin mining to much more nefarious means, such as stealing intellectual property or customer/employee data.

Like the public cloud, other ascendant technologies like SaaS, big data, machine learning, and increasingly connected Internet of Things devices, are today's double-edged sword: big benefits with big risks. This, in turn, has put great pressure on IT and security professionals to move quickly and embrace agility, while at the same time provide critical security safeguards. It's not easy. But it can be done.

Reject the Shiny Tool Syndrome

One of the big challenges in addressing these technologies is how quickly they are being implemented and how fast they are growing. Keeping up with the pace of innovation is becoming nearly impossible. Public-cloud feature development is a good example; AWS released over 497 features in their February 2018 quarterly launch.[1] And that's just one cloud provider.

Some security and IT professionals suffer from what I call the "shiny tool syndrome," while having a fear of missing out (FOMO) on all the new tools/features being developed. Unfortunately, the dirty little secret is that major cyberattacks happen due to poor cyber hygiene. Having legacy security architecture that is good on paper but doesn't prevent attacks, porous access control, and poor implementation of security controls will result in a broad attack surface that no new shiny tool will solve. Focusing first on basic blocking and tackling, like patch management, access control, service account rotation, certificate management, network segmentation, and others—while "uncool"—is a must. A strong, disciplined security process, coupled with an automated, software-based approach to security, one that is focused on solving for the right security outcomes will enable a stronger security posture and better position the company for today's and tomorrow's cybersecurity requirements.

Welcome to the Age of Software-Defined Security

Taking an automated, software-based approach to security is in keeping with one of the important trends rippling across the technology spectrum today, which is the shift to "software-defined" models. Software-defined is typically embodied as an algorithm or application programming interface. What we now call the "software economy," as well as traditional industries, is being disrupted by software-based approaches.

Industries thought to be untouchable, such as printing, taxi operations, hospitality, brick-and-mortar retail, and energy are being disrupted by the software economy. Traditional silicon-based approaches to security are being attacked as well. Having a software approach enables our two favorite requirements: speed and agility. Software-defined solutions can be deployed faster and provide organizations with the ability to deliver new business solutions in a more agile manner. And they provide additional important benefits, such as reduced reliance on Capex and a "light" management profile that doesn't require armies of technicians.

Today's cybersecurity solutions are fast joining the software-defined game, as well. Thanks to the development of powerful and adaptable machine learning tools based on the enormous amount of data being collected, cybersecurity defenses are increasingly shaped by software and the concepts of automation, integration, and cloud optimization. Software-defined security is designed and implemented with the understanding that automated, scalable, cloud-delivered security software now enables issues to be discovered and remediated in near real time. And as the incidences of zero-day attacks continue to increase, "real time" carries a whole new meaning and business impact. In addition, machine learning–based solutions are complementing rule-based software to further shorten the detection lifecycle of zero-day attacks and prevent them from causing havoc to our critical infrastructure. The futuristic vision of machines fighting machines may be a few years away, but it is increasingly advisable to choose a purely software-defined approach to security.

Software-defined security enables embedding security into the software lifecycle through automated security tests so development lifecycles can be iterative and fast. Additionally, Software-defined security empowers our employees to take more proactive roles in rooting out vulnerabilities and reducing risk. Our SOC team can do penetration testing to hunt for issues before they become problems and set up "honeypots" to attract threats and nip them in the bud. This is an entirely new model for cybersecurity—proactive, automated, and predictive, instead of reactive, manual, and based on "best estimates."

Another aspect of software-defined security is to buy security platforms that enable reinforced integrations (each integration improves the overall security posture), are scalable as companies grow, are consistent across cloud and on-premise implementation, and automate implementation, ongoing upgrade, and policy management.

By using software-defined security platform principles—which are going to be implemented in an agile, enterprise-wide platform, rather than a variety of point solutions for individual threats—organizations can scale security defenses in lockstep with the development of new environments for things like testing new business services or modeling assumptions on customer behavior or supply chain interruptions.

There's that speed and agility we talked about earlier. And that's what makes software-defined security a business issue, not just a technical issue. But it *is* really cool technology.

How Business Leaders Should Talk About Technology to the CISO

It's easy to equate business executives talking to technical leaders with what happens when we go to the doctor for a problem. When we experience sharp pain in our shoulder when working out at the gym, we don't want the orthopedist to give us the intimate details of the composition of the rotator cuff. We want to know how we can stop the pain and maintain our active lifestyles.

Business leaders obviously don't need to know—and certainly most of them don't want to know—about the technical underpinnings of their organizations' cyber defenses. They do want to know whether the CISO has taken the right defenses for known and anticipated risks, has the appropriate funding to ensure success, and has calibrated their cybersecurity with their risk/reward profile for new business opportunities.

When business executives talk with the CISO or CIO about cybersecurity technology, they shouldn't worry about which tools are being used as much as why and how those tools are delivering improved security outcomes. After all, business leaders understand risk, and they have all come around to the understanding that the right cybersecurity technology is an enabler to reduce risk while achieving strategic outcomes safely.

They also now know that the more manual your security processes are, it becomes exponentially harder to prevent new threat vectors from impacting the business, and it adds cost and complexity.

So, business leaders' conversations with CISOs—whether in the boardroom or impromptu in the hallway—should focus on issues like technical risk and technology process, rather than on trying to learn the language of bits, bytes, and bots.

For instance, business executives and board members should ask questions like:

- Do you believe you have the right security architecture in place for threats that have not yet impacted our business?

- Are your security teams embedded in the business and technology units, or are they sitting in ivory towers monitoring event logs?

- How are you quantifying risk, in terms of our core business assets? What is the financial impact of an hour of downtime after a hack?

- How are you minimizing the attack surfaces and points of compromise?

- What business service or product of ours are you most concerned about from a cybersecurity perspective (our crown jewels), and what are you doing about it?

- When we expand our corporate footprint through acquisition or market expansion, can we scale our existing security infrastructure without having to make huge new investments in Capex and staff?

- What is our optimal approach to adopting a new set of cybersecurity technologies—crawl, walk, or run? What are the trade-offs of each?

- Does our current security technology adequately protect us against potential problems with our cloud service providers or other third parties we connect with?

Conclusion

As I mentioned earlier in this chapter, organizations face an important challenge: how to achieve the goals of speed and agility, but in a safe and consistently secure manner. We all know that technology has become a critical catalyst for delivering speed and agility, as it has for ensuring rock-solid cybersecurity.

But can we use technology to achieve it all at the same time? Can we have our digital cake and eat it, too?

I believe we must. And, fortunately, I'm confident that we can. In fact, it's already happening at many enterprises around the world—enterprises whose business leaders and CISOs have modernized their approaches to cybersecurity technology in a software-defined, platform-driven model that prizes speed, agility, automation, and analytics.

Traditional approaches to cybersecurity—encounter a problem, buy some technology, plug the gap, then repeat—no longer work. They don't scale with the massive expansion of threats and vulnerabilities, and the resultant "security sprawl" is expensive, inefficient, and leaves too many gaps.

Organizations can move quicker and more securely than ever by re-imagining cybersecurity around software-based platforms that are easily deployed, cloud-powered for easy scalability and simple maintenance, and well-integrated into the core business processes.

And when they get to that state, they may even have gotten over the shiny object syndrome.

---

[1] "AWS Released 497 New Services And Features Last Quarter," AWS News, April 5, 2018

43

Harnessing the Power of Blockchain

Antanas Guoga — Member, European Parliament

Blockchain technology has the potential to change the world. It could be the foundation for building new levels of trust in elections, financial transactions, supply chain management, and the sharing of healthcare data. It could be used by political and government institutions to empower citizens. It could be, and probably should be, a vital part of the cybersecurity moonshot effort discussed by Mark McLaughlin at the beginning of this book.

A report from Santander InnoVentures predicts that blockchain technology could reduce the infrastructure costs of banks by up to $20 billion a year by 2022.[1] Capgemini has stated that blockchain technologies will enable consumers to reduce banking and insurance fees by $16 billion a year.[2] The market for blockchain in retail is expected to reach more than $2.3 billion in 2023, growing at a compound annual rate of 96.4%.[3] In the first five months of 2018, the dollar volume invested in blockchain companies reached nearly $1.3 billion, already surpassing the totals for the entire prior year.[4]

Clearly, the potential for blockchain is making it one of the most widely talked about technologies of our time. But it's one thing to talk about the potential of blockchain; we are approaching a new stage in the development of this exciting technol-

ogy. It is time to start adopting it into our lives—allowing it to shape today's digital economy into tomorrow's crypto economy and ensuring that blockchain can be used as a vital tool to build trust in applications and environments beyond the world of cryptocurrencies.

Understanding Blockchain Technology

Most people understand that blockchain is the technology behind Bitcoin. But, if asked to define what it actually is, they would be hard-pressed to give a clear answer. Here's a simple explanation, courtesy of *The New York Times*:

> The easiest and most basic way to think about the underlying technology is to think about a technology that keeps a master list of everyone who has ever interacted with it. It's a bit of an over-simplification, but if you've ever used Google Docs and allowed others to share the document so they can make changes, the programs keep a list of all the changes that are made to the document and by whom. Blockchain does that, but in an even more secure way so that every person who ever touches the document is trusted and everyone gets a copy of all the changes made so there is never a question about what hap-

pened along the way. There aren't multiple copies of a document and different versions—there is only one trusted document and you can keep track of everything that's ever happened to it.[5]

Blockchain as a distributed ledger technology, or DLT, when used properly, can have a profound impact on cybersecurity since it is, at its core, a secure database that is immutable and transparent. Bitcoin provides a perfect example of the potential: In the nine years of its formation, Bitcoin has successfully warded off all cybersecurity attacks—something no other online/digital entity can fully claim. Imagine how other industries can benefit from that level of trust and security in their transactions.

The Business Potential of Blockchain

Although the first historical use cases of blockchain have been the disintermediated exchange of virtual currencies, distributed ledger technologies can be applied to all industry and public sector activities. Multiple types of transactions can be recorded in a blockchain and various use cases can be implemented. For instance, it can be used:

- **In finance** for money transfer, peer-to-peer lending and transfer of securities.

- **By insurance companies** for automatic execution of contracts.

- **By governments** for citizens' ID management, taxation reporting, development aid management, e-voting, and regulatory compliance.

- **In healthcare** to track transactions on patients' health records and identification of access.

- **For media and intellectual property companies** to directly distribute loyalties to authors of music, videos, and other content.

- **For pharmaceutical companies** to verify the drug supply chain.

- **For retail companies** to verify proof of authenticity and origin, and to easily manage provenance supply chain.

The graphic below, from crowdfundinsider.com, provides a sense of the current use cases for blockchain technology.

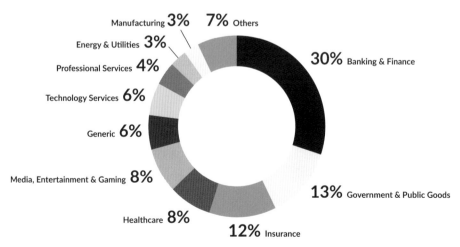

Manufacturing 3%   7% Others
Energy & Utilities 3%
Professional Services 4%
Technology Services 6%
Generic 6%
Media, Entertainment & Gaming 8%
Healthcare 8%
30% Banking & Finance
13% Government & Public Goods
12% Insurance

Note: This figure is based on a list of 132 use cases, grouped into industry segments, that have been frequently mentioned in public discussions, reports and press releases.

Figure 1: Breakdown of use cases of DTL (Real Estate applications fall under Others)

It is no surprise that banking and finance are leading the way in early adoption of blockchain technology. In the areas of banking, distributed ledger is incredibly useful because it keeps firms, individuals, and transactions on track and responsible. Blockchain provides financial institutions with a sense of security that was previously unattainable.

Blockchain Today

Blockchain is often compared to the beginning of the internet, when the potential was not fully understood or was subject to confusion by the large majority. Business models were unclear, regulatory frameworks were challenged by front-runners, and technical constraints hindered the uptake. Those who pioneered the internet and built long-term ecosystems, have been the big winners. That could be the case with blockchain now.

The biggest issue with blockchain today is scaling and cost. In order to better enable blockchain, we need to continue improving the technology. Blockchain is not a piece of code, it's an infrastructure and ecosystem of distributed applications as smart contracts. As long as it is built and audited properly and functions correctly, it will be successful. This includes the development of distributed information and communications technology (ICT) infrastructure and, most importantly, correct implementation to actually ensure that businesses remain compliant and aware of upcoming security issues.

Those provisos aside, there is a gold rush to blockchain because it has such vast potential to address today's most pressing cybersecurity challenges, creating a model for trust-based transactions that provide unmatched security to counter cyberattacks.

Moving Forward

I believe blockchain technology has much more to offer than just Bitcoin or cryptocurrencies. Apart from its main features of being efficient, transparent, secure and, more importantly, societal—its democratic aspects should be emphasized.

Blockchains bring to people the power to control data without the middlemen and cuts their service costs. Blockchain can also be a solution for secure and transparent e-voting, hence reducing the risk of ballot tampering or political persecution. This is the way that I believe the public's trust in governments and electoral systems can be restored.

We are already beginning to see how organizations plan to deploy blockchain technology in innovative use cases across the globe:

- In Australia, the Australian Securities Exchange is looking to replace its settlement system with a distributed ledger to improve efficiency and security in transmitting messages and accessing information. The managing director and CEO of the exchange's operator says moving to blockchain technology could save the exchange as much as $23 billion (AUS). The exchange is looking to roll out the system by the end of 2020.[6]

- In Canada, the National Research Council of Canada, through its Industrial Research Assistance Program, is already using blockchain technology to publish grant and contribution data. The government had identified a problem in that more than $300 million (CAN) worth of research grants were being issued every year. However, it was difficult to ensure that contracts were signed for each, to audit the total amount of grants issued, and make the information publicly accessible. Within the first week of launching the blockchain solution, the service had more than a million requests for information and, as of this writing, more than $500 billion of public spending has been disclosed.[7]

- In the Netherlands, numerous live projects have been presented, such as registering nursery childcare services on a blockchain; distributing and monitoring the use of the "Kindpakket," a social-benefit policy for children from low-income families; and trialing e-voting on a blockchain while keeping paper voting intact, in parallel.

- In my home country of Lithuania, the LB Chain initiative has been created by the Bank of Lithuania in response to demand for information and adoption. It will act as a safe technological sandbox environment, where domestic and foreign companies will be able to develop and test blockchain-based solutions in a regulatory and technological platform/service. The Bank of Lithuania has taken this strategic direction to accelerate development of a Fin-Tech-conducive regulatory and supervisory ecosystem, while still fostering innovation in the financial sector and positioning itself to be a world leader in FinTech.[8]

These are just few of many examples. A simple internet search will give you many more potential use cases to consider, as this innovative technology continues to roll out and make its impact around the world.

Advocacy for European Leadership

I have been, and continue to be, a strong advocate for Europe to take a leadership role in the development of blockchain. As of this writing we have more than 300 European startups in Europe, a number that will continue to grow as our ecosystem grows. The potential benefits for Europe are significant. In cooperation with the European Commission and other regulators we can:

- Support European industry, seizing the economic opportunity for more jobs and growth.

- Improve business processes in governments, companies, and organizations.

- Enable new, disintermediated business models based on direct peer-to-peer transactions, without the need for central platforms.

To achieve these benefits, the European Commission has already taken important actions, including:

- Active engagement in international standardization, such as the ISO technical Committee 307 on Blockchain and Distributed Ledger Technologies.

- Different H2020 Research & Innovation projects have been financed and will continue to be financed in different domains, such as eGovernment, eHealth, transport, energy, and finance. So far, 56M€ have been engaged by the EU in blockchain-related projects, and a potential of up to 340M€ could be engaged in 2018 and 2019.

- Proof-of-concept and pilot projects have been launched in the areas of regulatory compliance, tax and customs reporting, energy, and identity management.

In addition, during the first half of 2018, the European Commission has:

- Launched the EU Blockchain Observatory and Forum to map relevant blockchain initiatives, share experiences, and pool and develop expertise on blockchain at the EU level.

- Published the Fintech Plan, which aims to help the financial industry make use of rapid tech advancements, such as blockchain and other IT applications, and strengthen cybersecurity.

- Begun assessing the need for, and benefits of, an EU blockchain infrastructure. The feasibility study would be setting the right conditions for the advent of an open, innovative, trustworthy, transparent, and EU law-compliant data and transactional environment.

- Continued to engage with standards development organizations (ISO, ITU-T, potentially IETF, IEEE).

- Continued to support R&I projects in different areas.

- Supported other EU level projects: EFTG, Blockchain for Social Good Prize, PoC TAXUD (taxation and customs).

- Built on member states' initiatives to consolidate at the EU level.

A blockchain resolution was passed by the European Parliament's Industry, Research and Energy Committee on May 16, 2018. By the time this book is published, we hope it will have been approved by the entire Parliament. The motion for a resolution calls for open-minded, progressive, and innovation-friendly regulation of blockchain technology. The document looks at the implementation of blockchain technology, not only in the FinTech sector, but also at other sectors such as energy, healthcare, education, creative industries, and the public sector. This resolution is a strong position by the European Parliament, which shows that the EU wants to be a strong player in blockchain; therefore legal certainty is of utmost importance in order to secure blockchain-based projects and investments.

Numerous events on blockchain applications were organized at the European Parliament in 2018. And there is a great trend that the technology is acknowledged and better understood. The newest document to be discussed at the European Parliament is its own initiative report, "Blockchain: a Forward-Looking Trade Policy." Work on it is in progress in the International Trade Committee, as of this publication. The initiative report proposes to investigate in detail how trade agreements can facilitate the use of distributed ledger technologies and blockchain to underpin and streamline customs agreements. A key advantage of the application of blockchain in customs agreements is the potential to reduce fraudulent transactions. Therefore, the usage of a secure database could revolutionize the scope and security of international trade agreements. In addition, the report will assess the potential for the EU to use DLTs to develop secure "smart" contracts with trading partners in international trade agreements.

Even with all of that ongoing activity, I believe it is important to let the industry itself grow and see where it takes us. I am not a technologist, and neither are my fellow politicians. We don't know exactly where the technology will go. But we should all be open and aware—and we should definitely keep educating people on blockchain, cybersecurity, and related topics.

What's more, we should continue to fund these types of projects because it is more important to contribute than to actually make a profit. The smart young people who are creating and using this technology should be left alone and allowed to continue to advance the industry. Awareness should continue to be raised, and the technology should be given every opportunity to advance and flourish.

Conclusion

Blockchain technology has immense potential to solve real-world problems and create new types of organizational structures that can change the economic and power dynamics of traditional centralized bodies. The technology will give freedom to people's data and, therefore, stimulate new forms of democratic collective actions, security, trust, and transparency in daily activities. How far that potential and implementation goes is up to us and our ability to operate what the technology provides.

---

1 "Santander: Blockchain Tech Can Save Bands $20 Billion a Year," Coindesk, June 16, 2015

2 "How Blockchain is Changing Finance," Harvard Business Review, March 1, 2017

3 "Blockchain in Retail Market Worth 2339.0 Million USD by 2023," MarketsandMarkets, June 2018

4 "With at least $1.3 billion invested globally in 2018, VC funding for blockchain blows past 2017 totals," TechCrunch, May 20, 2018

5 "Dealbook: Demistifying the Blockchain," The New York Times, June 27, 2018

6 "ASX Head Says New DLT System Could Save Billions," Coindesk, August 16, 2018

7 Blockchain Conference: "Blockchain - Game Changer of the 4th Industrial Revolution," at the European Parliament https://www.youtube.com/watch?v=F7X9AS4AR9w&t=786s Intercontinental

8 "The Bank of Lithuania to launch blockchain sandbox platform-service," https://www.lb.lt/en/news/the-bank-of-lithuania-to-launch-blockchain-sandbox-platform-service

44

When It Comes to Shadow IT, What You Don't Know—and Don't Prepare for—Can Hurt You

Alice Cooper — Global Head of Derivative Trade Processing IT, BNP Paribas CIB

In a fast-paced and dynamic business environment, organizations depend more than ever on their IT teams as a source of growth, innovation, and competitive differentiation. With those escalating demands have come a tricky supply-and-demand balancing act: how to provide the IT services and resources needed by everyone, from business users all the way up to the corner office.

Many business users have grown frustrated and impatient because of a perceived inability of IT departments to meet their business needs with new systems, applications, and services in a timely, affordable manner. But the harsh truth is that everyone is clamoring for more support and collaboration from the IT organization at a time when IT budgets are not growing fast enough—and sometimes not at all—to keep up with skyrocketing and increasingly sophisticated user demands.

Perhaps even more important is the fact that IT hiring has flatlined in many industries, despite repeated requests for more programmers, application developers, systems analysts, data scientists, help-desk

technicians—and yes, more security professionals. So, since necessity is the mother of invention, the business users have come up with a simple solution: *"We'll do it ourselves."*

Why and How Shadow IT Took Hold

This trend, widely known as shadow IT, has become increasingly prevalent in enterprises of all sizes, industries, and geographies. Some organizations tacitly support the practice, while others are blithely unaware of its existence. Regardless, shadow IT has serious cybersecurity ramifications.

What exactly is shadow IT? Global IT consulting and research firm Gartner puts it succinctly:

"Shadow IT refers to IT devices, software, and services outside the ownership or control of IT organizations." [1]

Not that long ago, the notion of a shadow IT organization was preposterous. IT was a complicated discipline built upon in-depth, often arcane technical knowledge and access to expensive computing infrastructure. But that's changed dramatically. Today's workforce—and not just the millennials who were born seemingly tethered to their numerous Wi-Fi devices—is far more technologically adept and more comfortable writing applets, setting up wireless networks, deploying virtual machines, and putting in place digital sandboxes for short-term projects.

Then there's the cloud. Affordable, easily accessed cloud services have helped business users launch their own systems and procure IT services with a simple credit card transaction, all without the notice, review, approval, and control of the traditional IT organization.

As a result, shadow IT has not just become a big factor in how IT services are developed and deployed, but it also is an often-hidden development escaping the vision of IT and business executives. One study noted that 72% of companies don't know the scope of shadow IT at their organizations, *but want to.*[2] Another study pointed out a key reason for this disconnect: CIOs, on average, dramatically underestimate the number of cloud services running within their organizations. How dramatically? By a factor of more than 14 to 1.[3]

To many business executives and board members, the shadow IT movement seems like a smart, even necessary, workaround to a problem: the growing chasm between demand (for more IT services and solutions) and supply (of IT resources to get it all done). Initially, business leaders who were aware of this complaint from their business teams often applauded their creativity and innovation in finding organic, affordable solutions to their problem. This predisposition for "a bias for action" is, of course, widely supported and even encouraged by business leaders on their teams.

CIOs, CISOs, and other technical executives have been working feverishly to meet the growing demand for IT services and tools to help their organizations solve strategic problems, ranging from identifying new competitive threats and reducing global supply chain costs to mining troves of new data to make smarter, faster decisions. They want to help the organization succeed by leveraging technology for business benefit, and they want to collaborate with business colleagues to do that.

However, what once may have seemed like a creative way to bypass the IT bottleneck in the quest for digital transformation is now a problem. A big problem.

Shadow IT's Impact on Cybersecurity

Shadow IT dramatically expands an organization's cybersecurity threats in many ways and for many reasons. It's typically being done innocently enough, certainly without malevolent intent. But the impact can be really bad.

The reasons why shadow IT is so commonplace and so problematic today include:

- The dramatic growth of "bring your own device" policies (formal and otherwise), which have introduced a slew of unmanaged and either unprotected or under-protected devices on the wrong side of your firewalls.

- A lack of visibility into, and control of, inbound/outbound data traffic, often resulting in compromised data integrity and extensive data loss.

- The growing popularity of the Internet of Things, which manifests itself both in terms of new types of equipment that is often security-deficient and in "rogue" projects that, while exciting and full of business potential, can leak sensitive data like a sieve.

- An increasingly mobile/virtual workforce, where employees—as well as customers, suppliers, and partners—often access sensitive data over open networks that can easily be hacked.

As I mentioned earlier in this chapter, shadow IT often lurks under the radar of corporate IT, and thus is shielded from business executives and board members who ultimately bear responsibility for all cybersecurity problems.

Just how bad is the problem? I'll give you one example to let your imaginations run wild. A research study pointed out that 80% of IT professionals said their end users have gone around them to set up unapproved cloud services.[4] And do you want to know the really scary part? That data is five years old, taken at a time when cloud services were still in their infancy. You can only imagine how pervasive the problem is today—and will be in the future. The question is: What should you do about it?

Addressing the Cybersecurity Challenges of Shadow IT

Fortunately, there are some common-sense steps organizations can and should take to minimize the potential negative cybersecurity impact of shadow IT. While I don't think organizations should be taking draconian steps to curtail initiative and self-sufficiency of technically astute employees, there are some reasonable, collaborative approaches that can create stronger partnerships between enterprising business users and the security and IT professionals whose job it is to keep the organization's data and IT assets safe.

Of course, this also means that business leaders and boards must (A) acknowledge that the problem exists and that it has potentially devastating impact, and (B) lead the way in encouraging smart answers to the problem. Denial is not a solution.

But first, let's keep an important fact in mind: The end users themselves—your employees, primarily—are incredibly naïve as to the extent they are putting your organization at risk. They're not connecting the dots, despite the fact that this is a topic that is increasingly covered in news reports and is being talked about by others. Even though today's workers are very tech-savvy—especially the new generation of employees—they don't have a clue what happens when they open a gateway in any direction. It gives the bad guys the key to the house.

So, what is the best way to address this problem? Education? Audits? Penalties? Yes.

In my organization, we conduct mandatory cybersecurity training. That training has been extended to topics like shadow IT, so everyone knows when bad security hygiene is taking place and what its impact will be. Explain to your employees who are acting as "citizen developers" and are commissioning applications to be built what can happen.

I know that everyone will groan about adding training into employees' busy days, but those sessions don't have to be long. You can give people reading materials they can go through on their own time, but you have to have formal training programs on this, especially for new employees joining the organization. Testing is also a good step to ensure that users are fully conversant in policy goals and objectives.

There are times when penalties—such as shutting down rogue applications or access to certain cloud services—may be necessary. Your very clever people may know how to get around access controls or authentication, but do they know which actions are likely to open up the organization to bribery or blackmail threats? Do they realize the reputational damage that can result?

While we don't want to stifle innovation or discourage creative problem solving, organizations should send a zero-tolerance message. Your business units may be demonstrating initiative and even doing some very exciting work on their own, but if they are inviting in security risks, the downside can be much larger than the upside. Organizations can't afford to be naïve either about the incidence of shadow IT or its potentially catastrophic impact.

This should be part of every organization's risk tolerance profile: How much are we willing to let our employees do in order to get the work done?

Of course, that opens up another issue: The growing imbalance between what business units need in IT services and support, and what the IT organization is able to deliver. This is likely to raise some very challenging, yet important, discussions on budgets, manpower, use of outside contractors, and how to assess opportunity versus risk.

But we all have to understand and admit that until we address the root causes of shadow IT, we will never be able to solve the problem.

Conclusion

Despite many organizations' discomfort with shadow IT, I do not think executives should issue orders to outlaw the shadow IT. I know most organizations—if they are able to have very honest and open conversations with their teams—can highlight instances where enterprising employees working outside the sphere of the IT organization have done some things that resulted in a competitive advantage because they moved quickly and flexibly to take advantage of an opportunity.

Still, that doesn't mean you allow or look the other way on reckless behavior. You don't know for sure if it's reckless unless you understand what is happening and what the risk-to-reward ratio looks like. If you think you haven't been bitten by this problem yet, you either haven't been paying attention or you've been lucky. But I can promise you that your luck will not protect you from a data breach, a service interruption, a compliance violation, or a lawsuit.

As with so many things in today's business environment, it requires a real give-and-take among business users, IT, security, and business leaders. Once someone in your organization goes rogue and starts their own IT solution or service, it can lead to a lot of trouble if there is no discussion on the impact.

While it's true that talk is cheap, the cost of a cybersecurity problem is not.

---

1   Gartner IT Glossary, Shadow IT https://www.gartner.com/it-glossary/shadow

2   "Cloud Adoption Practices and Priorities," Cloud Security Alliance, 2015

3   "CIOs Vastly Underestimate Extent of Shadow IT," CIO magazine, 2015

4   "Security, Privacy, and the Shadowy Risks of Bypassing IT," Spiceworks, 2016

45

Unlocking Productivity With Security

Siân John, MBE — Chief Security Advisor, Microsoft

Mobile working has changed how organizations conduct business, from the development labs and the factory floor of the global supply chain all the way to the end customer. Mobile working and its facilitators—cloud computing, Internet of Things, and IT consumerization—have unleashed new waves of innovation that have resulted in new products and services, an empowered workforce, a streamlined global supply chain, and an engaged customer base.

But these and other mobile-centric developments have done something else: They've significantly expanded cybersecurity threat vectors and, in some cases, opened up vulnerabilities that are threatening to undermine our aspirations for agility, efficiency, and productivity. This is a common side effect of the move to a more digital and mobile world; we just need to be aware of and manage this risk if we are going to achieve our aspirations.

By now, you've undoubtedly picked up on the fact that I'm talking about "mobile working" rather than the more common "mobility" term. That's because I believe mobility has become synonymous with devices, and getting work done when away from a traditional fixed-point setting like an office is about much more than mobile devices.

For instance, so much of the flexibility, freedom, and balance now available to us in our work lives is driven not as much by small, lightweight devices as it is by the cloud. I'm sure that many of you reading this chapter were early adopters of tablets because they enabled you to leave your laptops at home when out and about while still remaining connected to business services. You could access your corporate email, search enterprise databases, or work on presentations or documents—thanks to the cloud.

So, as important as devices are in the overall process of mobile working, we must look at this trend as an ecosystem of devices, applications, workflows, and services.

Unfortunately, mobile working brings with it a host of new security threats that too many of our organizations have yet to confront, let alone overcome. It should surprise no C-level executive or board member to learn that Wi-Fi networks at the airport, sporting arena, or your local coffee shop are easy and frequent targets for cyber criminals.

Unless we commit to integrated security functionalities in our products, services, and workflows from the start, we will fail to achieve many of our most essential business goals. Conversely, if we pay attention to security from the start and design effective and efficient security safeguards into everything, we will unlock and unleash a wave of productivity never seen before.

Let me be clear about what I'm saying.

- Security is not an IT issue. It's a business issue, and it demands the support and leadership of business executives, IT and security professionals, board members, and end-user stakeholders.

- The financial cost of designing security into products, services, and workflows is far, far outweighed by both its long-term economic benefits and the resultant costs of remediating problems after the fact.

- Native security breeds confidence by all users, which in turn promotes productivity and delivers economic value.

We need to ensure we are living up to our own expectations of managing these issues.

What Secure Mobile Working Can Do for Productivity

It's important to understand and embrace the notion that you can't have productivity in mobile work without security—specifically, security integrated from the very beginning of product development or business-process creation.

Before mobile working became the accepted standard, employees were doing it any way they could to get the job done. But they did it by using personal email on personal devices, which do not have the same security levels as their work accounts. They could access sensitive data sent through email accounts or through personal subscriptions to public cloud services, for example looking at patient records over Gmail or searching intellec-

tual property drawings downloaded to a personal Dropbox account.

The ability to work anywhere at any time, to access data and applications from home or on the road, is central to worker productivity. We're now firmly entrenched in the era of non-traditional work hours, driven by such factors as a desire to juggle work and personal commitments, the realities of the global economy, and a need for many so-called knowledge workers to react instantaneously to a germ of an idea, to a spark of brilliance.

To do that, we must have native security in our devices, applications, and business processes. And if our organizations don't enact steps to bake in security from the start, the regulators will come knocking on our doors. The new Global Data Protection Regulation demands that we automatically do the things we should have been doing all along, in terms of protecting and managing personal information.

When it comes to secure mobile working, GDPR and other data protection mandates have simply increased the cost of doing nothing—which, in my view, is a very good thing.

Why You Can't Have Digital Transformation Without the Right Security for Mobile Work

If there's any term being bandied about by business executives more than "digital transformation," then I haven't heard it. By now, every business leader and board member has embraced the notion of using technology to further business goals, especially in retasking our bright, creative employees away from rote, repeatable activities that can easily be done by technology.

To further the goals of digital transformation, organizations should focus on three areas:

- More use of cloud platforms to accelerate the delivery of IT services for business aims.

- Customized, personalized computing built around mobile platforms to drive greater employee engagement.

- Improved productivity through the paradigm shift that is mobile working.

And to accomplish all of that, organizations must acknowledge that traditional security controls and procedures were not built in anticipation of digital transformation and all its components.

Too many organizations still cling to the concepts of strong physical boundaries that promote routing back through the physical network, rather than extending the perimeter to the cloud. By embracing the cloud as a tenet of mobile working, organizations optimize security risk management by leveraging the investments, knowledge, and ability to experiment—safely—of cloud service providers.

Done properly, digital transformation is more easily attained when security issues are anticipated and integrated in advance, rather than after a security problem arises. And it's important to keep in mind that organizations are only going to embrace digital transformation if their customers truly trust it. For this reason, the cybersecurity office should be considered an essential part of any digital transformation team; too often, they are left to the end of the process.

Enabling Security Professionals to Think About Mobile Work Outcomes, Not Security Outcomes

When security is baked into products, services, or business processes to support mobile working, everything starts with the consideration of how security affects business outcomes. Although we are fast moving away from old practices of "bolting on" security after the fact, it still happens far too often.

This is a crucial role for business leaders—to whom the CISO typically reports—and board members who naturally want to empower their employees to work in a way that engages them. And it all starts with analyzing business risk, though doing so can't be the sole domain of the business teams; it must include security professionals.

Business leaders need to consider the following steps (which your security team can definitely help accomplish):

- **Assess the possible threats that your industry and organization are exposed to.** A number of possible threats will already be known. However, executive support is needed to enable the security team to gain additional knowledge from cyber threat intelligence-sharing organizations (such as UK Cyber Information Sharing Partners and TruSTAR), as well as collaborating with law enforcement agencies.

- **Understand how identified threats could impact your intended business outcomes.** These could include flexible working arrangements, data analytics, global collaboration, productivity, employee empowerment, or more. It's essential to support your security teams' efforts in understanding how your business works; and in turn, how business units are affected by cyber risk, not just from a technical perspective but also from a user or operational standpoint.

- **Define how you can address the threats you are exposed to, whilst still achieving the business outcomes.** Ensure this happens from a people, process, and technology perspective and is articulated so all areas of the business can understand what they would need to do differently, and why.

- **Determine what type of digital transformation is needed for your security procedures so that your organization is protected as you change approaches.** If the suggestion is to buy more security products, ensure that you ask what impact they will have on your employees. Will it make it easier for them to follow procedures intuitively—has this been tested with users? Is there a cloud solution that can be deployed very quickly and easily maintained, rather than the protracted route of traditional software?

- **Ask how you can keep yourself up to date about the latest risks and threats and ensure that you are able to respond to them in a timely manner.** Make sure the previous four steps are a continuous loop to ensure that decisions are always being made to maintain security and risk management, as well as productivity.

Improving the Mobile User Experience With Security—Without Compromising Your Defenses

Striking the delicate balance between airtight security and worker flexibility and engagement is harder than ever in the era of mobile working. Users will look for the path of least resistance and for shortcuts to bypass what they consider to be cumbersome, annoying, and invasive procedures for authentication and access management. And they won't hold back in sharing that with their colleagues.

There are questions that board members and executives can ask to understand what can be done to strike the right balance between airtight security and mobile working within their own organization:

- **How easy is it for a user to access applications, services, and data?** You should find that by making user access simple and intuitive, you improve your security posture. More than likely, your CISO has deployed multifactor authentication (MFA) to reduce the risk of identity theft and ensure proper access to data. One key change could be to eliminate passwords as the authentication method of choice. While passwords may continue to be used in some MFA protocols, look at other approaches, such as biometrics or single sign-on using mechanisms such as Apple FaceID and Windows Hello.

- **What reasonable controls do we have in place to detect unusual and unusually high data movement?** This pattern could indicate that users are working outside of security controls. What type of data is it affecting and does that increase our risk exposure? Are there patterns in the type of data moved or applications being accessed that indicate users are working around security controls? What actions have we taken to mitigate that?

- **How do we enable collaboration while protecting information?** This is particularly important—given the widespread use of third-party relationships in daily business activities—in order to ensure that only the right people can access sensitive data.

- **Are we able to detect and respond to threats across the full enterprise ecosystem?** Devices, identities, cloud services, data, and more all must be protected in order to enable operational efficiencies and productivity, without introducing unacceptable levels of risk.

- **What security outcomes do we need to see?** Do we need to adjust our existing controls to enable productivity and mobile working, but still maintain our risk management levels?

- **What about our cloud service providers' risk management and security procedures?** With the continued uptick in cloud services adoption, organizations need to ensure that those providers have put in place the proper risk safeguards and strong controls to enable and protect identity, information, and the entire organization's digital profile.

Finally, ask your security team: Have you fully considered how cloud services and mobile working affects our risk and threat management models? Be sure your security team has tested its controls for usability on mobile devices and cloud services, and ask if they have taken all necessary steps to achieve the visibility and control needed for those environments, without impacting productivity.

In short, good security and a positive user experience are not mutually exclusive—not unless you make them so. Please don't.

Conclusion

We have only scratched the surface when it comes to the benefits of mobile working, and integrated, native security is a big reason why this trend will only accelerate. As we increasingly adopt over-the-top communications services, security will be assumed by users from the start. This will make mobile work a natural extension of the entire work experience and dramatically increase technology.

We must rapidly and zealously continue to move past the old paradigm when security—often in the form of frequent logins, repetitive identity verifications, and clunky passwords changed far too often—inhibits productivity. And adopting the right security practices and solutions for mobile working can prevent the need to lock down and route traffic in ways that result in unacceptable latency and deployment issues.

Instead, built-in security will make users—employees, customers, and all participants in the digital ecosystem—more confident in using technology for mobile working. And while this is great for our workers, it will undoubtedly be our enterprises that will benefit to the greatest extent.

Conclusion

46

How We Can Change Our Approach to Cybersecurity Today

Nir Zuk – Founder and Chief Technology Officer, Palo Alto Networks

One of the main goals of this book, *Navigating the Digital Age, Second Edition,* has been to foster a deeper understanding about cybersecurity between technical and non-technical executives. As the founder of several cybersecurity technology companies, including Palo Alto Networks, I have had the opportunity to straddle both worlds, coming from a background as a technologist and subsequently dealing with the challenges involved in building a successful business and creating a dynamic corporate culture.

When it comes to cybersecurity, I see the world from both the technology and business sides. From either perspective, I see challenges—and opportunities—when I look at the approach that most organizations take to cybersecurity today. The fundamental challenge is that our approach to cybersecurity is too reactive and the mechanisms we have in place are typically too slow and inefficient to react.

As our adversaries innovate faster, we fall behind, coming up with fixes for individual threats, but failing to create a sustainable platform to consume innovation quickly and efficiently. Our adversaries are innovating weekly, and it takes us months, if not years, to deploy a new reactive response. Too often, we maintain a mindset of using humans to fight machines, when we should have long since transitioned to a model of fighting machines with machines. If we don't address these challenges now, they will only get worse as our adversaries up the ante by using technology advances such as automation, machine learning, and artificial intelligence.

That's the bad news. The good news is that we can fix this. We can build cybersecurity into our technologies, products, services, and corporate cultures. We can make cybersecurity a business enabler. We can create a model of cybersecurity innovation that goes a long way toward addressing the "cybersecurity moonshot" challenges articulated at the start of this book by my friend and colleague, Mark McLaughlin.

We can fix it, and we will fix it. Here's how.

Challenge No. 1: Inefficient Consumption

The way cybersecurity has worked, thus far, is a vicious cycle that keeps adversaries one step ahead: Cybercriminals innovate quickly and come up with new mechanisms to cause more damage and make more money. Then cybersecurity companies, often led by innovative startups, develop solutions to stop those specific attack mechanisms. These new solutions usually take months to evaluate and deploy and, when they are finally deployed, they add to cybersecurity complexity.

As this cycle has evolved, our defense mechanisms have become cumbersome and inefficient. Companies now typically have dozens and sometimes hundreds of different cybersecurity solutions, which don't necessarily work in concert but rather in silos. The organization is paying to support and maintain these solutions, plus incurring costs to upgrade and replace them.

Challenge No. 2: Humans vs. Machines

Not only are we consuming cybersecurity innovation inefficiently; we continue to approach cybersecurity from the wrong mindset. In today's era, with automation, machine learning, and AI, if the battle is man against machine, machine will have the upper hand almost every time. We can't bring humans to that fight and expect to win.

Machines scale much quicker than humans. Whatever the human capacity may be—whether each person can deal with five security events, or 50 or 500—when the adversary is automated, it can always overcome that number simply by throwing more computing resources at the problem.

From the adversary's perspective, success is a function of compute, efficiency, automation, and ultimately money. As a defender, if you are relying on people to fight this battle, then you have to scale with people. So every time the adversaries add more compute power, you may need to increase the size of your team. Of course, then the adversaries just go out and spend a few more dollars to get more compute power.

There's no possible way to keep up, either logistically or financially. On the adversary side, growth is becoming exponential because of the easy availability of compute resources. Not only can they go to the public cloud to get compute resources; they are also stealing them from their victims, taking over our end-user machines, servers, or anything else they can use on the cheap and on the sly.

Today, we have humans in our security operations centers (SOCs), fighting machines with the help of machines. We have to shift the paradigm and have machines fighting against machines, with humans to help the machines. Whenever a machine can't do something, it can use a human.

The Opportunity: A Better Approach to Consuming Innovation

The technology to address these challenges is available today, right now. There are between 2,000 and 3,000 cybersecurity vendors out there and, contrary to popular wisdom, we don't need consolidation. Consolidation is not good for innovation. In fact, I would argue that we need *more* vendors and *more* innovation.

What we need is a better approach to *consuming* that innovation. And we need you, as a business executive, to demand it. *Now!* If your CISO or security team seeks to buy a cybersecurity solution that will be deployed in a few months or a year, you have to challenge their basic premise. Here's what CEOs, CIOs, and board members should demand:

1. Any new cybersecurity solution must be deployed in a day—preferably less than a day—across the entire infrastructure globally.

2. Any new cybersecurity solution cannot come with the requirement to hire more people.

3. Our entire cybersecurity team must demonstrate an accelerated rate of deploying innovation. The bad guys are moving fast; we must be moving just as fast.

At first, your CISO and security teams may be flustered because these demands fall so far out of the paradigm of how they've been doing things for so many years. That's okay, because the old paradigm is broken. Your cybersecurity professionals need to go to their vendors with the same demands: Find us a way to respond to this challenge, to deploy cybersecurity innovation quickly, efficiently, openly, and comprehensively.

Cybersecurity Innovation Through SaaS

What constitutes a better approach to consuming cybersecurity innovation? In today's world, software-as-a-service (SaaS) is the most efficient way to consume IT resources and innovation. We've seen the SaaS model work across many business functions: customer relationship management (CRM); salesforce management; human resources; enterprise resource planning; email; file sharing; and instant messaging.

All of these activities have either moved to a SaaS model or are moving quickly in that direction. That's because SaaS enables innovation to be consumed easily and quickly. Thus, the answer to the earlier question about addressing the challenges to our cybersecurity approach is the same for cybersecurity as it is for all of these

other business activities: We transform cybersecurity to a SaaS model.

If you look at most SaaS solutions, all you need to consume them is a web browser, and your access to innovation is immediate. Cybersecurity needs to be consumed just as easily. However, cybersecurity poses a different challenge than most of those other business activities because of the necessary evil of having the technology deployed within the infrastructure. The only way to get information from the infrastructure and to act on it, is to be part of the infrastructure. This goes for data centers, public clouds, and even end user-devices. So, whichever SaaS cybersecurity solutions are deployed, they have to be deployed simultaneously at every single location.

Cybersecurity as a Platform

The answer to that challenge is actually quite simple: Cybersecurity as a platform. Look at some of the most successful IT platforms: Apple, Windows, Facebook, Salesforce.com They provide a simple way to both provide and consume innovation by having an open platform that basically allows anyone with a good idea to come in and sell it. With a platform, the ability to deliver value and innovation becomes near instantaneous.

A platform is when the economic value of everybody that uses it exceeds the value of the company that creates it. Then, it's a platform. — Bill Gates

As our adversaries become better funded, more sophisticated, and more adept at leveraging automation, machine learning, and IT, we must fix the fundamental flaws in our security approach, and we must do it now. We must be able to consume cybersecurity in a way that enables us to deploy innovation quickly and fight machines with machines.

Cybersecurity has to become a set of services that you consume, rather than a set of technologies you deploy in networks, on endpoints, and in data centers. As we continue our journey in navigating the Digital Age, a platform is the path to get from here to there, to change forever the model for consuming cybersecurity services and innovation. It is the future of cybersecurity. And, as Pablo Emilio Tamez Lopez said so well at the beginning of this section: The future is now.

Looking Ahead

I am going to refrain from getting into the technical details of how a cybersecurity SaaS platform model can work. Your cybersecurity professionals should be able to explain the details to you. I will say this: Think about this with a sense of urgency. Your adversaries aren't waiting, so you can't afford to wait either.

We are now at the end of our book and, if you've read all, most, or even some of the preceding chapters, you can't help but conclude that cybersecurity is one of the defin-ing issues of our time, not just in business, but in the world at large. As Mark McLaughlin states in the opening chapter:

Whether we come from business and industry, academia or government, we all, as entrusted leaders, have a vested stake in protecting our way of life in the Digital Age. If we do our jobs well, we can change the world for the better.

You are on the frontlines. You are in a position to *take action:* whether it is setting the tone in your organization, pushing your teams to deploy a SaaS cybersecurity model, creating training and awareness programs, participating with government officials on regulation, or advocating for a cybersecurity moonshot.

There's much work to be done. Now is the time to act. In some ways, it seems like the Digital Age has been with us forever. In other ways, it seems all brand new. For all of us, there is still within our grasp the time and the opportunity to help build a better world. Let the journey continue.

Contributor Profiles

Contributor Profiles

Matt Aiello — United States of America
Partner
Heidrick & Struggles

Matt Aiello is Partner in Heidrick & Struggles' Menlo Park, California, office, where he specializes in the placement of senior-level technology, security, engineering, and operations executives. He leads the firm's Cybersecurity Practice and is a member of the Global Technology and Services Practice and the Global Information Technology Officers Practice.

Dr. Philipp Amann — Netherlands
Head of Strategy
Europol's European Cybercrime Centre (EC3)

Dr. Philipp Amann is Head of Strategy of Europol's European Cybercrime Centre (EC3), which is responsible for the delivery of strategic, situational, and tactical cyber-related products such as the Internet Organised Crime Threat Assessment. Prior to EC3, Philipp held management positions with the Organisation for Security and Cooperation in Europe, the Organisation for the Prohibition of Chemical Weapons, and the International Criminal Court.

Mark Anderson — United States of America
President
Palo Alto Networks

Mark Anderson is President of Palo Alto Networks, responsible for driving all sales, go-to-market, support, customer satisfaction, and business and corporate development. When he joined the company in 2012, and prior to becoming President in August 2016, Mark served as the company's Senior Vice President of Worldwide Field Operations. He has also held sales leadership positions at F5 Networks, Lucent Technologies, RadioFrame Networks, Cisco, and Comdisco.

Brad Arkin — United States of America
Vice President and Chief Security Officer
Adobe

Brad Arkin is Vice President and Chief Security Officer at Adobe, ultimately responsible for all security-related decisions and investments across the company. He previously held management positions at Symantec, @ Stake, and Cigital.

Kal Bittianda — United States of America
Head of North America Technology Practice
Egon Zehnder

Kal Bittianda heads Egon Zehnder's North American Technology Practice, where he works with companies in the mobility, communications, systems, software, and technology-enabled services sectors. Previously, he led business units at Kyriba, EXL, and Inductis.

Gary A. Bolles — United States of America
Chair, Future of Work at Singularity University;
Co-founder, eParachute.com; Partner, Charrette;
Speaker & Writer

Gary A. Bolles is an internationally recognized expert and lecturer on the future of work and learning. His focus is on strategies for helping individuals, organizations, communities, and countries to thrive in the digital work economy. He is a partner in the boutique consulting agency Charrette LLC, Chair for the Future of Work for Singularity University, and co-founder of eParachute.com.

Michal Boni — Belgium and Poland
Member
European Parliament

Michal Boni has been a Member of the European Parliament since 2014, and is currently Vice Chair of Delegation to the EU-Moldova Parliamentary Association Committee. He is an active member of several governmental committees, including: the Civil Liberties, Justice and Home Affairs; and the Constitutional Affairs and Delegation to the Euronest Parliamentary Assembly. Michal was Poland's Minister of Administration and Digitization from November 2011 to November 2013, has been a member of the Cabinet of Poland, and served in the lower house of the Polish Parliament and as the Minister of Labor and Social Policy.

Robert Boyce — United States of America
Managing Director, Accenture Security
Accenture

Robert Boyce is Managing Director of Accenture Security. Robert is responsible for the growth and development of Accenture's Cyber Threat Operations capabilities. He also provides hands-on consulting services to the Global 2000 in the areas of advanced security operations, crisis preparedness and response, and cyber defense and protection strategies.

Mario Chiock — United States of America
Schlumberger Fellow and CISO Emeritus
Schlumberger

Mario Chiock is a Schlumberger Fellow and former Chief Information Security Officer, where he was responsible for developing Schlumberger's worldwide cybersecurity strategy. He is widely recognized for his leadership and management in all aspects of cybersecurity. Mario serves on the advisory boards of Palo Alto Networks, Onapsis, and Qualys.

Gavin Colman — United Kingdom
Partner
Heidrick & Struggles

Gavin Colman is Partner in Heidrick & Struggles' London office and a member of the Cybersecurity and the Global IT Practices. He works with companies across various sectors to fill such senior roles as CISO, CIO, and CTO, and with technology companies to fill a broad range of executive roles.

Alice Cooper — United Kingdom
Global Head of Derivative Trade Processing IT
BNP Paribas CIB

Alice Cooper is Global Head of Derivative Trade Processing IT at BNP Paribas CIB. She has held a wide range of responsibilities at BNP Paribas across a number of IT functions for trades processing, credit, and equity. Previously, she worked at Mitsubishi Bank and Citibank.

Tom Farley — United States of America
Former President
New York Stock Exchange

Tom Farley is the former President of the NYSE Group. Tom joined the NYSE when ICE acquired NYSE Euronext in 2013, and served as its Chief Operating Officer. He has held several leadership positions, including Senior Vice President of Financial Markets at ICE, President and Chief Operating Officer of ICE Futures U.S., President of SunGard Kiodex, and various positions in investment banking at Montgomery Securities and in private equity at Gryphon Investors. Tom holds a BA degree in Political Science from Georgetown University and is a Chartered Financial Analyst.

George Finney — United States of America
Chief Security Officer
Southern Methodist University

George Finney is the Chief Security Officer for Southern Methodist University and the author of *No More Magic Wands: Transformative Cybersecurity Change for Everyone.* He previously worked with several startups and global telecommunications firms. George is a member of the Texas CISO Council, a governing body member of the Evanta CISO Coalition, a board member of the Palo Alto Networks FUEL User Group, and an advisory board member for SecureWorld.

Ryan Gillis — United States of America
Vice President for Cybersecurity Strategy and Global Policy
Palo Alto Networks

Ryan Gillis is Vice President for Cybersecurity Strategy and Global Policy at Palo Alto Networks. He has also held leadership positions in cybersecurity at the U.S. National Security Council and the Department of Homeland Security.

Marc Goodman — United States of America
Author and Global Security Advisor

Marc Goodman is the author of *Future Crimes: Everything Is Connected, Everyone Is Vulnerable and What We Can Do About It*. He is a leading speaker, author, and global strategist on the impact of technology on all aspects of our society. He also is a former law enforcement official and has consulted for such organizations as the FBI, Interpol, and NATO.

Mark Gosling — United States of America
Vice President, Internal Audit
Palo Alto Networks

Mark Gosling is Vice President of Internal Audit at Palo Alto Networks. He has previously held internal audit, compliance, and risk and controls leadership roles at Pricewaterhouse Coopers, Verisign, and NetApp.

Antanas Guoga — Belgium and Lithuania
Member
European Parliament

Antanas Guoga is a member of the European Parliament, EPP group, and a widely respected entrepreneur who has founded a number of successful international companies. He is also a committed philanthropist and former professional poker legend. He was a shadow rapporteur for the Network and Information Security Directive, organizing numerous events and consultations with stakeholders on cybersecurity in the European Parliament. With Blockchain Centre Vilnius, he was responsible for the first international blockchain technology center in Europe, connecting Asian and Australian blockchain centers.

Justin Harvey — United States of America
Managing Director, Accenture Security
Accenture

Justin Harvey is Managing Director of Accenture Security, with responsibilities for Global Incident Response and the Cyber Fusion Center Consulting Practice. In his role, he provides security thought leadership as a strategic advisor on cyber espionage, cyber war, and cybercrime. Justin previously held senior positions at Fidelis Cybersecurity, HP/ArcSight, CPSG Partners Consulting, and Mandiant/FireEye.

William Houston — United States of America
Advisor, Technology and Communications & Industrial Practices
Egon Zehnder

William Houston is an Advisor in Egon Zehnder's Technology and Communications & Industrial Practices. He previously worked in Google's Emerging Business Development Group and has held senior positions at the U.S. Department of Homeland Security and in U.S. Cyber Command.

Salim Ismail — Canada
Founder, ExO Foundation; Board Member, XPRIZE

Salim Ismail is the best-selling author of *Exponential Organizations*; he is also a sought-after business strategist and renowned entrepreneur with ties to Yahoo, Google, and Singularity University. Salim founded ExO Works in 2016 to transform global business by catapulting organizations into the world of exponential thinking.

Paul Jackson, GCFE — Hong Kong
Managing Director, Asia-Pacific Leader, Cyber Risk
Kroll

Paul Jackson is Managing Director and Asia-Pacific Leader for Cyber Risk at Kroll. He has worked in close concert with such leading organizations as Interpol, the U.S. Secret Service Electronic Crimes Task Forces, and Microsoft's Digital Crimes Consortium. Paul spent 22 years with the Hong Kong Police Force, eventually becoming Chief Inspector and Head of the IT Forensics Practice. He also has held leadership posts at J.P. Morgan Chase bank.

Siân John, MBE — United Kingdom
Chief Security Advisor
Microsoft

Siân John is Chief Security Advisor for the UK in the Enterprise Cybersecurity Group at Microsoft. She previously held a number of senior roles at the Houses of Parliament, Ubizen, and Symantec. She is the Chair of the Digital Economy Program Advisory Board for the Engineering and Physical Sciences Research Council and is Chair of the TechUK Cybersecurity Management Committee. Siân was made a Member of the Most Excellent Order of the British Empire (MBE) for Services to Cyber Security in the New Year's Honours List for 2018.

Ann Johnson — United States of America
Corporate Vice President, Cybersecurity Solutions
Microsoft

Ann Johnson is Corporate Vice President, Cybersecurity Solutions at Microsoft. She previously was CEO at Boundless, an open-source geospatial solutions company, and COO at Qualys, a leading supplier of cloud security and compliance solutions. She also has held executive positions at RSA and EMC.

John Kindervag — United States of America
Field Chief Technology Officer
Palo Alto Networks

John Kindervag is Field Chief Technology Officer at Palo Alto Networks. Previously, he was Vice President and Principal Analyst on the Security and Risk Team at Forrester Research. John is considered one of the world's foremost cybersecurity experts, and is best known for creating the revolutionary Zero Trust Model of Cybersecurity. John holds numerous industry certifications and a Bachelor of Arts degree in Communications from The University of Iowa.

Heather King — United States of America
Chief Operating Officer
Cyber Threat Alliance

Heather King is Chief Operating Officer for the Cyber Threat Alliance, a not-for-profit organization that brings together cybersecurity providers to improve the cybersecurity of the digital ecosystem. She also held senior roles for cybersecurity policy at the U.S. National Security Council and other federal agencies.

Mischel Kwon — United States of America
Founder and Chief Executive Officer
MKACyber

Mischel Kwon is Founder and Chief Executive Officer of MKACyber, a managed security operations provider and security consulting firm. Mischel has been in the IT and security field for 36 years. She has served as Vice-President for Public Sector Security at RSA Security, Director for US-CERT, and Deputy Director for IT Security Staff at the U.S. Department of Justice.

Selena Loh LaCroix — United States of America
Global Lead, Technology and Communications Practice
Egon Zehnder

Selena Loh LaCroix is the Global Lead of Egon Zehnder's Technology and Communications Practice, with a focus on semiconductors, smart devices, and cybersecurity. She previously practiced law in private practice at Gray Cary Ware & Freidenrich (now DLA Piper) and held legal leadership positions in-house at Texas Instruments and Honeywell International.

Gerd Leonhard — Switzerland
Author; Executive "Future Trainer;" Strategist;
Chief Executive Officer, The Futures Agency

Gerd Leonhard is an influential and best-selling author of *Technology vs. Humanity* and several other books. He is a sought-after executive "future trainer," a trusted strategic advisor to Fortune 1000 companies and government officials around the globe, and the CEO of The Futures Agency, a global network of over 30 leading futurists.

Pablo Emilio Tamez López — Mexico
Chief Information Security Officer
Tecnológico de Monterrey

As Chief Information Security Officer of Tecnológico de Monterrey, Pablo Tamez Lopez is responsible for the security of all its institutions, which includes Higher Education and Healthcare. Pablo has designed and led the organization's cybersecurity strategy, which includes workforce consolidation, security technologies and services, security operation center, and incident response.

Gary McAlum — United States of America
Chief Security Officer and Senior Vice President
for Enterprise Security
United States Automobile Association

Gary McAlum is Chief Security Officer and Senior Vice President for Enterprise Security at United States Automobile Association. He previously spent 25 years in the United States Air Force, where he held various staff and leadership positions in cybersecurity, information technology, telecommunications, and network operations.

Diane E. McCracken — United States of America
Banking Industry Executive Vice President and Chief Security Officer

Diane E. McCracken is the Executive Vice President and Chief Security Officer of a mid-sized bank located in the northeastern United States. Her office includes cyber, information, application, and physical security, as well as business continuity and disaster recovery. She moved to information security in 2004 as a security analyst with a super-regional bank and joined her current firm in 2011 as its information security leader.

Mark McLaughlin — United States of America
Vice Chairman
Palo Alto Networks

Mark McLaughlin is Vice Chairman of Palo Alto Networks, where he previously served as Chief Executive Officer and Chairman. He was previously President and CEO of Verisign and, prior to that, held senior positions at Signio and Gemplus. For nearly a decade, Mark has been a member of the National Security Telecommunications Advisory Committee, serving terms as Chairman and Vice-Chairman.

Danny McPherson — United States of America
Executive Vice President and Chief Security Officer
Verisign

Danny McPherson is Executive Vice President and Chief Security Officer at Verisign. Previously, he was Chief Security Officer at Arbor Networks, and he has held technical leadership positions at organizations such as Qwest Communications, MCI Communications, and the U.S. Army Signal Corps.

Stephen Moore — United States of America
Vice President and Chief Security Strategist
Exabeam

Stephen Moore is the Vice President and Chief Security Strategist at Exabeam, focused on driving solutions for threat detection/response and advising customers on breach response. Prior to joining Exabeam, Stephen has held a variety of cybersecurity practitioner and leadership roles. He spends his free time advising industry-leading organizations, mentoring, and helping those in need.

Robert Parisi — United States of America
Managing Director and U.S. Cyber Product Leader
Marsh

Robert Parisi is Managing Director and U.S. Cyber Product Leader for Marsh. Previously, he was Senior Vice President and Chief Underwriting Officer of eBusiness risk solutions at AIG, and was legal counsel for several Lloyds of London syndicates.

Sherri Ramsay — United States of America
Cybersecurity Consultant; Former Director of the U.S. National Security Agency / Central Security Service Threat Operations Center

Sherri Ramsay is the former Director of the U.S. National Security Agency / Central Security Service Threat Operations Center. She currently works as a consultant, engaged in strategy development and planning and development of security operations centers. She is a member of the Board of Advisors for the Hume Research Center at Virginia Tech and a member of the Board of Advisors for TruSTAR Technology.

Max Randria — Australia
Principal
Heidrick & Struggles

Max Randria is Principal in Heidrick & Struggles' Melbourne office and a member of the Global Technology and Services Practice. He is the Australia and New Zealand lead for Heidrick & Struggles' Cybersecurity Practice, having led numerous C-level searches across the cybersecurity landscape.

Mark Rasch — United States of America
Cybersecurity and Privacy Attorney

Mark Rasch is a cybersecurity and privacy attorney with more than 25 years of experience in corporate and government cybersecurity, computer privacy, regulatory compliance, probabilistic risk assessment, resilience, computer forensics, and incident response. Earlier in his career, Mark was with the U.S. Department of Justice, where he led the department's efforts to investigate and prosecute cyber and high-technology crime, starting the computer crime unit within the Criminal Division's Fraud Section.

Yorck O.A. Reuber — Germany
Head of Infrastructure Services & CTO, North Europe
AXA IT

Yorck O.A. Reuber is Chief Technology Officer for AXA IT, heading the domain Infrastructure in Northern Europe. His responsibilities include all central infrastructure, as well as the transformation to an agile, digital company that uses multi-cloud scenarios and services its IT globally. A certified Navy Chief Engineering Officer, Yorck formerly held senior-level positions at IBM, Verizon, and T-Systems.

Dr. Andreas Rohr — Germany
Chief Technology Officer
Deutsche Cyber-Sicherheitsorganisation GmbH (DCSO)

Dr. Andreas Rohr is Founding Manager and Chief Technology Officer at the Deutsche Cyber-Sicherheitsorganisation GmbH (DCSO). In this role, he leads cyber defense services and security engineering for the operative business. Previously, he worked in management positions at RWE, Volkswagen, and the German Federal Ministry of Defence.

John Scimone — United States of America
Senior Vice President and Chief Security Officer
Dell

John Scimone is Senior Vice President and Chief Security Officer at Dell. Previously, he was Senior Vice President and Chief Information Security Officer at Sony and Director of Security Operations at the U.S. Secretary of Defense Communications Office.

James Shira — United States of America
Network Chief Information Security Officer
PricewaterhouseCoopers

James Shira is Network Chief Information Security Officer at PricewaterhouseCoopers, where he has led an organization-wide information security transformation. Previously, he held executive positions at Zurich Insurance Group, including group CISO, and at American General Financial Services, where he was Chief Security Officer.

Justin Somaini — United States of America
Chief Security Officer
SAP

Justin Somaini heads the SAP Global Security (SGS) team. With more than 20 years of information security experience, he is responsible for SAP's overall security strategy. Before joining SAP in 2015, Justin was Chief Trust Officer at Box. Prior to Box, Justin held the role of Chief Information Security Officer (CISO) at Yahoo, Symantec, Verisign, and Charles Schwab.

Lisa J. Sotto — United States of America
Partner
Hunton Andrews Kurth LLP

Lisa Sotto chairs the top-ranked Global Privacy and Cybersecurity practice at Hunton Andrews Kurth. She is the managing partner of the firm's New York office and serves on the firm's Executive Committee. Lisa has received widespread recognition for her work in the areas of privacy and cybersecurity and was named among the *National Law Journal's* "100 Most Influential Lawyers." She also serves as Chairperson of the Department of Homeland Security's Data Privacy and Integrity Advisory Committee.

Jennifer Steffens — United States of America
Chief Executive Officer
IOActive

Jennifer Sunshine Steffens is the Chief Executive Officer of IOActive, a global consulting firm dedicated to making the world a safer place. She has received numerous industry awards for her leadership in the cybersecurity industry, including *CV Magazine*'s IT Security CEO of the Year award for 2018. Previously, she held leadership positions at groundbreaking cybersecurity companies such as Sourcefire and NFR Security.

Megan Stifel — United States of America
Attorney; Founder, Silicon Harbor Consultants;
Cybersecurity Policy Director, Public Knowledge

Megan Stifel is an Attorney and the Founder of Silicon Harbor Consultants, which provides strategic cybersecurity operations and counsel. She also is Cybersecurity Policy Director at Public Knowledge, and has held cybersecurity leadership posts at the U.S. National Security Council and the U.S. Department of Justice.

Ed Stroz — United States of America
Founder and Co-President
Stroz Friedberg, an Aon company

Ed Stroz is Founder and Co-President of Stroz Friedberg, an Aon company, a global leader in investigations, intelligence, and risk management. Previously, he was a Supervisory Special Agent for the U.S. Federal Bureau of Investigation, where he established the first Computer Crimes Squad in their New York Field Office.

Ria Thomas — United Kingdom
Partner and Global Co-Lead for Cybersecurity
Brunswick Group

Ria Thomas is the Global Co-Lead for Brunswick Group's cyber offering. She has almost 20 years of experience in private and public sector cybersecurity strategies and policies, including advising senior government leaders, board members and C-suite executives on cyber-focused crisis preparedness, enterprise-wide response, and corporate resilience strategies.

James C. Trainor — United States of America
Senior Vice President, Cyber Solutions Group
Aon

James C. Trainor is Senior Vice President within the Cyber Solutions Group at Aon, responsible for helping to shape the organization's overall cyber strategy. He previously led the Cyber Division at the Federal Bureau of Investigation, where he led agents and analytics in every major high-profile cyber investigation involving the FBI.

Rama Vedashree — India
Chief Executive Officer
Data Security Council of India

Rama Vedashree is Chief Executive Officer of the Data Security Council of India. She previously was Vice-President at NASSCOM, overseeing a wide range of initiatives, including domestic IT, eGovernance, smart cities, and healthcare. She also has held executive positions at Microsoft and General Electric.

Patric J.M. Versteeg, MSc — Netherlands

Patrick J.M. Versteeg has been a cybersecurity professional for more than 20 years. He works with organizations throughout the world on strategic cybersecurity planning, leadership engagement, and custom solutions that ensure organizations stay secure and safe in the ever-changing cyber landscape.

Nir Zuk — United States of America
Founder and Chief Technology Officer
Palo Alto Networks

Nir Zuk is Founder and Chief Technology Officer at Palo Alto Networks. Prior to co-founding Palo Alto Networks, Nir was CTO at NetScreen Technologies, which was acquired by Juniper Networks in 2004. Prior to NetScreen, Nir was co-founder and CTO at OneSecure, principal engineer at Check Point Software Technologies, and was one of the developers of stateful inspection technology.

Naveen Zutshi — United States of America
Senior Vice President and Chief Information Officer
Palo Alto Networks

Naveen Zutshi is Senior Vice President and Chief Information Officer at Palo Alto Networks, where he oversees the organization's IT solutions and strategy. Previously, he was Senior Vice President for Technology at Gap Inc., as well as Vice President for Technology and Operations at Encover, a SaaS-based CRM company. He also held senior technology positions at Cisco and Wal-Mart.